D1608984

Different Travellers,
Different Eyes:

Artists' Narratives of the

American West,

1820-1920

DIFFERENT

Artists' Narratives

TRAVELLERS,

of the American West,

DIFFERENT

1820-1920

EYES

Edited by

Peter Wild, Donald A. Barclay,

and James H. Maguire

Texas Christian University Press / Fort Worth

Library of Congress Cataloging-in-Publication Data

Different travellers, different eyes : artists' narratives of the
American West, 1820-1920 / edited by Peter Wild, Donald A.
 Barclay, and James H. Maguire.
   p. cm.
   Includes bibliographical references and index.
   ISBN 0-87565-242-5 (alk. Paper)
   1. Artists—Travel—United States—History—19th century.
2. Artists—Travel—United States—History—20th century.
Artists as authors—United States. 4. West (U.S.)—In literature. I. Wild,
Peter. II. Barclay, Donald A. III. Maguire, James H.
N6510.D465 2001
917.804'2'0887—dc21
2001033300

Book design by Barbara Mathews Whitehead

Contents

IV: After the Closing of the Frontier, 1891-1920 / 187

Introduction

But different travellers have different eyes!
—John James Audubon

This is not an art-history book. The authors of the passages anthologized here are not art historians. They are, instead, artists who experienced the western American frontier in the nineteenth and early twentieth centuries. The casual reader may recognize some of these artists' names because their paintings, sculptures, and photographs adorn the walls of museums, fill the pages of art books, fetch large sums at auction, and (as reproductions) illustrate histories of the early American West. Chances are slim, however, that the casual reader has read a word these artists wrote. That's because their literary artistry has been overshadowed by their visual artistry. This anthology brings the best of this literary art out of the shadows.

We believe the writings collected here stand on their own as feelingly written literature; moreover, these writings give us a fuller understanding of, and appreciation for, the artists as human beings. Nonetheless, we do not intend to downplay, much less ignore, the *artistic* merits and contributions of these artists. Indeed, what the artists write holds our interest not only because it entertains and often informs, but also because we sometimes find that what these artists *say* and what they *paint* are two different things. Often, it is as if they saw one set of "facts" when writing about the West and another when painting, sketching, or photographing it.

We learn, for example, that when John James Audubon wrote in the journal of his 1843 trip to the Upper Missouri, "But different travellers have different eyes!" he was referring specifically to the differences between his own perceptions of the Mandan villages and those of fellow artist George Catlin. To Audubon, the villages suggested a collection of potato sheds inhabited by mudsplattered sneak thieves, and he responded to his impressions with a warts-and-all verbal depiction that contrasts with the monumental and nationalistic portraits of birds that give him fame. To the romantic Catlin, who observed the Mandans thirteen years and at least one smallpox outbreak ahead of Audubon, the villages seemed a natural utopia peopled by a race of Noble Savages, a view expressed in both his painting and writing.

Among the artist/writers included in this volume, Audubon and Catlin are not alone in seeing the frontier West with different eyes, nor is Audubon the only one who presents in his writing a view of the West that contrasts with the scenes in his visual art. Father Nicolas Point, a Jesuit missionary, sees the West as a place of heavenly miracles, while painter and sculptor Frederic Remington describes a harsh landscape where no watchful God looks down on the puny struggles of Darwinian man. Yet Remington's written descriptions contrast with his carefully crafted drawings and his increasingly Impressionistic paintings. Mary Hallock Foote, a nationally known illustrator who gave up her genteel life in the East to follow her mining-engineer husband across the West, writes about hard life and hard dealings among the mining fraternity. She also admits to being sometimes overawed by the strangeness and sublimity of the West, a feeling that contrasts with the serenity and control apparent in her illustrations. Taking a quite different view of mining camp life, the youthful Frank Marryat, a well-born English illustrator, makes the California Gold Rush sound like non-stop hijinks.

German painter Balduin Möllhausen spins an improbable tale of isolation and murder on the frozen prairie, while Canadian artist Paul Kane relates an episode of Hawaiian dancing by Hudson's Bay Company trappers that oozes credibility. Titian R. Peale writes from a time when the appearance of a steamboat in western waters is something new and astounding, while Charles M. Russell recollects the vanished frontier at a time when the Model-T is fast replacing the oat burner.

For all their different ways of seeing, the artist/writers represented here are bound together by an uncommon common experience: each knew the frontier West first hand and each consciously chose to depict it both in words and images.

And what images. Peale's Indian, bow drawn tight to shoot a buffalo, sits as stiff as a twisted piece of wood atop an impossibly flying horse. Emily Carr's woman howls out of the fog-shrouded pines with a primordial cry that all but rings in our ears. Alfred Jacob Miller's hirsute trappers are one "WAUGH!!!" shy of leaping off the canvas into full-blown, unbridled life. Beneath a relentless Arizona sun, Remington's dusty troopers swig from life-giving canteens. Kicking Bear's pictograph of the fight at the Little Big Horn tells a familiar story in a language that seems to come from another planet.

The frontier experience that connects these artists creates a powerful bond, but it is not a bond of place. The territory covered was too vast and too varied for that. Rather, the frontier experience creates a bond of myth: the myth of the West.

≈

The myth began in Europe with the reports of the New World's first explorers. It grew and changed as the frontier started on the eastern shores of North America and moved westward. After the Lewis and Clark Expedition (1804-1806), when increasing numbers of Americans and Europeans crossed the Mississippi, they encountered a land of myth so large and varied that the mind reeled, and, unable to comprehend such dimensions, such bewildering variety, they turned the prospect into a wonderland reflecting the hopes and dreams of the culture from which they came. As art historian Brian W. Dippie notes, "Such is the nature of two-dimensional representation: art creates a separate reality reflecting the artist's cultural values" (*The Oxford History of the American West* 681).

Dippie adds, "Invention, repetition, and refinement define the western art tradition . . . " (676). In other words, struggling to comprehend this vast unknown and render it into image, frontier artists were myth makers whether they wanted to be or not. Nor could they help the fact that their work was fed by the existing mythology of the frontier West——a mythology based in part on paintings of the East's wilderness by artists such as Thomas Cole. Also beyond the control of the artists of the western frontier is the fact that their own work in turn fed, and still feeds, the imaginations of those who know the frontier only as an artistic creation. The paintings of Thomas Cole and the tales of James Fenimore Cooper influenced Frederic Remington. Remington's paintings influenced Hollywood director John Ford. Ford's films were key in creating the western icon known as John Wayne. And, eventually, reaction against the mythology of Cooper, Remington, Ford, and Wayne produced its own polar-opposite frontier mythology.

The process of creating this mythology-making art was much more complex than we have room to sketch here, so we refer readers to the selected bibliography (which lists some of the standard histories of "Western American Art") at the end of this anthology.

If the visual art of the frontier is a powerful force for myth making, then what artists write about their work, or about their experiences while creating their art, is of interest if it does nothing more than open up new, and sometimes surprising, dimensions of the paintings, drawings, and photographs. Looking at Thomas Moran's landscapes, a viewer can understand how they helped inspire the establishment of Yellowstone National Park, but reading Moran's account of his tough trip to Devil's Tower helps us to understand how the landscape of the Old West presented physical and psychological, as well as artistic, challenges to those who would create the images that have shaped our mythology.

Noticing the difference between Moran's visual and verbal responses to the West prompts us to ask: What are the ways in which an artist's written record complements his or her pictorial works and what are the ways in which it contradicts them? Robert Edson Lee's *From West to East: Studies in the Literature of the American West* (1966), suggests one possible answer to that question. Lee points out that Washington Irving's journal account of his travels in what is now Oklahoma differs significantly from his version of the trip in *A Tour of the Prairies* (1835). Lee says that discretion, romanticism, and use of literary rhetoric instead of the vernacular drained Irving's *Tour* of much of the vitality we find in his journal. In other words, Irving's descriptions changed as he tried to shape his view to meet audience standards and expectations. Probably audience expectations also account for the difference between the visual images and the written descriptions created by the artists and writers included here. Perhaps each form of expression released a different facet of the artist's creativity.

Whatever additional differences are to be found between these two ways of viewing and recreating the West, we must stress that this anthology's selections consist of words left by people accustomed to expressing themselves in visual images. We must reiterate, too, that with this book we are not trying to generate art history. We are, instead, trying to open yet another window on responses to the West, a window that opens on the work of people who are known for one sort of response but who have left another as well. Though whenever possible we chose writings that relate in some way to the creation of visual art, a text's readability was more important than any value it might have to an art historian or critic.

We have also included some selections that express objectionable views. The violence and prejudice apparent in some of the writing show not only that the actual Old West was no Garden of Eden, but also that some of the artists who painted the West's vistas had perceptions distorted by the cultural viruses of racism and sexism. In presenting an uncensored, un-bowdlerized version of artists' narratives, we share our view that we must know the whole truth about the past if we are to learn anything significant from it.

It is our hope that by giving readers a fuller understanding of the humanity of these artists, defects as well as virtues, we can contribute to our expanding sense of the western experience. Over the last half century, historians and literary critics have taught us that there are many Wests; and here we invite you to read about some of them as described by different travelers with different eyes.

A note on Organization and References

We have arranged the selections in chronological order based, as closely as is possible, on the dates of the events written about rather than dates of first publication. The selections are grouped into three sections, also chronologically arranged, and a short introduction prefaces each section. Instead of saturating the pages with footnotes that would make the anthology seem more a ponderous dissertation than a selection of narratives meant to be read as literature, we have chosen to provide a context for the readings by giving each selection a brief introduction and suggestions for further reading. Even so, in an anthology of this length, it is impossible to answer all the questions readers might have. For answers to such questions, we advise readers to consult the works listed in the selected bibliography at the end of the book.

Acknowledgments

Jim Maguire thanks his family, the librarians at Boise State University, and Judy Alter, Tracy Row and Vickie Lea Hardie at Texas Christian University Press for helping to make this book a reality.

Donald A. Barclay thanks his colleagues at the Houston Academy of Medicine—Texas Medical Center Library. And Jim, Peter and Darcie.

I.

"Virgin Land," 1820-1848

When Meriwether Lewis, William Clark, and the others in their expedition floated down the Missouri River in 1806, they met a party of fur trappers headed upstream. This event showed many Americans east of the Mississippi that the West had become a land of golden opportunities. In the next four decades, entrepreneurs by the thousands took advantage of those opportunities. John Jacob Astor founded the American Fur Company in 1808; William Becknell, following Major Stephen H. Long's 1820 exploring expedition, opened the Santa Fe Trail in 1821; and William Ashley organized the first mountain-man rendezvous in 1825.

These advance parties of America's westward movement did not, however, enter uninhabited territory. Although smallpox and other diseases brought to North America by Europeans had decimated native peoples in the West even before Lewis and Clark arrived on the scene, hundreds of thousands of American Indians lived throughout almost all of the lands beyond the hundredth meridian. Decades, in some cases even centuries, earlier Spanish missionaries and settlers had displaced many Indians in what is Arizona, New Mexico, Texas, and California. Many of the Spanish missions and settlements were still going concerns when Lewis and Clark led their expedition.

Though Lewis and Clark did not have a trained artist with them, later government expeditions routinely included an artist hired to make a visual record of the West's strange sights and vast vistas. In "The Visual West," a chapter in *The Oxford History of the American West* (edited by Clyde A. Milner, et al.), Brian W. Dippie explains that these artists' work was shaped in part by their preconceptions and that it changed as their experience in the West and the fashions in art changed. Pointing out that their art "was a kind of visual naming" and that it reflected their cultural values, he adds:

> American exploration artists, [William H.] Goetzmann notes, shifted from the exotic and pastoral to the sublime and picturesque, keeping apace with the spirit of different ages of discovery. The pastoral mode was appropriate to the earliest phase of exploration, when the West seemed a remote wonderland full of possibilities; the sublime reinvigorated interest in exploration, an activity that had become predictable by the middle of the nineteenth century. (681-682)

Of course not all artists in the West worked for the government. Some came west as retainers of wealthy European travelers. Alfred Jacob Miller, for example, was hired by Sir William Drummond Stewart to make a record in paintings of the Scottish nobleman's adventures among mountain men and Indians. The enterprising George Catlin, on the other hand, took himself up the Missouri to paint Indians in 1832. Other artists could be found among the missionaries who began arriving in the Northwest in 1834.

Not surprisingly, many artists chose to write about their experiences. If you have read few or none of these writings, it is probably for the reason Peter Matthiessen points out in his 1989 edition of Catlin's *North American Indians:*

> George Catlin's splendid *"Letters and Notes" on the North American Indians* has always been overshadowed by the paintings, and this undue neglect has certainly been worsened by the nineteenth-century rhetoric and repetitions with which he encumbered his otherwise excellent prose. (xxi)

We invite you to sample not only the best of Catlin's writing but also the best passages from the western narratives of his contemporaries. In that by-gone era, American Indians still seemed exotic to other Americans, and this fascination for all things native accounts for the Indian presence in so many artists' narratives.

Events of the 1840s would start bringing to a close the time when the West could still be seen as a "virgin land" (to use the phrase made famous in Henry Nash Smith's book of the same title). As the shine wore off Eden, the West's different cultures increasingly clashed, often violently. A year after the annexation of Texas in 1845, the United States went to war with Mexico, and by 1848 U.S. territory expanded to include the Northwest and Southwest. In 1847 the Latter-Day Saints (Mormons) arrived at the shores of the Great Salt Lake. And in 1848 James Marshall's discovery of gold at Sutter's Mill in California turned the trickle of westward migration into a steady flow. The West had been changed, not only as a subject for the paintbrush, but also as the site of adventures recorded by the pen.

I.

"Virgin Land"

American Buffaloe by Titian Ramsay Peale (reproduced from *Titian Ramsay Peale, 1799-1885, and His Journals of the Wilkes Expedition* [Philadelphia: The American Philosophical Society, 1961]).

~

Titian R. Peale (1799-1885)

In the spring of 1819, a dragon with raised head belched its way, with great effect, up the Missouri River. Indians ran terrified from the creature steaming out of a nightmare, while the few settlers along the banks stood awed at the wonder.

The monster was the *Western Engineer,* the first steamboat to ascend this important route into the unknown. Designed by Major Stephen H. Long both to intimidate tribes resentful of the invasions of whites and to navigate a capricious waterway choked with sandbars and downed trees, the boat heralded Long's major penetration of the Far West. With its serpent's head at the prow, its churning engine, and shallow draft, the craft might be taken as a symbol of coming technological triumph over the wilds. Certainly, one would get that impression from reading the weighty, two-volume *Account of an Expedition from Pittsburgh to the Rocky Mountains* authored by Edwin James, a member of the Long party.

Progress rarely is a smooth affair, however. In the months ahead, Long's expedition, striking out on horseback across the plains to study the Front Range of the Rocky Mountains, would flounder badly. Understandably confused by a vastness untamed by maps, the explorers took wrong turns, mistook one river for another, and nearly starved before staggering back to civilization. Nonetheless, although the theatrics of the dragon were quickly forgotten, the nation would marvel at what Long brought back—the first widely distributed images of those strange mountains and swallowing spaces which would soon bewilder westering Americans.

Sometimes awkward in their attempts to convey the inenarrable in paint, these images were the work of two men. Or, rather, a man and a youth. The expedition's senior artist was English-born Samuel Seymour, whose diary of the trip, if, indeed, he wrote one, no longer exists. The junior artist was a remarkable teenager, Titian Ramsay Peale. Only a fragment of Peale's journal recounting the trip exists, but pieced together with his other writings, these provide an impressive context for the daily, grinding drudgery pulling down the artist striving to record bright visions.

As to a different kind of context, "Wunderkind" would be too narrow a term applied to young Peale. What he brought West with him matched the wonder of what he saw. His father, Charles Willson Peale, was a patriot in the Revolutionary War, a naturalist, a portrait painter, the founder the nation's first museum, and the sire of two further generations of excited artists and naturalists. A friend of Thomas Jefferson, the elder Peale displayed the candescence that quickened the intellectual life of the young Republic, a hopeful verve perhaps burning never so brightly since. Jessie Poesch describes this blend of neoclassicism laced with a romantic spirit as producing a "joyful excitement about the world and God's creatures" (43). It was just such, in Poesch's words, "loving awe" (*Titian Ramsay Peale and His Journals* 18) that drove Titian Peale far from his hometown of Philadelphia, the nation's cultural center at the time, out on various expeditions and, despite the hardships, infused his work.

What survives of Peale's journal from the Long expedition is but a fragment, taking us barely to where the wild life of the venture begins. But Peale's first entry catches his ebullience as the youth sets out into the intriguing unknown, a headiness we'll see again nearly twenty years later as another young artist, Alfred Jacob Miller, is about to take his first steps into the beckoning frontier. After the trek with Major Long, Peale spent a great deal of his life as an artist and illustrator for government-sponsored explorations. In the second selection, Peale, now in his forties, trudges from Oregon to California on a grueling side trip of the famed Wilkes expedition to the South Seas. As the account opens, Peale has already lost one journal in a shipwreck and now faces yet a greater shock for any painter, the loss of the very materials necessary to practice his art.

Through all the labors of the tramp, artist Peale, pained as he may be, doesn't overlook the bird's nest built in an Indian's skull or fail to record a macabre night of marching punctuated by the "rattleing" of bones breaking beneath his horse's hooves. Nor does he miss the wonder of a tree whose fragrance perfumes the air all about him. *Sic itur ad astra.*

Further Reading

Elam, Charles H. *The Peale Family: Three Generations of American Artists.* Detroit: The Detroit Institute of Arts, 1967.

James, Edwin. *Account of an Expedition from Pittsburgh to the Rocky*

Mountains Performed in the Years 1819 and 1820. 2 vols. Philadelphia: H. C. Carey and I. Lea, 1822-1823.

    Poesch, Jessie. *Titian Ramsay Peale and His Journals of The Wilkes Expedition.* Philadelphia: The American Philosophical Society, 1961.

    Sellers, Charles Coleman. *Mr. Peale's Museum: Charles Willson Peale and the First Popular Museum of Natural Science and Art.* New York: W. W. Norton, 1980.

    Weese, Asa Orrin. "The Journal of Titian Ramsay Peale, Pioneer Naturalist." *Missouri Historical Review* 47 (1947): 147-163, 266-284.

Titian
R.
Peale

~

From "The Journal of Titian Ramsay Peale"

Departure for the Rocky Mountains

May 3, 1819. Left the garrison 2 miles from Pittsburg on the Alleghany River at 4 o'clock in the afternoon after firing a salute of 22 guns which were answered with as many from the arsenal. As we steered for Pittsburgh our appearance attracted great numbers of spectators to the banks of the River. We fired a few guns and were cheered in return from the shore. Our boat appears to answer very well, but being quite new, the machinery is rather stiff. Our party are all in excellent spirits, but Dr. Baldwin who is rather unwell. Our party consist of Major Long, commandant of the expedition, Lieutenant Graham, and Cadet Swift, his assistants, Maj. Thomas Biddle, journalist and historian, Dr. Baldwin, botanist and surgeon, Mr. Say, zoologist, Mr. Jessup, geologist, Mr. Seymour, landscape painter, and myself, assistant naturalist and painter of natural history. Mr. O'Fallen is to accompany us. He is Indian Agent. Our boat is built in the most convenient manner for the purpose. She draws about two feet and a half water, the wheels placed in the stern in order to avoid trees, snags and sawyers, etc. On the quarter deck there is a bullet proof house for the steersmen. On the right hand wheel is *James Monroe* in capitals, and on the left, *J. C. Calhoun,* they being the two propelling powers of the expedition. She has a mast to ship and unship at pleasure, which carries a square and topsail, on the bow is carved the figure of a large serpent, through the gapping mouth of which the waste steam issues.

It will give, no doubt, to the Indians an idea that the boat is pulled along by this monster. Our arms consist of one brass four pounder mounted on the bow, four brass 2 7/8 inch howitzers, two on swivels, and two on field carriages, two wolf pieces carrying four once balls; twelve muskets, six rifles, and several fowling pieces, besides an air gun, twelve sabers, pistols, and a quantity of private arms of various sorts and a great sufficiency of ammunition of all kinds for our purposes. This evening, we sent up a few rockets.

Overland Trip from Oregon to California

September 1841

Wednesday 22d Crossed the Umpqua mountains, they are about 3000 feet elevation (from the plaines), very steep and covered with Spruce and Lamberts pine trees, with a thick undergroth of Arbutus, Dogwood (Cornus Nuttallii), etc.

The days Journey was a most arduous one although we gained but 16 or 18 miles. One or two horses fell down the steep side of the mountains with their packs but were recovered with some little delay. The bag containing my bedg and wardrobe was torn open by the brush and carelessness of the men in charge, and the case containing my drawing instruments was broken and all the instruments, my sketch book and Journal lost—with all my notes and drawings from the time of our landing in Oregon after the wreck of the Peacock; a loss the more serious by reason of my being destitute of the materials to continue my observations.

Encamped on the south side of the mountains before night, at which time only I became acquainted with my loss; the men restoring a boot picked up in the road.

Thursday 23d The party were delayed today, to allow me time to try and recover my Journal, etc. I returned over the mountains with two men (Wood & Black). I succeeded in finding my camera lucida only, and continued searching untill afternoon, when meeting some Indians in the path concluded it was useless to search further, and that my books and the remaining instruments and paint-box were irrecoverably lost. We searched the quivers and baskets of the Indians who were much alarmed; but their language being unintelligable to us, it was requisite. These

Indians are known by the name of "Rascals," and were the first of the tribe we saw. They have always been considered hostile to the Whites. . . .

Saty 25th Being imprudently encamped on the banks of the creek the Indians last night approached within a few yards of our tents, under cover of the bushes. In their retreat a small, neatly wrought net bag was left. It contained cooked roots.

Started at 9 A.M. and continued our course over burned woods and small patches of prairie, abounding in black tail Deer, which we could not succeed in killing notwithstanding there was much firing at them. Indian tracks numerous though but few were seen. Reached and crossed "Rogues river" before night, pitching our tents on it South bank. Some Indians approached in canoes, but were not suffered to enter the camp. The river was at the camp about 90 yards Wide, and three feet deep with a gentle current, and an even, gravelly bottom.

Ignace (an Irraquois Ind) went out to hunt, and killed a buck; but while he was busy skinning it, he was attacked by about 20 Indians, with arrows, which he described as striking all round him. He remounted his horse, firing a shot from his rifle amongst them first, and then retreated at full speed to camp, arrivg just at dark. . . .

Monday 27th The night passed off quietly, although the yells of Indians close by us were constant untill midnight. . . .

Tuesday Sept. 28th Soon after starting this morning Messrs Rich and Colvocoresses were both taken sick, with fever. Mr. C. became delirious, and was unable to ride. Dr. Whittle and a small party of us remained with them as a guard, this being the most dangerous part of the country— where the natives are most numerous and avowedly hostile. It was necessary to deprive Mr. C. of his arms, and to proceed in very short and easy stages untill we overtook Mr. Emmons at night. . . .

October 1841

Wednesday 13th The wolves were so bold last night that they entered our camp and carried off a fresh bear skin from the side of a fire, and within a few feet of a tent. . . .

Monday 18th . . . At the junction of Feather river, and the Sacramento we saw the remains of an Indian town, which a few years since contained several hundred natives, all of whom perrished in one season by a tertian fever. Their bones now are bleaching on the ground, strewed in all directions—in one of the skulls a bird has built its nest. . . .

Tuesday Octr 19th We started at the usual hour and traveled over the same perfet level to the American river which was forded and here met Capt Sutter of "Nueva Helvetia" who came to meet us and conduct us to his house where we arrived about 2 oclock, and partook of some refreshment; then proceeded two miles further to the Sacramento and encampd, Capt Sutter accepting our invitation to sup with us.

The Mexican government has made a conditional grant of 30 square leagues of land to Capt Sutter, a Swiss gentleman, for the purpose of Settling this portion of California. He commenced about two years since, and is now building extensive corrals and houses of adobes, by Indian labor for which he pays in goods. He has now 1000 horses, 3000 cattle, and 800 sheep; all in a thriving condition. . . .

Saty Oct 23d Started early, crossed the same kind of level prairie, to rio Joaquin, which is not usually fordable but the season being unusually dry, we succeeded in crossing without damage, though some few packs got wet. At about 11 a.m. reached a lagoon filled with geese & Ducks, once surrounded by Antelopes & sandhill cranes. Here our guide proposed that we should halt for the day, stating that we should find no more water or grass in a long days Journey; but it was concluded notwithstanding to push on; about the middle of the afternoon we arrived at a range of naked hills through the valies of which we threaded our way meeting a few springs of water, but no wood, once but little grass. Several strata of sandstone appeared in the hills abounding in organic remains, and the fragments of an enormous species of oyster (fossil) were strewed about the surface of the ground. (Subsequently we learned that fossil fish were common here.) At night having crossed the hills & again reached the plain we were unable to find grass for the horses, and had to push on until 9 p.m. when reaching a swamp abounding in geese, ducks, & Sandhill Cranes, we halted for the night, but it was too dark to find the water; consequently we had to go to bed, dinner & supperless. The bed however, was better than usual, being rushes, & we were tired enough after a 45 miles ride to enjoy it.

In the course of the day we saw several herds of Wild horses, Elk, and Antelopes.

Sunday, Octr 24th The innumerable geese & Sandhill Cranes we disturbed last night kept up a racket that would effectually have kept awake any other persons who might not have made such a Journey as we did yesterday. Killed a Bullock and with a few geese made a meal which would astonish people who eat more than once in 24 hours!! After it we set off on our course over naked hills or rather mountains. The road became plainer as we advanced, and the number of Indians increased. They were all clean and well dressed, most of them spoke Spanish, they told us they were returning from Mass at the Mission of San José. Each was loaded with beef, which is issued to them at the Mission in weekly rations. Once per annum they are allowed a recess to return to their native wilds to gather acorns, etc. now ripe, which accts for our meeting them away from the restraints of the Mission. Many had horses.

Arrived at the Mission of San José a little past noon. Our reception was rather inhospitable, notwithstanding we had letters of introduction; but fortunately we were lucky enough to meet an agent of the H B Company, Mr. Forbes, who invited us to his farm 6 miles further on our road, to which the party conducted by Mr. Forbes went while Mr. Eld & I having found a countryman of ours in the Tailor of the Mission (Ephraim Travel, formerly of Philadelphia) we staid to see the Church and Gardens—the former contains some good oil paintings, and the walls are rather neatly painted in distemper [tempera] by a wandering Italian.

The gardens are extensive, and contain some good fruits, Peaches, Pears, Apples, Figs, Grapes, Olives.

40 bbls of wine were made this season, although a large portion of the grapes were improvidentially consumed by the Indians.

Dormitorys in two or three paralel lines, forming a hollow square, with the Church in the center, flanked by the officers & priests quarters.

1600 was the number of natives here in 1832, but now there is less than 600. It is the principal Mission of California & the priest is Vicar General.

Passed a rancho, on our way to Mr. Forbes's around which were walls built of Bullocks skulls. Plaines in all directions covered with carcases in different stages of decomposition, the hides and tallow only being preserved. As we traveled in the dark last night, the continued rattleing and breaking of bones under our horses feet had a most singular and unpoetic effect; any but Californian horses would have been frightened by it.

Monday Octr 25th Slept in a bed last night, under roof, for the first time since leaving fort Vancouver in August. Mr. Forbes accompanied us a short distance on our road this morning untill we came in sight of the Mission of Sta Clara. We then sent on the men and horses to a place some 10-15 miles beyond called San Francisquito, where there was a little grass, our horses having had little or nothing to eat these two days.

The rest of us visited the Mission, and were hospitably recd by the padre dressed in the gray Capote & cord of St. Francis. He conducted us over the church and burial grounds, etc.

On expressing a wish to see the gardens we were conducted to the superintendent who was probably judging by our appearance (we were dressed in deer skin shirts & trowsers, mockassins, etc. with plentiful mostacios and beards none the cleaner for exposure to weather) he took us to be some vagabond trappers wanting to eat fruit, and recd us rather rudely; but being reproved by Mr. Rich in good Spanish, his conduct so completely altered, that we not only visited the garden to see peach, pear, apple & olive besides fig trees, but he insisted on our coming to his rooms, to eat the fruit, and drink a sample of the spirit distilled from the pears.

Reached San Francisquito before dark, after riding 20 miles.

Tuesday Octr 26th The grass being good, and none to be had further on the road, it was concluded best to remain in camp today to recruit the horses for a "long camp" tomorrow. Hunted & botanized.

Killed several geese, but having plenty of beef no one would eat them, and the wolves entered the camp during the night and carried them off. Found another species of Tobacco (Nicotia _____) and obtained the ripe fruit of a very fragrant species of Laurus. It is a beautiful tree 30-40 ft. high, regularly formed and close in foliage. Packed some of the nuts with dry clay in a goose skin, hoping to introduce it at home. We found it first in the valley of the Umpqua river, and in the mountains where it must endure considerable cold in the winters. The foliage is so fragrant as to perfume the air to a considerable distance when heated by the sun. At dark it commenced raining and caused us to spend a wet night. We had guarded against the decending torrents of rain but forgot that we were on level ground & without floor to our tent.

Wednesday Octr 27th Started early in a heavy rain, some over a level marshy prairie passing several Ranchos. A high wooded range of hills to our left, course about N. We were in hopes to have completed our Journey today but several horses gave out about the middle of the afternoon, and we had to halt on the borders of a marshy prairie between two ranges of hills about 12 miles short of our destination.

Having no more beef, we had to kill some Geese and Ducks for our supper. They are fortunately for us very abundant. The weather cleared a little, but not long enough to dry our blankets. It was chilly & we had a wet bed and but little food.

Thursday 28th Started a little after sunrise and in four hours reached "Yerba-buena," stopping at the Mission of Dolores by the way. It is a mission truly of Sorrow, and is nearly all in ruins, but 50 Indians are left in it who are the "picture of poverty." Yerba buena on the contrary presents quite a prosperous appearance having several neatly built frame houses & Stores—all English or American.

We found a boat waiting for us, and before night reached the Vincennes at Sausalito where the Brigs Oregon & Porpoise also lay. . . .

Titian R. Peale

George Catlin's *Keokuk* (Smithsonian American Art Museum [gift of Mrs. Joseph Harrison, Jr.], Washington, D.C.).

~

George Catlin (1796-1872)

"In the beginning all the world was America," rhapsodized seventeenth-century English philosopher John Locke. Hundreds of years before him, at least as far back as Roman historian Tacitus, thinkers in Western Civilization had imagined that less technologically advanced peoples lived closer to the bosom of God. When John Locke gazed across the seas at the New World, he thought he could see an Edenic land, a new continent of ultimate potential inhabited by tribes of savage Adams and Eves all but untainted by the corruptions of getting and spending.

This was a rosy if tremendously powerful concept, one no better stated, or painted, than by George Catlin, a man who devoted most of his adult life to preserving what he perceived as a bright but threatened reality of pristine glory. In the course of things, such willful iridescence drove him to create a forceful art transcending the enthusiastic fantasy lying at its roots.

Born in Wilkes-Barre, Pennsylvania, shortly after the Revolutionary War, George Catlin grew up fascinated with Indians—in part due to family stories of his mother's brief captivity among the Iroquois. Though Catlin eventually followed his father's wishes and became an attorney, the young lawyer found his mind wandering, found himself doodling with a penknife even while judges droned on. In a sudden change, he sold his law books and moved to Philadelphia, the nation's cultural center at that time. There, completely untrained in art, he surprised himself by becoming a successful portrait painter.

Even at that, he wasn't satisfied. Finally he realized what was eating at his soul. In 1830 he packed up a few belongings, left his new wife, and plunged off into the wild lands beyond St. Louis. There, on a number of trips over the next several years, Catlin lived among the free-roaming tribes of the Great Plains, painting a hunter's way of life then at its apex. The result was not only a book about his travels but hundreds of paintings capturing a buffalo culture soon about to pass. This grand gallery he took on tour to Europe; today, it forms a striking legacy in the Smithsonian Institution, though it nearly perished from long neglect.

Rarely in art do we find, as in Catlin's book, such a detailed record both of the life and concepts involved in producing canvases. At first, it may seem a record laced with contradictions. The Indians Catlin labels as "knights of the forest" and "chivalrous" also treated their women as slaves and took delight in the cruelest tortures. Yet these produced no contradictions in Catlin's mind. In the tradition of Tacitus, Catlin divided society into two groups: the intellectually refined but vice-ridden civilization of his own origins and the unsophisticated peoples living close to nature. As condescending as it may seem today, under this classification it was thought that those people living close to nature had no laws, that no cares wrinkled their beaming faces. The violent aspects of their cultures were seen as part of their harmonious moral dimness.

Yet nowhere is it written that great art must consort with objective reality, and Catlin did not allow reality to get in the way of his vision. As Catlin painted, often working among jostling crowds of curious Indians, he was able to incarnate his ideas in the figures standing compellingly, even nobly, before us. The unschooled Catlin painted quickly, and if a certain awkwardness is the result, it is one nonetheless that impresses with directness and vitality. And all this led, given the complex interweavings behind social changes, to the first appeal for a national park.

Further Reading

Catlin, George. *Letters and Notes on the Manners, Customs, and Conditions of the North American Indians.* 1844. 2 vols. New York: Dover, 1973.

Hassrick, Royal B. *The George Catlin Book of American Indians.* New York: Watson-Guptill, 1977.

Locke, John. *Two Treatises of Government.* 1690. Peter Laslett, ed. Cambridge: Cambridge University Press, 1960. 319.

McCracken, Harold. *George Catlin and the Old Frontier.* New York: Dial, 1959.

$\sim$

From *Letters and Notes on the Manners,*
Customs, and Conditions of the
North American Indians

After I had done with the chiefs and braves, and proposed to paint a few of the women, I at once got myself into a serious perplexity, being heartily laughed at by the whole tribe, both by men and by women, for my exceeding and (to them) unaccountable condescension in seriously proposing to paint a woman; conferring on her the same honour that I had done the chiefs and braves. Those whom I had honoured, were laughed at by hundreds of the jealous, who had been decided unworthy the distinction, and were now amusing themselves with the very enviable honour which the great white medicine-man had conferred, especially on them, and was now to confer equally upon the squaws!

The first reply that I received from those whom I had painted, was, that if I was to paint women and children, the sooner I destroyed their pictures, the better; for I had represented to them that I wanted their pictures to exhibit to white chiefs, to shew who were the most distinguished and worthy of the Sioux; and their women had never taken scalps, nor did anything better than make fires and dress skins. I was quite awkward in this dilemma, in explaining to them that I wanted the portraits of the women to hang under those of their husbands, merely to shew how their women looked, and how they dressed, without saying any more of them. After some considerable delay of my operations, and much deliberation on the subject, through the village, I succeeded in getting a number of women's portraits, of which the two above introduced are a couple.

The vanity of these men, after they had agreed to be painted was beyond all description, and far surpassing that which is oftentimes immodest enough in civilized society, where the sitter generally leaves the picture, when it is done to speak for, and to take care of, itself; while an Indian often lays down, from morning till night, in front of his portrait, admiring his own beautiful face, and faithfully guarding it day to day, to save it from accident or harm.

This watching or guarding their portraits, I have observed during all of my travels amongst them as a very curious thing; and in many instances, where my colours were not dry, and subjected to so many accidents, from the crowds who were gathering about them, I have found this peculiar guardianship of essential service to me—relieving my mind oftentimes from a great deal of anxiety.

I was for a long time at a loss for the true cause of so singular a peculiarity, but at last learned that it was owing to their superstitious notion, that there may be life to a certain extent in the picture; and that if harm or violence be done to it, it may in some mysterious way, affect their health or do them other injury.

I cannot help but repeat . . . that the tribes of the red men of North America, as a nation of human beings, are on their wane; that (to use their own very beautiful figure) "they are fast travelling to the shades of their fathers, towards the setting sun;" and that the traveller who would see these people in their native simplicity and beauty, must needs be hastily on his way to the prairies and Rocky Mountains, or he will see them only as they are now seen on the frontiers, as a basket of dead game,—harassed, chased, bleeding and dead; with their plumage and colours despoiled; to be gazed amongst in vain for some system of moral, or for some scale by which to estimate their true native character, other than that which has too often recorded them but a dark and unintelligible mass of cruelty and barbarity.

I have for a long time been of opinion, that the wilderness of our country afforded models equal to those from which the Grecian sculptors transferred to the marble such inimitable grace and beauty; and I am now more confirmed in this opinion, since I have immersed myself in the midst of thousands and tens of thousands of these knights of the forest; whose whole lives are lives of chivalry, and whose daily feats, with their naked limbs, might vie with those of the Grecian youths in the beautiful rivalry of the Olympian games.

No man's imagination, with all the aids of description that can be given to it, can ever picture the beauty and wildness of scenes that may be daily witnessed in this romantic country; of hundreds of these graceful youths, without a care to wrinkle, or a fear to disturb the full expression of pleasure and enjoyment that beams upon their faces—their long black hair mingling with their horses' tails, floating in the wind, while they are flying over the carpeted prairie, and dealing death with their spears and arrows, to a band of infuriated buffaloes; or their splendid procession in a war-parade, arrayed in all their gorgeous colours and trappings, moving with most exquisite grace and manly beauty, added to that bold defiance which man carries on his front, who acknowledges no superior on earth, and who is amenable to no laws except the laws of God and honour. . . .

[O]ne at a time of the young fellows, already emaciated with fasting, and thirsting, and waking, for nearly four days and nights, advanced from the side of the lodge, and placed himself on his hands and feet, or otherwise, as best suited for the performance of the operation, where he submitted to the cruelties in the following manner:—An inch or more of the flesh on each shoulder, or each breast was taken up between the thumb and finger by the man who held the knife in his right hand; and the knife, which had been ground sharp on both edges, and then hacked and notched with the blade of another, to make it produce as much pain as possible, was forced through the flesh below the fingers, and being withdrawn, was followed with a splint or skewer, from the other, who held a bunch of such in his left hand, and was ready to force them through the wound. There were then two cords lowered down from the top of the lodge (by men who were placed on the lodge outside, for the purpose), which were fastened to these splints or skewers, and they instantly began to haul him up; he was thus raised until his body was suspended from the ground where he rested, until the knife and a splint were passed through the flesh or integuments in a similar manner on each arm below the shoulder (over the brachialis externus), below the elbow (over the extensor carpi radialis), on the thighs (over the vastus externus), and below the knees (over the peroneus).

In some instances they remained in a reclining position on the ground until this painful operation was finished, which was performed, in all instances, exactly on the same parts of the body and limbs; and which, in its progress, occupied some five or six minutes.

Each one was then instantly raised with the cords, until the weight of his body was suspended by them, and then, while the blood was streaming down their limbs, the bystanders hung upon the splints each man's appropriate shield, bow and quiver, etc.; and in many instances, the skull of a buffalo with the horns on it, was attached to each lower arm and each lower leg, for the purpose, probably, of preventing by their great weight, the struggling, which might otherwise have taken place to their disadvantage whilst they were hung up.

When these things were all adjusted, each one was raised higher by the cords, until these weights all swung clear from the ground, leaving his feet, in most cases, some six or eight feet above the ground. In this plight they at once became appalling and frightful to look at—the flesh, to support the weight of their bodies, with the additional weights which were attached to them, was raised six or eight inches by the skewers; and their heads sunk forward on the breasts, or thrown backwards, in a much more frightful condition, according to the way in which they were hung up.

The unflinching fortitude, with which every one of them bore this part of the torture surpassed credulity; each one as the knife was passed through his flesh sustained an unchangeable countenance; and several of them, seeing me making sketches, beckoned me to look at their faces, which I watched through all this horrid operation, without being able to detect anything but the pleasantest smiles as they looked me in the eye, while I could hear the knife rip through the flesh, and feel enough of it myself, to start involuntary and uncontroullable tears over my cheeks.

When raised to the condition above described, and completely suspended by the cords, the sanguinary hands, through which he had just passed, turned back to perform a similar operation on another who was ready, and each one in his turn passed into the charge of others, who instantly introduced him to a new and improved stage of their refinements in cruelty.

Surrounded by imps and demons as they appear, a dozen or more, who seem to be concerting and devising means for his exquisite agony, gather around him, when one of the number advances towards him in a sneering manner, and commences turning him around with a pole which he brings in his hand for the purpose. This is done in a gentle manner at first; but gradually increased, when the brave fellow, whose proud spirit can controul its agony no longer, burst out in the most lamentable and heart-rending cries that the human voice is capable of producing, crying forth a prayer to the Great Spirit to support and protect him in this dreadful trial; and continually repeating his confidence in his protection. In this condition he is continued to be turned, faster and faster—and there is no hope of escape from it, nor chance for the slightest relief, until by fainting, his voice falters, and his struggling ceases, and he hangs, apparently, a still and lifeless corpse! When he is, by turning, gradually brought to this condition, which is generally done within ten or fifteen minutes, there is a close scrutiny passed upon him among his tormentors, who are checking and holding each other back as long as the least struggling or tremour can be discovered, lest he should be removed before he is (as they term it) "entirely dead."

When brought to this alarming and most frightful condition, and the turning has gradually ceased, as his voice and his strength have given out, leaving him to hang entirely still, and apparently lifeless; when his tongue is distended from his mouth, and his medicine-bag, which he has affectionately and superstitiously clung to with his left hand, has dropped to the ground; the signal is given to the men on top of the lodge, by gently striking the cord with the pole below, when they very gradually and carefully lower him to the ground.

In this helpless condition he lies, like a loathsome corpse to look at, though in the keeping (as they call it) of the Great Spirit, whom he trusts will protect him, and enable him to get up and walk away. As soon as he is lowered to the ground thus, one of the bystanders advances, and pulls out the two splints or pins from the breasts and shoulders, thereby disengaging him from the cords by which he has been hung up; but leaving all the others with their weights, etc. hanging to his flesh.

In this condition he lies for six or eight minutes, until he gets strength to rise and move himself, for no one is allowed to assist or offer him aid, as he is here enjoying the most valued privilege which a Mandan can boast of, that of "trusting his life to the keeping of the Great Spirit," in this time of extreme peril.

As soon as he is seen to get strength enough to rise on his hands and feet, and drag his body around the lodge, he crawls with the weights still hanging to his body, to another part of the lodge, where there is another Indian sitting with a hatchet in his hand, and a dried buffalo skull before him; and here, in the most earnest and humble manner, by holding up the little finger of his left hand to the Great Spirit, he expresses to Him, in a speech of a few words, his willingness to give it as a sacrifice; when he lays it on the dried buffalo skull, where the other chops it off near the hand, with a blow of the hatchet!

Polygamy is countenanced amongst all of the North American Indians, so far as I have visited them; and it is no uncommon thing to find a chief with six, eight, or ten, and some with twelve or fourteen wives in his lodge. Such is an ancient custom, and in their estimation is right as well as necessary. Women in a savage state, I believe, are always held in a rank inferior to that of the men, in relation to whom in many respects

George Catlin

they stand rather in the light of menials and slaves than otherwise; and as they are the "hewers of wood and drawers of water," it becomes a matter of necessity for a chief (who must be liberal, keep open doors, and entertain, for the support of his popularity) to have in his wigwam a sufficient number of such handmaids or menials to perform the numerous duties and drudgeries of so large and expensive an establishment.

There are two other reasons for this custom which operate with equal, if not with greater force than the one above assigned. In the first place, these people, though far behind the civilized world in acquisitiveness, have still more or less passion for the accumulation of wealth, or, in other words, for the luxuries of life; and a chief, excited by a desire of this kind, together with a wish to be able to furnish his lodge with something more than ordinary for the entertainment of his own people, as well as strangers who fall upon his hospitality, sees fit to marry a number of wives, who are kept at hard labour during most of the year; and the avails of that labour enable him to procure those luxuries, and give to his lodge the appearance of respectability which is not ordinarily seen. Amongst those tribes who trade with the Fur Companies, this system is carried out to a great extent, and the women are kept for the greater part of the year, dressing buffalo robes and other skins for the market; and the brave or chief, who has the greatest number of wives, is considered the most affluent and envied man in the tribe; for his table is most bountifully supplied, and his lodge the most abundantly furnished with the luxuries of civilized manufacture, who has at the year's end the greatest number of robes to vend to the Fur Company. . . .

There are other and very rational grounds on which the propriety of such a custom may be urged, one of which is as follows:—as all nations of Indians in their natural condition are unceasingly at war with the tribes that are about them, for the adjustment of ancient and never-ending feuds, as well as from a love of glory, to which in Indian life the battle-field is almost the only road, their warriors are killed off to that extent, that in many instances two and sometimes three women to a man are found in a tribe. In such instances I have found that the custom of polygamy has kindly helped the community to an evident relief from a cruel and prodigious calamity.

The instances of which I have above spoken, are generally confined to the chiefs and medicine-men; though there is no regulation prohibiting a poor or obscure individual from marrying several wives, other than the personal difficulties which lie between him and the hand which he wishes in vain to get, for want of sufficient celebrity in society, or from a still more frequent objection, that of his inability (from want of worldly goods) to deal in the customary way with the fathers of the girls whom he would appropriate to his own household.

In traversing the immense regions of the classic West, the mind of a philanthropist is filled to the brim with feelings of admiration; but to reach this country, one is obliged to descend from the light and glow of civilized atmosphere, through the different grades of civilization, which gradually sink to the most deplorable condition along the extreme frontier; thence through the most pitiable misery and wretchedness of savage degradation; where the genius of natural liberty and independence have been blasted and destroyed by the contaminating vices and dissipations introduced by the immoral part of civilized society. Through this dark and sunken vale of wretchedness one hurries, as through a pestilence, until he gradually rises again into the proud and chivalrous pale of savage society, in its state of original nature, beyond the reach of civilized contamination; here he finds much to fix his enthusiasm upon, and much to admire. Even here, the predominant passions of the savage breast, of ferocity and cruelty, are often found; yet restrained and frequently subdued, by the noblest traits of honour and magnanimity,—a race of men who live and enjoy life and its luxuries, and practice its virtues, very far beyond the usual estimation of the world, who are apt to judge the savage and his virtues from the poor, degraded, and humbled specimens which alone can be seen along our frontiers. From the first settlements of our Atlantic coast to the present day, the bane of this blasting frontier has regularly crowded upon them, from the northern to the southern extremities of our country; and, like the fire in a prairie, which destroys everything where it passes, it has blasted and sunk them, and all but their names, into oblivion, wherever it has travelled. It is to this tainted class alone that the epithet of "poor, naked, and drunken savage," can be, with propriety, applied; for all those numerous tribes which I have visited, and are yet uncorrupted by the vices of civilized acquaintance, are well clad, in many instances cleanly, and in the full enjoyment of life and its luxuries. It is for the character and preservation of these noble fellows that I am an enthusiast; and it is for these uncontaminated people that I would be willing to devote the energies of my life. It is a sad and melancholy truth to contemplate, that all the numerous tribes who inhabited our vast Atlantic States have not "fled to the West;"—that they are not to be found here—that they have been blasted by the fire which has passed over them—have sunk into their graves, and everything but their names travelled into oblivion.

The distinctive character of all these Western Indians, as well as their traditions relative to their ancient locations, prove beyond a doubt, that they have been for a very long time located on the soil which they now possess; and in most respects, distinct and unlike those nations who formerly inhabited the Atlantic coast, and who (according to the erroneous opinion of a great part of the world), have fled to the West.

It is for these inoffensive and unoffending people, yet unvisited by the vices of civilized society, that I would proclaim to the world, that it is time, for the honour of our country—for the honour of every citizen of the republic—and for the sake of humanity, that our government should raise her strong arm to save the remainder of them from the pestilence which is rapidly advancing upon them. We have gotten from them territory enough, and the country which they now inhabit is most of it too barren of timber for the use of civilized man; it affords them, however, the means and luxuries of savage life; and it is to be hoped that our government will not acquiesce in the continued wilful destruction of these happy people.

My heart has sometimes almost bled with pity for them, while amongst them, and witnessing their innocent amusements, as I have contemplated the inevitable bane that was rapidly advancing upon them; without that check from the protecting arm of government, and which alone could shield them from destruction.

What degree of happiness these sons of Nature may attain to in the world, in their own way; or in what proportion they may relish the pleasures of life, compared to the sum of happiness belonging to civilized society, has long been a subject of much doubt, and one which I cannot undertake to decide at this time. I would say this much, however, that if the thirst for knowledge has entailed everlasting miseries on mankind from the beginning of the world; if refined and intellectual pains increase in proportion to our intellectual pleasures, I do not see that we gain much advantage over them on that score; and judging from the full-toned enjoyment which beams from their happy faces, I should give it as my opinion, that their lives were much more happy than ours; that is, if the word happiness is properly applied to the enjoyments of those who have not experienced the light of the Christian religion. I have long looked with the eye of a critic, into the jovial faces of these sons of the forest, unfurrowed with cares—where the agonizing feeling of poverty had never stamped distress upon the brow. I have watched the bold, intrepid step—the proud, yet dignified deportment of Nature's man, in fearless freedom, with a soul unalloyed by mercenary lusts, too great to yield to laws or power except from God. As these independent fellows are all joint-tenants of the soil, they are all rich, and none of the steepings of comparative poverty can strangle their just claims to renown. Who (I would ask) can look without admiring, into a society where peace and harmony prevail—where virtue is cherished—where rights are protected, and wrongs are redressed—with no laws, but the laws of honour, which are the supreme laws of their land. Trust the boasted virtues of civilized society for awhile, with all its intellectual refinements, to such a tribunal, and then write down the degradation of the "lawless savage," and our trancendent virtues.

As these people have no laws, the sovereign right of summary redress lies in the breast of the party (or friends of the party) aggrieved; and infinitely more dreaded is the certainty of cruel revenge from the licensed hands of an offended savage, than the slow and uncertain vengeance of the law.

If you think me enthusiast, be it so; for I deny it not. It has ever been the predominant passion of my soul to seek Nature's wildest haunts, and give my hand to Nature's men. Legends of these, and visits to those, filled the earliest page of my juvenile impressions.

The tablet has stood, and I am an enthusiast for God's works as He left them.

This strip of country, which extends from the province of Mexico to lake Winnepeg on the North, is almost one entire plain of grass, which is, and ever must be, useless to cultivating man. It is here, and here chiefly, that the buffaloes dwell; and with, and hovering about them, live and flourish the tribes of Indians, whom God made for the enjoyment of that fair land and its luxuries.

It is a melancholy contemplation for one who has travelled as I have, through these realms, and seen this noble animal in all its pride and glory, to contemplate it so rapidly wasting from the world, drawing the irresistible conclusion too, which one must do, that its species is soon to be extinguished, and with it the peace and happiness (if not the actual existence) of the tribes of Indians who are joint tenants with them, in the occupancy of these vast and idle plains.

And what a splendid contemplation too, when one (who has travelled these realms, and can duly appreciate them) imagines them as they might in future be seen, (by some great protecting policy of government) preserved in their pristine beauty and wildness, in a magnificent park, where the world could see for ages to come, the native Indian in his classic attire, galloping his wild horse, with sinewy bow, and shield and lance, amid the fleeting herds of elks and buffaloes. What a beautiful and thrilling specimen for America to preserve and hold up to the view of her refined citizens and the world, in future ages! A nation's Park, containing man and beast, in all the wild and freshness of their nature's beauty!

I would ask no other monument to my memory, nor any other enrolment of my name amongst the famous dead, than the reputation of having been the founder of such an institution.

Such scenes might easily have been preserved, and still could be cherished on the great plains of the West, without detriment to the country or its borders; for the tracts of country on which the buffaloes have assembled, are uniformly sterile, and of no available use to cultivating man.

It is on these plains, which are stocked with buffaloes, that the finest specimens of the Indian race are to be seen. It is here, that the savage is decorated in the richest costume. It is here, and here only, that his wants are all satisfied, and even the luxuries of life are afforded him in abundance. And here also is he the proud and honourable man (before he has had teachers or laws), above the imported wants, which beget meanness and vice; stimulated by ideas of honour and virtue, in which the God of Nature has certainly not curtailed him.

Alfred Jacob Miller's *The Lost Greenhorn* (The Warner Collection of Gulf States Paper Corporation, Tuscaloosa, Alabama).

~

Alfred Jacob Miller (1810-1874)

It wasn't long before painting the West turned into an industry. Eager for fantastic possibilities, the public was electrified to see— and pay good money for—canvases of the shining peaks and brilliant savagery beyond the Mississippi. In 1851, Alfred Jacob Miller received the then respectable sum of $230 for three pictures: *Drink to Trapper, Watering Horses,* and *Fort Laramie Indian Camp* (*Alfred Jacob Miller* 67). Through income earned from his paintings and shrewd investments, Miller would die a rich man. But unlike later artists such as Albert Bierstadt and Charles M. Russell, Miller would never receive tens of thousands for a single work; and unlike artists such as Catlin and Audubon, Miller would never catch the cultural froth and put on glittering, profitable shows where the citizenry stood agog. Whatever idealism one might ascribe to these performers, in essence they were barkers. Rarely is fame a product of humility.

Still, we might wish that Alfred Jacob Miller had been possessed of at least a modest dose of his fellow artists' knack for self-promotion, for though he was among the finest to wield a brush on the frontier, his gentle nature and cautious estimate of his own talents left him nearly forgotten. And had it not been for a stroke of luck—one of those stellar moments in American art—his powers may well have taken the usual path into oblivion.

The son of a prosperous Baltimore businessman, Miller enjoyed early travel to Europe and training at the École des Beaux-Arts in Paris. At the age of twenty-four he was back in Baltimore, setting up shop as a portrait painter and landscapist. Shortly after, the family suffered a series of setbacks, including the deaths of his father and mother, and although the nature of other misfortunes is unclear, by late 1836 Miller was struggling to make a living in New Orleans.

One day in the following spring an imperious gentleman walked into Miller's studio. Captain William Drummond Stewart was a hero of Waterloo, and, like many another lusty nobleman, he was back in America for yet another extended hunting lark on the frontier. Would Miller like to go along and paint some pictures of the expedition to hang in Stewart's castle back in Scotland? The artist's excited letter to a friend, seen in the second selection, shows the naïveté of Miller, a youth of twenty-seven about to leap off into the unknown and face one of the most rambunctious and bone-crushing experiences available to that day's adventurers.

Whatever his sensitive nature, the young artist not only survived, he throve artistically out there among the uproars on the frontier. Months later, he returned to civilization with a couple of hundred paintings and drawings. These, and the many others based on them, were the first to show the mountain men, the first to depict the wild rendezvous of the trappers, and, more generally, among the first to show Americans the soaring Rocky Mountains—in short, historically nonpareil in their priceless scope.

And what wonders the fluid wrist and fingers worked with paint. The vital result reminds the Goetzmanns of the haunting mistiness of Turner's canvases married to the swirling figures of Delacroix (*The West of the Imagination* 59). That may be putting too lavish a point on work whose genius needs no comparison. Art historian Ron Tyler observes that, in contrast to Catlin and others, with Miller "there was no sense of driving personal quest or national mission." Rather, avoiding such clamor, Miller's work comes from that rich, placid center of an artist, humility at its creative best, "meant to serve personal enjoyment" (*Alfred Jacob Miller* 5). Supporting this view are Miller's own notes on his paintings, made long after the events of their subjects. Forming charming vignettes of the wild life, they stand easily on their own, as if the artist were savoring in another way, in the quite different medium of prose, what had so delighted his painter's eye.

Further Reading

Goetzmann, William H., and William N. Goetzmann. *The West of the Imagination*. New York: W. W. Norton, 1986.

Miller, Alfred Jacob. *The West of Alfred Jacob Miller: From the Notes and Water Colors in The Walters Art Gallery*. Marvin C. Ross, ed. 1951. Rev. ed. Norman: University of Oklahoma Press, 1968.

Tyler, Ron, ed. *Alfred Jacob Miller: Artist on the Oregon Trail*. Fort Worth: Amon Carter Museum, 1982.

Warner, Robert Combs. *The Fort Laramie of Alfred Jacob Miller: A Catalogue of All the Known Illustrations of the First Fort Laramie.* University of Wyoming Publications 43.2. Laramie: University of Wyoming, 1979.

Alfred Jacob Miller

∼

From *The West of Alfred Jacob Miller,* pages xvi-xviii

First Meeting with Captain Stewart

One day while busily engaged on a picture in my room on Chartres St. New Orleans. A gentleman walked in & after nodding to me,—commenced examining the pictures on the walls,—consisting of Portraits and Landscapes, framed & otherwise.—At first glance he seemed to me to be a Kentuckian,—he had on a grey suit with a black stripe worked on the seam of his pantaloons, & held himself as straight as an arrow,—to be sure there was no Bowie knife peeping out at the top of his vest,—this formed very fashionable jewelry at that time on the lower border of the Mississippi;—he had a military air.

Giving no farther attention to my visitor, I proceeded on with my work at the easel:—after a certain time he came where I stood & pointing to a view of the City of Baltimore said—"I like the management of that picture & the View"—he then left the room. (It is as well to digress here a moment to explain the treatment of this picture—it may be constructive to some young artist should he happen to read;—the size of the picture was about 5 ft by 3 1/2 ft, & the original sketch was drawn from what was then called Laudenslager's hill, on the eastern confines of the City of Balto.—at about 5 o'clock, the sun would be (as it were) behind the city, throwing a mysterious haze over every object, & producing a truly charming effect,—Now—the thing for me to do was to reach this glorious & brilliant appearance; after getting in the sky, I then commenced the detail of buildings—Churches, Exchange, Town Clock, Monument, Cathedral etc—these "I kept down" to use a professional phrase, and approached the tint as nearly as I could,—but I found after finishing my foreground that a great heaviness hung over the City, with too much detail in the buildings, considering that they were two miles distant,—in going out on the hill several times;—I saw that there was no detail, that a general mist rested

31

over everything & gave the imagination full swing,—Now I read of "dry scrumbling,"—but had never tried it practically, there was the subject to try it on—so mixing on my palette portions of white, blue, vermillion & black until I had attained what I conceived might be the colour,—I then took a large brush & with this mixture covered thinly all the buildings in the distance,—the effect was like magic,—it destroyed the detail,— massed all of a general tint, & made it appear as if you were looking through a hazy atmosphere,—no amount of labor with solid colour could have produced it.

This mistiness was pleasing to the observer because it leaves his imagination full play. . . .

Turner was lavish in his misty effects—& no doubt he produced them as here described but was reticent & would tell nobody how his marvelous mists were effected.)

But to resume,—the gentleman mentioned previous, in a few days after, called again—This time he was more sociable,—took a chair & after a little conversation handed me a "card" on which was engraved "Capt. W. D. Stewart British Army"—he then told me "that he was making preparations for another journey to the Rocky Mountains,—(he had already made 2 or 3) and wished to have a competent artist,—to sketch the remarkable scenery & incidents of the journey,—now (he said) as I am very well satisfied with your work I should like you to accompany me,— take a little time to think over it, & you can also call on the British Consul here, Mr. Crawford,—he will give you any information that you may require as regards myself—also consult your friends"—I called on Mr. Crawford & he gave me to understand that Capt. Stewart was next heir to the vast estate of Murthly in Scotland,—that he made these journeys for his pleasure & instruction, & advised me by all means to accept his kind offer,—which I eventually did.

He had Antoine with him—a famous Western hunter & on visiting Capt. S. at his residence sometimes of an evening—have seen him play cards with Antoine in order to amuse that wild child of the Prairie who was like a fish out of water in N. Orleans—I learned afterwards that he was instrumental in saving Capt. S.'s life on one or two occasions in the mountains.

From Robert Combs Warner,
The Fort Laramie of Alfred Jacob Miller

A Letter to a Baltimore Friend
St. Louis Ap 23rd 1837
Brantz Mayer Esq
Dear Sir.—

. . . I have much gratification in informing you, that I am at present under engagement to proceed with Capt W. Stewart, (an affluent gentleman,) on an expedition to the Rocky Mountains, (professionally) the tour to occupy six months,—and I speak candidly & truthistically when I say, that I wish you were with us—it's a new and wider field both for the poet & painter—for if you can weave such beautiful garlands with the simplest flowers of Nature—what a subject her wild sons of the West present, intermixed with their legendary history.—Washington Irving has done nothing of moment thus far,—one would think at first sight from want of Material—but Catlin's (the painter's) letters, prove the contrary—by the way (to make a small digression) I'm told his pictures are as especially bad, as his letters are admirable,—I've not seen them.

What a thriving little place St Louis is:—and then a man has only to buy a lot—descend into his cellar—and gives it a "blowing up"—and "presto"—his house is as good as "being built." Now that's what I call fertility of soil; for to let you into a secret, a person who buys a lot is furnished with as much stone on the ground as will build his house.—What liberality?—but the hotels are abominable,—at the "City" which is considered to be the best, imagine a rush of two hundred persons who have been waiting for 1/2 an hour at the entrance of a small door,—the servants wisely locking the entrances an hour previous—and too!—to the unlucky wight who either stumps his toe, or loses his reckoning—he is either thrown on Scylla or Charybdis, with an addition of a punch in the ribs, as "in duty bound," and the victorious Army march over him;—after getting through & securing a seat—such a man instinctively examines his coat—there happy is he to find that it has clung to him through his pressing difficulties—he then gives a long breath in order to find that his "pipes" are all clear, he congratulates himself, or if of a serious disposition, a short prayer is the consequence;—scratches and bruises are not taken into consideration;—the worthy man considers that now he is to enjoy the fruits of his labors;—fatal mistake.

—The soup is brought to him, and he becomes Shakespearean—with hands uplifted towards the waiter he pronounces with a trembling voice "more in sorrow than in anger,"—"Angels and ministers of grease,— defend us"—at this time a universally clatter & din fills the room,— mouths are open & eyes goggling,—he seizes a servant (stalking is out of the question) & demands Beef, Roast Beef,—the waiter in order to be very accommodating this time—brings him six pounds on his plate; (neither more nor less)—looking on wistfully, he utters a sniffled groan and inwardly wishes that "this too solid flesh would melt,—thaw & resolve itself;" & that "t'were done,"—a chicken follows out, and in trying to dis-locate its shoulder, he has nearly broken his wrist—throwing down his knife, he utters in voice of dispair "O sides, you are too tough" and rush-es out of the room!

—reports saith that "bodies" are seen floating on the Mississippi in the afternoon—but whether of the animal or vegetable trunk—it's thought not prudent to investigate.

I expect to depart from St. Louis on Tuesday next 25 inst and join Capt S above fort Independence,—I am told by the gentleman who trans-acts his business, that the fitting out this year has Cost him above $20,000.—

I shall be happy to show you my sketches when I return, and tender you my warmest wishes for your health and prosperity, in the interval—If you find my communication tedious,—there is one consolation—it is this—I cannot trouble you again for the next six months.—

I remain truly Yr obliged frnd

Alfred J. Miller

Comps to Your brother

From *The West of Alfred Jacob Miller,*
pages 11, 69, 141, 163, 188, 192

A Young Woman of the Flat Head Tribe

This young girl was quite a belle. A young gentleman, Mr. P., of hand-some face and figure, who journeyed with us, was quite enamoured of her;

he exerted himself with all his persuasive powers and insinuative address to render himself agreeable. She would have none of him; of course, this only gave our hero more ardor. What! with such a charming moustache and such eyes, that had caused such mischief in his native City, to be rejected and slighted by a poor Indian girl. Zounds! it was not to be thought of;—he renewed his visits, but all to no purpose, each interview was more discouraging than the former, he became crest-fallen and melancholy. We tried to console him with some lines written 200 years ago, and offered them as a specific.

> Quit, Quit, for shame; this will not move
> This cannot take her
> If of herself she will not love
> Nothing will make her;—
> The devil take her!

Now ordinarily, he was fond of both poetry and music, witness ye artless trappers for whose delectation we used to sing at the camp fire (P——— taking second), "I know a bank whereon the wild thyme grows," but the scene had changed. Instead of thanking us, P——— gave us a hearty cursing all round, himself included. Seeing our good offices so ill received, we left him to "Chew the cud of sweet and bitter fancy." A short time gave us a clew to the mystery,—a stalwart trapper with brawn like an ox had been beforehand with our poor friend P.——— and he (the trapper) soon carried her off with him on a beaver expedition;—as soon as the cause was removed, the effect ceased, and our friend recovered his usual serenity.

Rock of Independence

On approaching this famous land-mark, when within 10 miles of it, we were struck with its resemblance to a huge tortoise sprawling on the prairie;—this appearance lessening in proportion as we came nearer. We found it composed of granite or coarse porphyry, from 5 to 600 ft. in height, and in a prominent part were inscribed the names of the pioneers of the Rocky Mountains, among others the names of Sublette, Wyeth, Campbell, Bonneville, Pitcher, &c., many carved deep into the stone. The temptation was too strong not to add our own;—to make amends for this assumption, and show our zeal for others, we found a man by the cognomen of Nelson had carved his name, and to insure him immortality we added to it, "Of the Nile!" "Odds chisels and hammers" (as Bob Acres would say), what a pity it is he will never know his benefactors.

When we first came in view of the Rock, Buffalo were feeding under its shadow, and the swift-footed Antelope bounding along so fleetly and so phantom like that we almost imagined them to embody the spirit of departed Indians, again visiting their beautiful hunting grounds and scenes of former exploits.

The Lost "Green-Horn"

On reaching the Buffalo District, one of our young men began to be ambitious, and although it was his first journey, boasted continually of what he would do in hunting Buffalo if permitted. This was John (our cook), he was an Englishman and did no discredit to that illustrious nation in his stupid conceit and wrong-headed obstinacy. Our Captain, when any one boasted, put them to the test, so a day was given to John and he started off early alone. The day passed over, night came,—but so did not John. Another day rolled over, the hunters returning at evening without having met him. The next morning men were dispatched in different quarters, and at about two o'clock, one of the parties brought in the wanderer—crest fallen and nearly starved;—he was met by a storm of ridicule and roasted on every side by the Trappers. Thus carrying out that ugly maxim of Rochefoucault's "There is always something in the misfortune of our friends not disagreeable to us."

Afterwards he described to us his adventures. In about an hour's ride from the camp, he encountered a large herd of Buffalo, but found his trepidation and excitement so great that although in running them he approached near enough, he could not shoot one;—in the meantime, they had led him off so far that he had lost his reckoning, and wandered about until night, completely bewildered;—he laid down on the prairie hungry and exhausted, and tried to sleep. As he began to doze, he was awakened by a great noise, raising his head he found a large herd of Buffalo making directly towards him: by his shouting and action they swerved, and passed him without injury. The next morning he was fortunate enough to find some wild plums and berries, and on these he had subsisted until our hunters discovered him.

John gave no further trouble after this, but attended to his duty as cook with becoming resignation.

Free Trappers in Trouble

The sketch illustrates an incident of two mountain Trappers, found near Independence Rock, in a starving condition. Our Caravan's reaching them, it was discovered that their ammunition was completely exhausted,—but on that morning one of them had succeeded in killing two rattle snakes, which were in the process of cooking on the fire. Our Captain's question to them was, "Good God! how can you eat such disgusting food?" One of them answered "This child doe'st savez what disgustin' is"—Wagh! in consideration of their weak state, a soup was first prepared for them, which they ate with a will. This was followed by some bottled porter—and then came the substantials in the shape of humpribs &c.

On parting with them, our Captain presented each with a horse, a supply of powder and shot, & a blanket, sending them on their way rejoicing, and with an equipment better than ever.

Indian Women

The foreground of this sketch presents some Indian women in repose;—they have dismounted from their horses near a stream, where the Caravan will halt for a "nooning."

Much cannot be said in favor of the manner in which the female part of the community are treated by the Indians,—they are mere "hewers of wood and drawers of water."—the North American savage entertaining, we fear, a kindred opinion with the Turks, id est—that they have no souls. When the grande Seigneur arrives,—they set up his lodge, spread his robes, unladen the horses & mules, make his fire, and prepare his meat.

One might suppose that this would entitle them to some little acknowledgement,—but if they receive a grunt of acquiescence it is more than is always accorded. This trait does not solely belong to our Indians,—it may be observed in all barbarous countries, and civilization here presents a glorious and shining contrast. Indeed the rise and progress of the latter may be graduated by the estimation in which women are held, and her appreciation as a companion and faithful friend of man, even when all others discard him.

The Scalp-Lock

There was a laughing devil in his sneer,
That raised emotions both of rage and fear;
And where his frown of hatred darkly fell,
Hope withering fled,—and Mercy sighed farewell.

To a people who delight in war, and who are instructed from youth in its principles, and practice, it is almost useless to preach the blessings of peace. If you attempt to explain the benefits that may accrue to them from the observance of the latter, they have a ready answer: "If we make peace how shall we employ our young men?" They point out to you their scalps and arms, and ask—"Shall we throw these away, and become women?"

If a relative or member of their tribe is killed, they will listen to neither palliation or justification, but pursue relentlessly any member of the offender's company, to have their revenge. This perhaps forms one of their worst traits, and cannot be defended, yet it is characteristic of the whole of them.

In the sketch, an Indian has secured the scalp-lock of his enemy, and is making good his escape,—for this honor awaits him in his camp, and it often presents a strong claim for the post of a chief or brave.

John James Audubon's *Buffalo* (University of Arizona Special Collections, Tucson).

~

John James Audubon (1785-1851)

In June 1826, John James Audubon set out on the riskiest journey of his life. This excursion took him not to the wilds of the American frontier, but to the drawing rooms of upper-class Britain where he hoped to bag subscribers for his proposed book of bird paintings. At the time a complete unknown, and so poor that his devoted wife, Lucy, had to stay behind and work as a governess to support their young family, Audubon was taking a huge gamble in going abroad. Fortunately for him it paid off. Audubon not only captivated the British with his wildlife paintings, he also charmed them by playing the part of the rugged and simple frontiersman, donning a fringed leather shirt and allowing his long hair to flow to his shoulders. In one wealthy Liverpool home, Audubon writes:

> I was asked to imitate the Wild Turkey call, I did, to the surprise of all the circle. Hooted like a Barred Owl, and cooed like the doves. . . .
> [T]hey all seem very much surprised that I have no wonderful tale to relate; that, for instance, I, so much in the woods, have not been devoured at least six times by tigers, bears, wolves, foxes, or—a rat. . . . (*Audubon Reader* 201)

If Audubon did in fact refrain from telling wonderful tales to his hosts, it would have been out of character for a man who invented so many tales about himself. Born Jean Rabine in Sainte-Domingue (later Haiti) in 1785, Audubon would hide the fact that he was the illegitimate son of a French naval officer and a Creole woman. Raised in France and sporadically schooled, he dodged the Napoleonic draft by emigrating to Pennsylvania in 1803. Once in America, young Rabine took the name John James Audubon, married English-born Lucy Bakewell, failed repeatedly in business, and tirelessly drew and painted birds. Frustration over the failure to secure an American publisher for his bird paintings drove Audubon to Britain in 1826. Nonetheless he returned to his adopted homeland in 1829—a homecoming made no doubt sweeter by the celebrity the artist had earned abroad as well as by the fact that his successful *Birds of America* (1827-1838) was in production.

Audubon continued to paint and make collecting trips after his return to the United States. He also began to write for publication. In 1831 Audubon published the first volume of *Ornithological Biography* (1831-1839), the accompanying text for *Birds of America*. Besides chapters about birds, *Ornithological Biography* includes fanciful narratives of the author's adventures and travels. The year 1831 also saw Audubon writing to Lucy of his strong desire to see the American West.

It would be 1843 before Audubon made his western visit. By that time he was the best-known man of science in North America and, as such, was able to make the journey in considerable style. Instead of traveling the wilds as a solitary wanderer, he was accompanied by a team of assistants that included Edward Harris, a close friend and amateur ornithologist; John G. Bell, a hunter and specimen preparer; Lewis Squires, who served as Audubon's secretary; and Isaac Sprague, an adventurous young man of Audubon's acquaintance. Audubon's pockets were filled not with the hardtack and hand-molded bullets of the frontiersman, but with letters of introduction from President John Tyler, half of Tyler's cabinet, and General Winfield Scott. Instead of scrambling for a publisher when the western trip ended in September 1843, Audubon had the luxury of returning to Minnie's Land, his Manhattan estate where he could devote himself entirely to work on a book about North American quadrupeds. Once home, however, Audubon's health slowly began to deteriorate. His sons John and Victor eventually took over the work on *Viviparous Quadrupeds of North America* (1852-1854), with most of the text being written by John Bachman. Audubon died in January 1851.

As an artist, Audubon achieved realism by working from specimens, many of which he collected himself. Yet critics point out that Audubon would often heighten a painting's artistic impact by posing his specimens in unrealistic positions. The same criticism may be leveled at much of Audubon's published writing. In his popular *Ornithological Biography* (a book that influenced Charles Darwin and Henry David Thoreau, among others), Audubon based his writings on observed experience but was not above repositioning the facts if they stood in the way of a good story, as evidenced by such passages as his improbable account of a meeting with legendary frontiersman Daniel Boone. Audubon's diaries, on the other hand, bring readers closer to the genuine thoughts and experiences of the artist (this despite the fact that Audubon's granddaughter heavily edited and bowdlerized the diaries prior to their publication in 1897). The selection included here is from the diary Audubon kept during his time on the Upper Missouri. These diary passages show us much: A nineteenth-century scientist and artist engaged in intense field work. A possibly envious artist belittling the work of his predecessor, George Catlin. A careful observer recording his impressions of western lands and people. A naturalist concerned about the fate of vanishing wild creatures. And, not least, a mature man enjoying one last romp on the frontier before it, and he, vanished from the face of the earth.

In the text that follows, Alexander Culbertson, James Kipp, and Etienne Provost were all agents of the American Fur Company. Mrs. Culbertson refers to Natawista Ikasana, a Blood Indian woman whom Alexander Culbertson married in 1840 (when she was approximately fifteen years old).

Further Reading

Audubon, John James. *Audubon And His Journals.* Maria R. Audubon, ed. 2 vols. New York: Scribner's, 1897.

_____. *Audubon Reader: The Best Writings of John James Audubon.* Scott Russell Sanders, ed. Bloomington: University of Indiana Press, 1986.

_____. *Delineations of American Scenery and Character.* New York: G. A. Baker, 1926.

_____. *Ornithological Biography, or An Account of the Habits of the Birds of the United States of America.* 5 vols. Philadelphia: J. Dobson, 1831 (vol. 1); Boston: Hilliard, Gray & Co. (vol. 2); Edinburgh: A. & C. Black, 1835-1839 (vols. 3-5).

Audubon, John James, and John Bachman. *Viviparous Quadrupeds of North America.* 5 vols. New York: V. G. Audubon, 1852-1854.

Branch, Michael. "Indexing American Possibilities: The Natural History Writing of Bartram, Wilson, and Audubon." *The Ecocriticism Reader: Landmarks in Literary Ecology.* Cheryll Glotfelty and Harold Fromm, eds. Athens: University of Georgia Press, 1996. 282-302.

McDermott, John Francis, ed. *Audubon in the West.* Norman: University of Oklahoma Press, 1965.

~

From *Audubon and His Journals*

June 7, Wednesday. We had a vile night of rain and wind from the northeast, which is still going on, and likely to continue the whole of this blessed day. Yesterday, when we had a white frost, ice was found in the kettles of Mr. Kipp's barges. We reached Fort Clark [on the Missouri River] and the Mandan Villages at half-past seven this morning. Great guns were fired from the fort and from the "Omega," as our captain took the guns from the "Trapper" at Fort Pierre. The site of this fort appears a good one, though it is placed considerably below the Mandan Village. We saw some small spots cultivated, where corn, pumpkins, and beans are grown. The fort and village are situated on the high bank, rising somewhat to the elevation of a hill. The Mandan mud huts are very far from looking poetical, although Mr. Catlin has tried to render them so by placing them in regular rows, and all of the same size and form, which is by no means the case. But different travellers have different eyes! We saw more Indians than at any previous time since leaving St. Louis; and it is possible that there are a hundred huts, made of mud, all looking like so many potato winter-houses in the Eastern States. As soon as we were near the shore, every article that could conveniently be carried off was placed under lock and key, and our division door was made fast, as well as those of our own rooms. Even the axes and poles were put by. Our captain told us that last year they stole his cap and his shot-pouch and horn, and that it was through the interference of the first chief that he recovered his cap and horn; but that a squaw had his leather belt, and would not give it up. The appearance of these poor, miserable devils, as we approached the shore, was wretched enough. There they stood in the pelting rain and keen wind, covered with Buffalo robes, red blankets, and the like, some partially and most curiously besmeared with mud; and as they came on board, and we shook hands with each of them, I felt a clamminess that rendered the ceremony most repulsive. Their legs and naked feet were covered with mud. They looked at me with apparent curiosity, perhaps on account of my beard, which produced the same effect at Fort Pierre. They all looked very poor; and our captain says they are the *ne plus ultra* of thieves. It is said there are nearly three thousand men, women, and children that, during winter, cram themselves into these miserable hovels. Harris and I walked to the fort about nine o'clock. The walking was rascally, passing through mud and water the whole way. The yard of the fort itself was as bad. We entered Mr. Chardon's own room, crawled up a crazy ladder, and in a low garret I had the great pleasure of seeing alive the Swift or Kit Fox which he has given to me. It ran swiftly from one corner to another, and, when approached, growled somewhat in the manner of a common Fox. Mr. Chardon told me that good care would be taken of it until our return, that it would be chained to render it more gentle, and that I would find it an easy matter to take it along. I sincerely hope so. Seeing a remarkably fine skin of a large Cross Fox which I wished to buy, it was handed over to me. After this, Mr. Chardon asked one of the Indians to take us into the village, and particularly to show us the "Medicine Lodge." We followed our guide through mud and mire, even into the Lodge. We found this to be, in general terms, like all the other lodges, only larger, measuring twenty-three yards in diameter, with a large squarish aperture in the centre of the roof, some six or seven feet long by about four wide. We had entered this curiosity shop by pushing aside a wet Elk skin stretched on four sticks. Looking around, I saw a number of calabashes, eight or ten Otter skulls, two very large Buffalo skulls with the horns on, evidently of great age, and some sticks and other magical implements with which none but a "Great Medicine Man" is acquainted. During my survey there sat, crouched down on his haunches, an Indian wrapped in a dirty blanket, with only his filthy head peeping out. Our guide spoke to him; but he stirred not. Again, at the foot of one of the posts that support the central portion of this great room, lay a parcel that I took for a bundle of Buffalo robes; but it moved presently, and from beneath it half arose the emaciated body of a poor blind Indian, whose skin was quite shrivelled; and our guide made us signs that he was about to die. We all shook both hands with him; and he pressed our hands closely and with evident satisfaction. He had his pipe and tobacco pouch by him, and soon lay down again. We left this abode of mysteries, as I was anxious to see the interior of one of the common huts around; and again our guide led us through mud and mire to his own lodge, which we entered in the same way as we had done the other. All these lodges have a sort of portico that leads to the door, and on the tops of most of them I observed Buffalo skulls. This lodge contained the whole family of our guide—several women and children, and another man, perhaps a son-in-law or a brother. All these, except the man, were on the outer edge of the lodge, crouching on the ground, some suckling children;

John
James
Audubon

and at nearly equal distances apart were placed berths, raised about two feet above the ground, made of leather, and with square apertures for the sleepers or occupants to enter. The man of whom I have spoken was lying down in one of these, which was all open in front. I walked up to him, and, after disturbing his happy slumbers, shook hands with him; he made signs for me to sit down; and after Harris and I had done so, he rose, squatted himself near us, and, getting out a large spoon made of boiled Buffalo horn, handed it to a young girl, who brought a great rounded wooden bowl filled with pemmican, mixed with corn and some other stuff. I ate a mouthful or so of it, and found it quite palatable; and Harris and the rest then ate of it also. Bell was absent; we had seen nothing of him since we left the boat. This lodge, as well as the other, was dirty with water and mud; but I am told that in dry weather they are kept cleaner, and much cleaning do they need, most truly. A round, shallow hole was dug in the centre for the fire; and from the roof descended over this a chain, by the aid of which they do their cooking, the utensil being attached to the chain when wanted. As we returned towards the fort, I gave our guide a piece of tobacco, and he appeared well pleased. He followed us on board, and as he peeped in my room, and saw the dried and stuffed specimens we have, he evinced a slight degree of curiosity. Our captain, Mr. Chardon, and our men have been busily engaged in putting ashore that portion of the cargo designed for this fort, which in general appearance might be called a poor miniature representation of Fort Pierre. The whole country around was over-grown with "Lamb's quarters" *(Chenopòdium album),* which I have no doubt, if boiled, would take the place of spinach in this wild and, to my eyes, miserable country, the poetry of which lies in the imagination of those writers who have described the "velvety prairies" and "enchanted castles" (of mud), so common where we now are. We observed a considerable difference in the color of these Indians, who, by the way, are almost all Riccarees; many appeared, and in fact are, redder than others; they are lank, rather tall, and very alert, but, as I have said before, all look poor and dirty. After dinner we went up the muddy bank again to look at the corn-fields, as the small patches that are meanly cultivated are called. We found poor, sickly looking corn about two inches high, that had been represented to us this morning as full six inches high. We followed the prairie, a very extensive one, to the hills, and there found a deep ravine, sufficiently impregnated with saline matter to answer the purpose of salt water for the Indians to boil their corn and pemmican, clear and clean; but they, as well as the whites at the fort, resort to the muddy Missouri for their drinking water, the only fresh water at hand. Not a drop of spirituous liquor has been brought to this place for the last two years; and there can be no doubt that on this account the Indians have become more peaceable than heretofore, though now and then a white man is murdered, and many horses are stolen. As we walked over the plain, we saw heaps of earth thrown up to cover the poor Mandans who died of the small-pox. These mounds in many instances appear to contain the remains of several bodies and, perched on the top, lies, pretty generally, the rotting skull of a Buffalo. Indeed, the skulls of the Buffaloes seem as if a kind of relation to these most absurdly superstitious and ignorant beings. I could not hear a word of the young Grizzly Bear of which Mr. Chardon had spoken to me. He gave me his Buffalo head-dress and other trifles—as he was pleased to call all of which will prove more or less interesting and curious to you when they reach Minniesland. He presented Squires with a good hunting shirt and a few other things, and to all of us, presented moccasins. We collected a few round cacti; and I saw several birds that looked much the worse for the cold and wet weather we have had these last few days. Our boat has been thronged with Indians ever since we have tied to the shore; and it is with considerable difficulty and care that we can stop them from intruding into our rooms when we are there. We found many portions of skulls lying on the ground which, perhaps, did at one period form the circles of them spoke of by Catlin. All around the village is filthy beyond description. Our captain tells us that no matter what weather we may have to-morrow, he will start at daylight, even if he can only go across the river, to get rid of these wolfish-looking vagabonds of Indians. I sincerely hope that we may have a fair day and a long run, so that the air around us may once more be pure and fresh from the hand of Nature. After the Riccarees had taken possession of this Mandan Village, the remains of that once powerful tribe removed about three miles up the river, and there have now fifteen or twenty huts, containing of course, only that number of families. During the worst periods of the epidemic which swept over this village with such fury, many became maniacs, rushed to the Missouri, leaped into its turbid waters, and were seen no more. Mr. Primeau, wife, and children, as well as another half-breed, have gone to the fort, and are to remain there till further orders. The fort is in a poor condition, roofs leaking etc. Whilst at the fort this afternoon, I was surprised to see a tall, athletic Indian thrashing the dirty rascals about Mr. Chardon's door most severely; but I

John
James
Audubon

47

found on inquiry that he was called "the soldier," and that he had authority to do so whenever the Indians intruded or congregated in the manner
this *canaille* had done. After a while the same tall fellow came on board
with his long stick, and immediately began belaboring the fellows on the
lower guards; the latter ran off over the planks, and scrambled up the
muddy banks as if so many affrighted Buffaloes. Since then we have been
comparatively quiet; but I hope they will all go off, as the captain is going
to put the boat from the shore, to the full length of our spars. The wind
has shifted to the northward, and the atmosphere has been so chilled that
a House Swallow was caught, benumbed with cold, and brought to me by
our captain. Harris, Bell, and I saw a Cliff Swallow take refuge on board;
but this was not caught. We have seen Say's Flycatcher, the Ground Finch,
Cow Buntings, and a few other birds. One of the agents arrived this afternoon from the Gros Ventre, or Minnetaree Village, about twelve miles
above us. He is represented as a remarkably brave man, and he relates
some strange adventures of his prowess. Several *great warriors* have con-
descended to shake me by the hand; their very touch is disgusting—it will
indeed be a deliverance to get rid of all this "Indian poetry." We are, nevertheless, to take a few to the Yellowstone. Alexis has his wife, who is, in
fact, a good-looking young woman; an old patroon, Provost, takes one of
his daughters along; and we have, besides, several red-skinned single gentlemen. We were assured that the northern parts of the hills, that form a
complete curtain to the vast prairie on which we have walked this afternoon, are still adorned with patches of snow that fell there during last
winter. It is now nine o'clock, but before I go to rest I cannot resist giving
you a description of the curious exhibition that we have had on board,
from a numerous lot of Indians of the first class, say some forty or fifty.
They ranged themselves along the sides of the large cabin, squatting on
the floor. Coffee had been prepared for the whole party, and hard sea-bis-
cuit likewise. The coffee was first given to each of them, and afterwards the
biscuits, and I had the honor of handing the latter to the row on one side
of the boat; a box of tobacco was opened and laid on the table. The man
who came from the Gros Ventres this afternoon proved to be an excellent
interpreter; and after the captain had delivered his speech to him, he spoke
loudly to the group, and explained the purport of the captain's speech.
They grunted their approbation frequently, and were, no doubt, pleased.
Two individuals (Indians) made their appearance highly decorated, with
epaulets on the shoulders, red clay on blue uniforms, three cocks' plumes

in their head-dress, rich moccasins, leggings, etc. These are men who, though in the employ of the Opposition company, act truly as friends; but who, meantime, being called "Braves," never grunted, bowed, or shook hands with any of us. Supper over and the tobacco distributed, the whole body arose simultaneously, and each and every one of these dirty wretches we had all to shake by the hand. The two braves sat still until all the rest had gone ashore, and then retired as majestically as they had entered, not even shaking hands with our good-humored captain. I am told that this performance takes place once every year, on the passing of the Company's boats. I need not say that the coffee and the two biscuits apiece were gobbled down in less than no time. The tobacco, which averaged about two pounds to each man, was hid in their robes or blankets for future use. Two of the Indians, who must have been of the highest order, and who distributed the "rank weed," were nearly naked; one had on only a breech-clout and one legging, the other was in no better case. They are now all ashore except one or more who are going with us to the Yellowstone; and I will now go to my rest. Though I have said "Goodnight," I have arisen almost immediately, and I must write on, for we have other scenes going on both among the trappers below and some of the people above. Many Indians, squaws as well as men, are bartering and trading, and keep up such a babble that Harris and I find sleep impossible; needless to say, the squaws who are on board are of the lowest grade of morality. . . .

July 17, Monday. A beautiful day, with a west wind. Sprague, who is very industrious at all times, drew some flowers, and I have been busy both writing and drawing.

In the afternoon Bell went after Rabbits, but saw one only, which he could not get, and Sprague walked to the hills about two miles off, but could not see any portion of the Yellowstone River, which Mr. Catlin has given in his view, as if he had been in a balloon some thousands of feet above the earth. Two men arrived last evening by land from Fort Pierre, and brought a letter, but no news of any importance; one is a cook as well as a hunter, the other named Wolff, a German, and a tinsmith by trade, though now a trapper.

July 18, Tuesday. When I went to bed last night the mosquitoes were so numerous downstairs that I took my bed under my arm and went to a room above, where I slept well. On going down this morning, I found two other persons from Fort Pierre, and Mr. Culbertson very busy reading and writing letters. Immediately after breakfast young McKenzie and another man were despatched on mules, with a letter for Mr. Kipp, and Owen expects to overtake the boat in three or four days. An Indian arrived with a stolen squaw, both Assiniboins; and I am told such things are of frequent occurrence among these sons of nature. Mr. Culbertson proposed that we should take a ride to see the mowers, and Harris and I joined him. We found the men at work, among them one called Bernard Adams, of Charleston, S. C., who knew the Bachmans quite well, and who had read the whole of the "Biographies of Birds." Leaving the men, we entered a ravine in search of plants, etc., and having started an Owl, which I took for the barred one, I left my horse and went in search of it, but could not see it, and hearing a new note soon saw a bird not to be mistaken, and killed it, when it proved, as I expected, to be the Rock Wren; then I shot another sitting by the mouth of a hole. The bird did not fly off; Mr. Culbertson watched it closely, but when the hole was demolished no bird was to be found. Harris saw a Shrike, but of what species he could not tell, and he also found some Rock Wrens in another ravine. We returned to the fort and promised to visit the place this afternoon, which we have done, and procured three more Wrens, and killed the Owl, which proves to be precisely the resemblance of the Northern specimen of the Great Horned Owl, which we published under another name. The Rock Wren, which might as well be called the Ground Wren, builds its nest in holes, and now the young are well able to fly, and we procured one in the act. In two instances we saw these birds enter a hole here, and an investigation showed a passage or communication, and on my pointing out a hole to Bell where one had entered, he pushed his arm in and touched the little fellow, but it escaped by running up his arm and away it flew. Black clouds now arose in the west, and we moved homewards. Harris and Bell went to the mowers to get a drink of water, and we reached home without getting wet, though it rained violently for some time, and the weather is much cooler.

July 20, Thursday. We were up early, and had our breakfast shortly after four o'clock, and before eight had left the landing of the fort, and were fairly under way for the prairies. Our equipment was much the same as before, except that we had two carts this time. Mr. C. drove Harris, Bell, and myself, and the others rode on the carts and led the hunting horses, or runners, as they are called here. I observed a Rabbit running across the road, and saw some flowers different from any I had ever seen. After we had crossed a bottom prairie, we ascended between the high and rough ravines until we were on the rolling grounds of the plains. The fort showed well from this point, and we also saw a good number of Antelopes, and some young ones. These small things run even faster than the old ones. As we neared the Fox River some one espied four Buffaloes, and Mr. C., taking the telescope, showed them to me, lying on the ground. Our heads and carts were soon turned towards them, and we travelled within half a mile of them, concealed by a ridge or hill which separated them from us. The wind was favorable, and we moved on slowly round the hill, the hunters being now mounted. Harris and Bell had their hats on, but Owen and Mr. Culbertson had their heads bound with handkerchiefs. With the rest of the party I crawled on the ridge, and saw the bulls running away, but in a direction favorable for us to see the chase. On the word of command the horses were let loose, and away went the hunters, who soon were seen to gain on the game; two bulls ran together and Mr. C. and Bell followed after them, and presently one after another of the hunters followed them. Mr. C. shot first, and his bull stopped at the fire, walked towards where I was, and halted about sixty yards from me. His nose was within a few inches of the ground; the blood poured from his mouth, nose, and side, his tail hung down, but his legs looked as firm as ever, but in less than two minutes the poor beast fell on his side, and lay quite dead. Bell and Mr. Culbertson went after the second. Harris took the third, and Squires the fourth. Bell's shot took effect in the buttock, and Mr. Culbertson shot, placing his ball a few inches above or below Bell's; after this Mr. Culbertson ran no more. At this moment Squires's horse threw him over his head, fully ten feet; he fell on his powder-horn and was severely bruised; he cried to Harris to catch his horse, and was on his legs at once, but felt sick for a few minutes. Harris, who was as cool as a cucumber, neared his bull, shot it through the lungs, and it fell dead on the spot. Bell was now seen in full pursuit of his game, and Harris joined Squires, and followed the fourth, which, however, was soon out of my sight. I saw Bell shooting two or three times, and I heard the firing of Squires and perhaps Harris, but the weather was hot, and being afraid of injuring their horses, they let the fourth bull make his escape. Bell's bull fell on his knees, got up again, and rushed on Bell, and was shot again. The animal stood a minute with his tail partially elevated, and then fell dead; through some mishap Bell had no knife with him, so did not bring the tongue, as is customary. Mr. Culbertson walked towards the first bull and I joined him. It was a fine animal about seven years old; Harris's and Bell's

*John
James
Audubon*

51

were younger. The first was fat, and was soon skinned and cut up for meat. Mr. Culbertson insisted on calling it my bull, so I cut off the brush of the tail and placed it in my hat-band. We then walked towards Harris, who was seated on his bull, and the same ceremony took place, and while they were cutting the animal up for meat, Bell, who said he thought his bull was about three quarters of a mile distant, went off with me to see it; we walked at least a mile and a half, and at last came to it. It was a poor one, and the tongue and tail were all we took away, and we rejoined the party, who had already started the cart with Mr. Pike, who was told to fall to the rear, and reach the fort before sundown; this he could do readily, as we were not more than six miles distant. Mr. Culbertson broke open the head of "my" bull, and ate part of the brains raw, and yet warm, and so did many of the others, even Squires. The very sight of this turned my stomach, but I am told that were I to hunt Buffalo one year, I should like it "even better than dog meat." Mr. Pike did not reach the fort till the next morning about ten, I will say *en passant*. We continued our route, passing over the same road on which we had come, and about midway between the Missouri and Yellowstone Rivers. We saw more Antelopes, but not one Wolf; these rascals are never abundant where game is scarce, but where game is, there too are the Wolves. When we had travelled about ten miles further we saw seven Buffaloes grazing on a hill, but as the sun was about one hour high, we drove to one side of the road where there was a pond of water, and there stopped for the night; while the hunters were soon mounted, and with Squires they went off, leaving the men to arrange the camp. I crossed the pond, and having ascended the opposite bank, saw the bulls grazing as leisurely as usual. The hunters near them, they started down the hill, and the chase immediately began. One broke from the rest and was followed by Mr. C. who shot it, and then abandoned the hunt, his horse being much fatigued. I now counted ten shots, but all was out of my sight, and I seated myself near a Fox hole, longing for him. The hunters returned in time; Bell and Harris had killed one, but Squires had no luck, owing to his being unable to continue the chase on account of the injury he had received from his fall. We had a good supper, having brought abundance of eatables and drinkables. The tent was pitched; I put up my mosquito-bar under the wagon, and there slept very soundly till sunrise. Harris and Bell wedged together under another bar, Mr. C. went into the tent, and Squires, who is tough and likes to rough it with the hunters, slept on a Buffalo hide somewhere with Moncrévier, one of the most skillful of the hunters. The horses were all hoppled and turned to grass; they, however, went off too far, and had to be sent after, but I heard nothing of all this. As there is no wood on the prairies proper, our fire was made of Buffalo dung, which is so abundant that one meets these deposits at every few feet and in all directions.

July 21, Friday. We were up at sunrise, and had our coffee, after which Lafleur a mulatto, Harris, and Bell went off after Antelopes, for we cared no more about bulls; where the cows are, we cannot tell. Cows run faster than bulls, yearlings faster than cows, and calves faster than any of these. Squires felt sore, and his side was very black, so we took our guns and went after Black breasted Lark Buntings, of which we saw many, but could not near them. I found a nest of them, however, with five eggs. The nest is planted in the ground, deep enough to sink the edges of it. It is formed of dried fine grasses and roots, without any lining of hair or wool. By and by we saw Harris sitting on a high hill about one mile off, and joined him; he said the bulls they had killed last evening were close by, and I offered to go and see the bones, for I expected that the Wolves had devoured it during the night. We travelled on, and Squires returned to the camp. After about two miles of walking against a delightful strong breeze, we reached the animals; Ravens or Buzzards had worked at the eyes, but only one Wolf, apparently, had been there. They were bloated, and smelt quite unpleasant. We returned to the camp and saw a Wolf cross our path, and an Antelope looking at us. We determined to stop and try to bring him to us; I lay on my back and threw my legs up, kicking first one and then the other foot, and sure enough the Antelope walked towards us, slowly and carefully, however. In about twenty minutes he had come two or three hundred yards; he was a superb male, and I looked at him for some minutes; when about sixty yards off I could see his eyes, and being loaded with buck-shot pulled the trigger without rising from my awkward position. Off he went; Harris fired, but he only ran the faster for some hundred yards, when he turned, looked at us again, and was off. When we reached camp we found Bell there; he had shot three times at Antelopes without killing; Lafleur had also returned, and had broken the foreleg of one, but an Antelope can run fast enough with three legs, and he saw no more of it. We now broke camp, arranged the horses and turned our heads towards the Missouri, and in four and three-quarter hours reached the landing. On entering the wood we again broke branches of service-berries, and carried a great quantity over the river. I much enjoyed the trip; we had our

*John
James
Audubon*

53

supper, and soon to bed in our hot room, where Sprague says the thermometer has been at 99° most of the day. I noticed it was warm when walking. I must not forget to notice some things which happened on our return. First, as we came near Fox River, we thought of the horns of our bulls, and Mr. Culbertson, who knows the country like a book, drove us first to Bell's, who knocked the horns off, then to Harris's, which was served in the same manner; this bull had been eaten entirely except the head, and a good portion of mine had been devoured also; it lay immediately under "Audubon's Bluff" (the name Mr. Culbertson gave the ridge on which I stood to see the chase), and we could see it when nearly a mile distant. Bell's horns were the handsomest and largest, mine next best, and Harris's the smallest, but we are all contented. Mr. Culbertson tells me that Harris and Bell have done wonders, for persons who have never shot at Buffaloes from on horseback. Harris had a fall too, during his second chase, and was bruised in the manner of Squires, but not so badly. I have but little doubt that Squires killed his bull, as he says he shot it three times, and Mr. Culbertson's must have died also. What a terrible destruction of life, as it were for nothing, or next to it, as the tongues only were brought in, and the flesh of these fine animals was left to beasts and birds of prey, or to rot on the spots where they fell. The prairies are literally *covered* with the skulls of the victims, and the roads the Buffalo make in crossing the prairies have all the appearance of heavy wagon tracks. We saw young Golden Eagles, Ravens, and Buzzards. I found the Short-billed Marsh Wren quite abundant, and in such localities as it is found eastward. The Blackbreasted Prairie-bunting flies much like a Lark, hovering while singing, and sweeping round and round, over and above its female while she sits on the eggs on the prairie below. I saw only one Gadwall Duck; these birds are found in abundance on the plains where water and rushes are to be found. Alas! alas! eighteen Assiniboins have reached the fort this evening in two groups; they are better-looking than those previously seen by us.

July 22, Saturday. Thermometer 99°—102°. This day has been the hottest of the season, and we all felt the influence of this densely oppressive atmosphere, not a breath of air stirring. Immediately after breakfast Provost and Lafleur went across the river in search of Antelopes, and we remained looking at the Indians, all Assiniboins, and very dirty. When and where Mr. Catlin saw these Indians as he has represented them, dressed in magnificent attire, with all sorts of extravagant accoutrements, is more than I can divine, or Mr. Culbertson tell me.

July 23, Sunday. Thermometer 84°. I had a very pleasant night, and no mosquitoes, as the breeze rose a little before I lay down; and I anticipated a heavy thunder storm, but we had only a few drops of rain. About one o'clock Harris was called to see one of the Indians, who was bleeding at the nose profusely, and I too went to see the poor devil. He had bled quite enough, and Harris stopped his nostrils with cotton, put cold water on his neck and head—God knows when they had felt it before—and the bleeding stopped. These dirty fellows had made a large fire between the walls of the fort, but outside the inner gates, and it was a wonder that the whole establishment was not destroyed by fire. Before sunrise they were pounding at the gate to be allowed to enter, but, of course, this was not permitted. When the sun had fairly risen, some one came and told me the hill-tops were covered with Indians, probably Blackfeet. I walked to the back gate, and the number had dwindled, or the account been greatly exaggerated, for there seemed only fifty or sixty, and when, later, they were counted, there were found to be exactly seventy. They remained a long time on the hill, and sent a youth to ask for whiskey. But whiskey there is none for them, and very little for any one. By and by they came down the hill leading four horses, and armed principally with bows and arrows, spears, tomahawks, and a few guns. They have proved to be a party of Crees from the British dominions on the Saskatchewan River, and have been fifteen days in travelling here. They had seen few Buffaloes, and were hungry and thirsty enough. They assured Mr. Culbertson that the Hudson's Bay Company supplied them all with abundance of spirituous liquors, and as the white traders on the Missouri had none for them, they would hereafter travel with the English. Now ought not this subject to be brought before the press in our country and forwarded to England? If our Congress will not allow our traders to sell whiskey or rum to the Indians, why should not the British follow the same rule? Surely the British, who are so anxious about the emancipation of the blacks, might as well take care of the souls and bodies of the redskins. After a long talk and smoking of pipes, tobacco, flints, powder, gun-screws and vermilion were placed before their great chief (who is tattooed and has a most rascally look), who examined everything minutely, counting over the packets of vermilion; more tobacco was added, a file, and a piece of white cotton with which to adorn his head; then he walked off, followed by his son, and the whole posse left the fort. They passed by the garden, pulled up a few squash vines and some turnips, and tore down a few of the pickets on their way elsewhere. We all

John James Audubon

turned to, and picked a quantity of peas, which with a fine roast pig, made us a capital dinner. After this, seeing the Assiniboins loitering about the fort, we had some tobacco put up as a target, and many arrows were sent to enter the prize, but I never saw Indians—usually so skillful with their bows—shoot worse in my life. Presently some one cried there were Buffaloes on the hill, and going to see we found that four bulls were on the highest ridge standing still. The horses being got in the yard, the guns were gathered, saddles placed, and the riders mounted, Mr. C., Harris, and Bell; Squires declined going, not having recovered from his fall, Mr. C. led his followers round the hills by the ravines, and approached the bulls quite near, when the affrighted cattle ran down the hills and over the broken grounds, out of our sight, followed by the hunters. When I see game chased by Mr. Culbertson, I feel confident of its being killed, and in less than one hour he had killed two bulls, Harris and Bell each one. Thus these poor animals which two hours before were tranquilly feeding are now dead; short work this. Harris and Bell remained on the hills to watch the Wolves, and carts being ordered, Mr. C. and I went off on horseback to the second one he had killed. We found it entire, and I began to operate upon it at once; after making what measurements and investigations I desired, I saved the head, the tail, and a large piece of the silky skin from the rump. The meat of three of the bulls was brought to the fort, the fourth was left to rot on the ground. Mr. C. cut his finger severely, but paid no attention to that; I, however, tore a strip off my shirt and bound it up for him. It is so hot I am going to sleep on the gallery again; the thermometer this evening is 89.

July 24, Monday. I had a fine sleep last night, and this morning early a slight sprinkling of rain somewhat refreshed the earth. After breakfast we talked of going to see if Mr. Culbertson's bull had been injured by the Wolves. Mr. C., Harris, and I went off to the spot by a roundabout way, and when we reached the animal it was somewhat swollen, but untouched, but we made up our minds to have it weighed, *coute qui coute.* Harris pro-posed to remain and watch it, looking for Hares meantime, but saw none. The Wolves must be migratory at this season, or so starved out that they have gone elsewhere, as we now see but few. We returned first to the fort, and mustered three men and Bell, for Sprague would not go, being busy drawing a plant, and finding the heat almost insupportable. We carried all the necessary implements, and found Harris quite ready to drink some claret and water which we took for him.

To cut up so large a bull, and one now with so dreadful an odor, was no joke; but with the will follows the success, and in about one hour the poor beast had been measured and weighed, and we were once more *en route* for the fort. This bull measured as follows: from end of nose to root of tail, 131 inches; height at shoulder, 67 inches; at rump, 57 inches; tail vertebrae, 15 1/2, inches, hair in length beyond it 11 inches. We weighed the whole animal by cutting it in parts and then by addition found that this Buffalo, which was an old bull, weighed 1777 lbs. avoir-dupois. The flesh was all tainted, and was therefore left for the beasts of prey. Our road was over high hills, and presented to our searching eyes a great extent of broken ground, and here and there groups of Buffaloes grazing. This afternoon we are going to bring in the skeleton of Mr. Culbertson's second bull. I lost the head of my first bull because I forgot to tell Mrs. Culbertson that I wished to save it, and the princess had its skull broken open to enjoy its brains. Handsome, and really courteous and refined in many ways, I cannot reconcile to myself the fact that she partakes of raw animal food with such evident relish. Before our departure, in came six half-breeds, belonging, or attached to Fort Mortimer; and understanding that they were first-rate hunters, I offered them ten dollars in goods for each Bighorn up to eight or ten in number. They have promised to go to-morrow, but, alas! the half-breeds are so uncertain I cannot tell whether they will move a step or not. Mrs. Culbertson, who has great pride in her pure Indian blood, told me with scorn that "all such no-color fellows are lazy." We were delayed in starting by a very heavy gale of wind and hard rain, which cooled the weather considerably; but we finally got off in the wagon, the cart with three mules following, to bring in the skeleton of the Buffalo which Mr. Culbertson had killed; but we were defeated, for some Wolves had been to it, dragged it about twenty-five feet, and gnawed the ends of the ribs and the backbone. The head of Harris's bull was brought in, but it was smaller; the horns alone were pretty good, and they were given to Sprague. On our return Mrs. Culbertson was good enough to give me six young Mallards, which she had caught by swimming after them in the Missouri; she is a most expert and graceful swimmer, besides being capable of remaining under water a long time; all the Blackfoot Indians excel in swimming and take great pride in the accomplishment. We found three of the Assiniboins had remained, one of whom wanted to carry off a squaw, and probably a couple of horses too. He strutted about the fort in such a manner that we watched him pretty closely. Mr. Culbertson took his

John
James
Audubon

gun, and a six-barrelled pistol in his pocket; I, my double-barrelled gun, and we stood at the back gate. The fellow had a spear made of a cut-and-thrust sword, planted in a good stick covered with red cloth, and this he never put down at any time; but no more, indeed, do any Indians, who carry all their goods and chattels forever about their persons. The three gentlemen, however, went off about dusk, and took the road to Fort Mortimer, where six half-breeds from the Northeast brought to Fort Mortimer eleven head of cattle, and came to pay a visit to their friends here. All these men know Provost, and have inquired for him. I feel somewhat uneasy about Provost and La Fleur, who have now been gone four full days. The prairie is wet and damp, so I must sleep indoors. The bull we cut up was not a fat one; I think in good condition it would have weighed 2000 lbs.

July 25, Tuesday. We were all rather lazy this morning, but about dinner-time Owen and his man arrived, and told us they had reached Mr. Kipp and his boat at the crossings within about half a mile of Fort Alexander; that his men were all broken down with drawing the cordelle through mud and water, and that they had lost a white horse, which, however, Owen saw on his way, and on the morning of his start from this fort. About the same time he shot a large Porcupine, and killed four bulls and one cow to feed upon, as well as three rattlesnakes. They saw a large number of Buffalo cows, and we are going after them to-morrow morning bright and early. About two hours later Provost and La Fleur, about whom I had felt some uneasiness, came to the landing, and brought the heads and skins attached to two female Antelopes. Both had been killed by one shot from La Fleur, and his ball broke the leg of a third. Provost was made quite sick by the salt water he had drunk; he killed one doe, on which they fed as well as on the flesh of the "Cabris [antelope]." Whilst following the Mauvaises Terres (broken lands), they saw about twenty Bighorns, and had not the horse on which Provost rode been frightened at the sight of a monstrous buck of these animals, he would have shot it down within twenty yards. They saw from fifteen to twenty Buffalo cows, and we hope some of the hunters will come up with them to-morrow. I have been drawing the head of one of these beautiful female Antelopes; but their horns puzzle me, and all of us; they seem to me as if they were new horns, soft and short; time, however, will prove whether they shed them or not.

Father Nicolas Point's *Indian Woman* (Special Collections, Washington State University, Pullman).

≈

Father Nicolas Point (1799-1868)

In Father Nicolas Point's introduction to the six manuscript volumes that comprise his *Souvenirs des Montagnes Rocheuses,* he modestly offers this self-assessment of his skills as a painter and sketcher:

> Should this collection be appraised by a connoisseur, he would say, I know, "This is the work of neither a painter nor even a doodler." And he would be right, for I have no formal training in painting or sketching. But with this collection, such as it is, I do homage to you, dear reader, and were it to do nothing more than to give you an agreeable diversion from your serious occupations, I should be grateful to God for that. If it should, however, accomplish more, that is, if it should prompt you to do for the poor savages even the hundredth part of the good I wish for you, then, certainly, you would receive a hundredfold [blessing] in this world and in the next. If, on the contrary, my production only bores you, pray for me, as I do for you, in order that God, Who alone does not err, may judge both of us only in the light of His most sweet mercy. (*Wilderness Kingdom* 13)

Far from boring, Father Point's work has, since the 1967 publication of his manuscript, paintings, and sketches, entranced readers and viewers. In addition to having a rawness of vision, some of Point's work is also reminiscent of the colorful surrealistic art of Marc Chagall, the twentieth-century Russian painter. This is not to say that his art is the work of a polished professional. Father Point could fairly be called the Grandma Moses of the Rocky Mountain frontier.

Born at the end of the eighteenth century, Nicolas Point dreamed of becoming a missionary to native peoples. His dream became reality but not before his life had almost gone in other directions. In spite of strong anti-clericalism in his native France, he attended a church school in Rocroy where the French Marshal Michel Ney saw the boy and offered to adopt him. Point's parents refused, and in 1819, their son entered St. Acheul, a Jesuit college near Amiens. Although illness delayed his studies and he had to resume them at Brigg after an anti-clerical mob burned St. Acheul to the ground in 1828, he became a Jesuit priest in 1831.

The young priest's first assignments took him to Switzerland and then to Spain. In 1835 he sailed for New York, a voyage that took four months and almost cost him his life because an incompetent captain didn't know how to navigate stormy seas. After teaching for a year at a Jesuit school in Kentucky, Father Point went next to Louisiana where, on January 5, 1838, he opened St. Charles College. He might have remained the administrator of the college for the rest of his life if his superior had not assigned him to accompany Father Pierre Jean De Smet on the famous Jesuit missionary expedition to the Northwest. Point, De Smet, and four other Jesuits left Westport, Missouri, on April 30, 1841, bound for the Rocky Mountains.

During his stay in an area now spread across the boundaries of northern Idaho and northern Montana, Father Point lived among or encountered many groups of natives, including the Coeur d'Alenes, the Flatheads, the Nez Percés, the Crows, and the Blackfeet. Although he enjoyed his missionary service among these peoples, poor health forced him to ask that he be transferred to a settled area in Canada. His request granted in 1847, he spent the last twenty-one years of his life in Canada, dying in Quebec in 1868.

Although Nicolas Point and George Catlin were exact contemporaries, virtually only the Jesuits knew of Father Point for the first century after his death. Then, in 1967, Father Joseph P. Donnelly's translation of Point's manuscript was published along with Point's sketches and full-color reproductions of his paintings. That Father Point remains so little known even after the publication of his book can be attributed to the absence of his art in museums. If ever the manuscript finds a place among a great museum's exhibits (an event that its translator inexplicably hoped would "forever be averted"), "a page of Point's manuscript," Father Donnelly says, "will be nearly as much a treasure as a page of a medieval manuscript on vellum is today."

Father Point's narratives deserve as much consideration as do the pages of his manuscript, for he describes with great clarity the lifestyles of the Indians, the beauty of the landscape, and the Edenic abundance of the wildlife.

Buckley, Cornelius M. *Nicolas Point, S.J.: His Life and Northwest Indian Chronicles.* Chicago: Loyola University Press, 1989.

Point, Nicolas, S.J. *Wilderness Kingdom: Indian Life in the Rocky Mountains: 1840-1847; The Journals and Paintings of Nicolas Point, S.J.* Joseph P. Donnelly, S.J., trans. New York: Holt, Rinehart and Winston, 1967.

~

From *Wilderness Kingdom: Indian Life in the Rocky Mountains: 1840-1847; The Journals and Paintings of Nicolas Point, S.J.*

Second Summer Hunt with the Flatheads: From mid-July 1846

The Flatheads had left for their summer hunt at least fifteen days before and we, Father De Smet and I, were still with the Coeur d'Alenes, twenty-five days' journey from their camp. We reached St. Mary's in time to celebrate the Feast of the Assumption, the patronal feast of the Flatheads, and left on the evening of that great day, so eager were we to join the hunters. Since we were obliged to travel through enemy territory, our escort consisted of eight men, of whom four were half-breeds; one, a Flathead; two, young Blackfeet; and one who left us near Hell Gate.

Nothing remarkable happened en route which has not been presented in previous descriptions, except that we found a great abundance of fruit of the berry variety. The largest of the berries we saw was scarcely as big as our little wood cherries. The cherries were in bunches like our currants. The pears were in clusters like our cherries. The bilberries, more tasty than our own, are also more pleasing to the eye. They are a brilliant violet color, like the red of the currant. Another fruit which resembles it, and which is called buffalo berry because these animals are very fond of it, was more abundant than all the others. I believe that it is unknown in Europe. When cooked in grease, it is an Indian delicacy. Civilized epicures add sugar and cream to it whenever they can.

What struck me in the area of the Three Forks [of the Missouri] was the great variety of flowers. Big timber also thrives in this region and the beaver finds many a beautiful home there. As we reached Blackfoot territory, the thick brush offered ideal refuge for wolves and mountain lions. Bears were so numerous that, the year before, our people had killed as many as a dozen of them in less than two hours. But we, poor hunters that we were, could only travel in silence, even during the night, because of the war parties which were constantly crossing through this territory.

Thank God, we were on the trail of the Flatheads. What pleased our companions of the Little Robe was that they recognized the poles used as a means of transport by their tribe. There were also pickets which were used only by the Nez Percés. Thus, we could be certain that we were on the trail of the Flatheads. A party of Nez Percés, together with the tribe of the Little Robe, had joined the Flatheads. This fact was all the more favorable for all concerned because the Crows, who were very numerous, seemed disposed to anything but peaceful relations. We took a short cut, but, instead of gaining, we lost ground. Toward midday our horses were so oppressed by the suffocating heat that we were forced to halt in a spot where there was no water. It was decided that we would wait there while two of the best riders scouted ahead. But in which direction ought one to go? At that moment fleeing buffalo gave us the information we needed and our scouts set out. They returned on the twenty-seventh, accompanied by our good Flathead friend, Pierre Jean.

During their absence Providence had led us to a Nez Percé camp. Because of the great danger of being in enemy territory, they were no less eager than we to join the Flatheads. The first question of all was, therefore, "What news?"

"We are on the point of fighting with the Crows."
"Are they there in large numbers?"
"They are five times our number."

While I was absent, Father De Smet decided that I could remain until the next day and baptize a few people. He left with the others who forgot, no doubt, that there was no one left with us. Nevertheless, the following day, after a ceremony in which nine souls were placed on the road to Heaven, and after eight hours of hard riding, we saw in the distance something which looked like a camp. But was it the camp of the Flatheads or that of the Crows? Before us lay the Square Buttes, so famous in the history of the *Voyageurs*. These appeared to be many forts, drawn up in echelons one behind the other. On the right side of the river was a succession of ravines, elevations, recesses, and projections resembling a vast system of fortifications. Nevertheless, we advanced, and as we did so, the sharp eyes of our companions discovered something which stilled our fears. Coming in our direction, armed to the teeth, was a warrior of the first rank. It was George, the Flathead. We were delighted to see each other. He was very silent, as though he doubted whether what he had done was good or bad. The night before his tribe had won a great victory over the Crows. But did not this victory retard their [the Crows'] conversion? It was this fear which could be seen in his modest gaze. I noticed the same attitude in all who had accounted for themselves most nobly in this affair. That evening, reunited with our neophytes, we heard from them the details of the battle. Since we could not but praise their good conduct, all the clouds disappeared from their faces, in spite of the fact that any moment a new attack might be made by the Crows, who were only three miles away.

There are among the Crows, as among all people who wage war, really brave men. But to hear those who are, perhaps, the least brave, there are no people under the sun comparable to them in point of warlike courage. They compare themselves to an angry buffalo, which never retreats, which nothing can stop, and which overthrows whatever it finds in its way. They liken their enemies to slaves who only tremble.

Though the Crows heaped opprobrium on the Flatheads, this had not prevented the latter from harboring the remnants of the Little Robe tribe, half of whose members had been massacred by these brutal people, or from pursuing buffalo right up to the neighborhood of their camp. For, said the Flatheads, the Crows must not think that, because we have the true prayer, we fear them the more. God knows that we want only peace, but if they attack us unjustly, we will know how to defend ourselves. Such was the attitude of the Flatheads when the Crows, under pretext of a friendly visit, poured into their camp like an overflowing torrent, and pushed insult so far as to say that one Crow, armed with a stick, would be enough to make a hundred Flatheads flee. And despite their chiefs, who were less unreasonable, these great braggarts, adding insult to injury, acted as though they were about to plunder the camp. Separating the branches which formed a palisade around the lodges, some Crows were aiming with their rifles at the bravest of the Flatheads. With their patience thus taxed to the extreme, the Flatheads were on the point of giving the war cry when, fortunately, our scouts arrived. One of them, seeing what was in the wind, as soon as he was within earshot, cried out, "The Blackrobes are coming and with them the Nez Percés and the Pend d'Oreilles."

At this cry, the Crows hesitated, and their chiefs, knowing better than the others what they had to fear, shouted, "Amaraba, amaraba!" which means, "Off with you." To their commands they added vigorous blows with the rod, so that even the most obstinate were obliged to retreat without striking another blow. The Crow word amaraba had been repeated so often that even the Flathead children were still repeating it when we arrived.

The Flatheads spent the night thanking Heaven for such a happy outcome. But the next day the Crows, having undoubtedly learned that the re-enforcements had not arrived, stole thirty horses in plain daylight, right from under the noses of the Flatheads. And, as when an innocent person is mistakenly punished in place of the guilty, nothing more was required to rekindle the fires of war. Toward ten o'clock in the morning, in the midst of a cloud of dust, the Crows came at full gallop, under the false impression that nothing could stand in the face of the suddenness of their attack. But the Flatheads, forseeing such an effort, were waiting in solid formation, ranged in a line outside of the camp.

When the attackers were within rifle range, Titiche Loutso, surnamed the Bravest of the Brave, after making the little vanguard pray, rose up and said, "My friends, if God wishes that we be victors, we shall be victors. If He does not, then may His will be done. Meanwhile, courage!"

He and his men then opened fire so effectively that the Crows immediately changed their plan of attack into a boastful display of horsemanship which only served to tire their horses. Victor, observing this, cried, "Now, my children, forward!" Each of the Flathead warriors rode so skillfully that the enemy horsemen were forced to retreat more than two miles from the point of attack. Nevertheless, taking courage in numbers, the Crows came up for the attack time after time. This lasted until evening.

During the fighting the youngest of the warriors displayed a fearlessness which astonished the elders. Several women rivaled the bravest of the men in courage. In the midst of the fray an elderly woman, hatchet in hand, hurled herself so violently between her son, whose horse was tiring, and a Crow on the point of reaching him, that the pursuer, despite his giant stature, judged it prudent to move away. Another younger woman went about on the battlefield gathering up arrows for those of her warriors who had run out of them. Another, who had advanced too far in pursuit of the enemy, made such a swift about face, at the very moment several arms were outstretched to grab her, that she galloped back to her own lines leaving the enemy stupified. Still another, after having spent some time pursuing several Crows, returned saying, "I thought these great talkers were men, but I was wrong. They are not even worth pursuing."

Indian fights are very similar to a *jeu de barres* [mock battle], and for this reason last a long time without spilling much blood. Thus, instead of saying, "We shall fight," they say, "We shall have sport." In this fight, which lasted nine hours, there were only ten killed and fourteen wounded, all on the side of the Crows, with the single exception of a Nez Percé. Why had this one man been killed? In answer to this question, the people of the Little Robe replied that it was because he had not made the sign of the cross before going into battle.

On leaving the field of battle, which had become for seventy-six of their members the cradle of a new life, the Little Robe warriors ranged themselves in an extended line. Behind them came some distinguished women, led by the woman calumet bearer. All of them, both men and women, were dressed in their finest garb. The costume of the chief was red. Everyone carried a green branch in his hand and, at intervals, there were flags of various colors and shapes. As the phalanx started to march, the triumphal chant began, accompanied by the drums. The high voices of the women mingled pleasingly with the bass voices of the men. Each phrase ended in a sharp cry of joy. Excited by the warlike music, the horses advanced proudly along the river, the banks of which resembled the towers and fortresses of medieval times.

When the multitude arrived at camp, there was talk of holding a scalp dance. As the sun was still smiling down with all of its force, they held their meeting in a place where great trees afforded a pleasant, deep shade. These old giant trees served as a grandstand for the spectators who formed a vast audience. Those not lucky enough to find a place in the trees or in the first row, watched from horseback behind the others. The same horse sometimes offered a vantage point for two people, one sitting in the usual fashion and another standing erect, with his hands resting on the shoulders of his seated companion. In the middle of the natural arena, women were dancing. Off to one side were the musicians whose instruments were piercing whistles and drums, beaten more or less rapidly depending on the nature of the presentation. Among the dancers were members from every lodge. Some carried the weapons which had contributed to victory; others were rigged out grotesquely, wearing outlandish costumes or ornaments of honor. These fantastic decorations were never once taken off. The choicest costumes were those which combined with bizarre form and brilliance of color a system of rattles or bells of many tones. But in the eyes of the Indian nothing could compare with the headdress made of eagle plumes and purple bands. The truth is that the undulating movements of such headgear harmonized with those of the dance and the music, having about them something magical, not always found amid the luxuries of civilization.

Perhaps for the first time crowns of greenery or green branches had taken the place of bloody scalps. Hence this dance, which is, in any event, more religious than profane, offered nothing the least bit offensive or painful. The particular characteristic of the dance was a little hop, more or less lively, depending on the tempo set by the drum or by the chant. The drum was beaten only by the great men, but the chant, which was the soul of the occasion, was participated in by all. From time to time, to break the monotony of the chant, the sharper sound of the whistles could be heard. If, in spite of this stimulation, the action appeared to be slowing down, to liven it, there were harangues accompanied by great gestures, by burlesque grimaces, and by broken cries produced by striking the mouth with the hand.

All this could be seen in our dance. We even saw old women who, to achieve greater effect, abandoned the staffs with which they were supporting their trembling hops, and swung their arms about with all the force they could muster, leaping until they were exhausted. As the movement was a circular one, and the dancers tended to approach the center, it would happen that the circle became too tight and even little hops were no longer possible. Then the dancers would turn about, reform their circle, and begin again with renewed vigor.

After the dance ceremony came the procession of the calumet, which went in a circle to the left until it had reached its point of departure. This procession was made up of three officiating priestesses of distinction, led by a high and powerful personage whose function was to control the speed of the group. The principal priestess was in the middle, bearing the calumet. The one to her right carried a fan, and the third, to her left, bore a kind of cymbal. The whole thing together seemed to express the thought that *peace, concord, and harmony ought to be the fruits of victory.*

On September 9, the north wind, which was blowing in our faces, became so sharp that, in spite of our desire to hurry, we were obliged to call a halt sooner than usual. In the evening a Nez Percé accompanied by three Blackfeet, entered the camp. This Nez Percé presented himself as a great friend of the white men, almost believing himself to be white because, instead of plucking his beard as the Indians do, he shaved it as we do. The youngest of his companions, whose features were most interesting, had lost his parents so early that he did not remember them. His mother, who had been carrying him in her arms when she was captured by the Blackfeet, died a few days later. Whereupon, his father, becoming the mortal enemy of his new masters, virtually ceased to exist for him. But the orphan was adopted by an Indian woman who wished to be a mother to him and who, until just recently, had, indeed, been one. She had told him, the young man said, that she was not really his mother and that his father, who was in our camp, would be glad to see him. The father, touched by what he learned, but still unconvinced, remembered that his child had a pronounced birth mark. He looked for the mark and so assured himself that this was indeed his son.

The following scene took place in the Blackrobe's lodge: "I am very rich in horses," said the father, in an effort to attach his son to him. "The fastest horse in the tribe is mine and I will give it to you."

"My father, I should be very happy to follow you," replied the young man, "but only after I have introduced the Blackrobe to my adoptive country."

This was such an exceptional remark that Father De Smet gave the youth permission to visit our lodge whenever he might wish to do so. But many days later the young man assured us that the Nez Percé chief was not his father. Others told us that the supposedly touching scene had been faked only in the hope of swindling the Nez Percé out of a good horse.

With good reason the Nez Percés disliked the Blackfeet. In spite of the esteem in which the Flatheads held the Little Robe people, the Nez Percés conducted themselves so poorly toward them that, if on two or three occasions they did not take leave of the Flatheads, it was only because of the missionaries. On the tenth, when the Nez Percés announced that they were going to leave us, everybody rejoiced. But scarcely had they gone a mile when, justly fearing an encounter with the Crows, they thought only of retracing their steps. This made the Little Robe people, and consequently also the missionaries, decide to say adieu to the Flathead camp. The Flatheads had given sufficient proof that they did not fear war. But they loved peace and everything that might contribute to maintaining it. Thus, as they gave us their hands, perhaps for the last time, it was easy to see that this separation was costing them a great deal. A goodly number of them conducted us for some distance. To spend still one more night with us, five or six of them accompanied us as far as our campsite. The void caused by the absence of our best converts and the recollection of what the Blackfeet were still like contributed to make us gloomy. Also, while skirting the chain of mountains that lay to our left, it seemed to us that the masses of desolate rock, whose ghostly configurations were multiplied by the heavy shadows as we marched along, were the openings of so many caverns ready to spew forth at us all the brigands of the country.

En route, one of the distinguished horsemen fell from his mount and our efforts to revive him were unavailing. He was the first baptized of his nation, a chief who, for five years, had been preparing the way in his country for the preaching of the Gospel. He was a warrior who, in the last battle, had been a prodigy of valor; a Christian who, only the night before, had rejoiced in the hope that his fondest prayers were about to be answered. In a word, it was Nicolas, our precursor, who had fallen at the very moment we were setting foot in his country. What a tragedy for us, for his tribe, and for his son, who was our interpreter! Ordinarily the Blackfeet express their grief in cries and by inflicting on themselves more or less serious wounds. But Sata, this good son, remembering that his father and he had become the servants of a Master who regards sacrifices of the heart more highly than any others, recommended to his wife and his children that they forget the cries, the tears, and the useless blood in order the better to help their dear departed ascend into Heaven. They all passed the night in prayer. At the funeral, Sata himself, whose heart was almost failing him, pronounced the eulogy of his father. Scarcely had the mortal remains descended into the grave when it was announced that the great tribe of the Piegans, the tribe of Nicolas himself, was advancing to meet us.

Paul Kane's *Cun-na-wa-bum* (Royal Ontario Museum, Toronto, Ontario).

~

Paul Kane (1810-1871)

Paul Kane's father, a former British soldier turned wine merchant in crude and muddy Little York (later Toronto), Canada, could give his son few advantages. Lacking resources, Paul joined many a talented youth of his day optimistically determined to be an artist: He painted furniture and signs to earn his keep. Then, becoming an itinerant portrait painter, he lived from hand to mouth, wandering from Detroit to Mobile to New Orleans.

In the days before cameras, drawing likenesses of those who could afford the indulgence could be at least moderately profitable for a skilled and amiable man with a brush. By 1841, Kane had earned enough to take the obligatory pilgrimage to Europe, where in Rome and other art centers he marveled, studying the geniuses who had gone before him. Still, he was poor and lacked artistic focus. A chance meeting with George Catlin, who was touring London with his Indian paintings, set Kane on fire. He would paint Indians, too, but he would capture those far beyond the Great Plains of the United States where Catlin had ranged. Kane borrowed the fare for the trip back across the Atlantic, turned out more portraits to earn himself a grubstake, then plunged off into the wilds of far-western Canada and the Pacific Northwest. Between 1845 and 1848 he produced hundreds of sketches and paintings.

Kane soon became famous because of his art. In fact, Kane would find Canada more conducive to the artistic life than Catlin had found the United States where, despite his glad showmanship, Catlin had almost starved while touring his gallery of Indian portraits. Conditions were truly better in Canada, where a general quickening sparked interest in political change, transportation, and geography. Part of the intellectual ferment included a new look at Canada's native peoples, now pushed far enough west to be seen as fascinating human beings rather than as threats. As a result, the thoroughly organized and efficient Hudson's Bay Company eased Kane's way across its vast trading empire, providing him with transportation, refuge, and protection under its flag. Kane's paintings were displayed in Toronto's city hall, and Canada's legislature hailed Kane's artistic revelations of life on the frontier.

There are more reasons than topical fame to gaze once again at Paul Kane's work. Catlin's chiefs stand before us with the awkward grandeur of wooden gods making temporary appearances on earth. Although Kane could struggle with perspective and with animals on the move, his artistic acumen is far more subtle than Catlin's and his range of subject far wider, running from a detailed, realistic Walla Walla calumet, to a pleasantly curved canoe, to landscapes so airy that, at times, the mountains and valleys before him seem sculpted from an ice so delicate that they will start to evaporate into the atmosphere the instant after we blink.

Further Reading

Harper, J. Russell. *Paul Kane: 1810-1871.* Fort Worth: Amon Carter Museum of Western Art, and Ottawa: The National Gallery of Canada, 1971.

Kane, Paul. *Paul Kane's Frontier: Including Wanderings of an Artist among the Indians of North America.* J. Russell Harper, ed. Austin: The University of Texas Press, 1971.

∾

From *Paul Kane's Frontier:*
Including Wanderings of an Artist among the Indians of North America

On my return to Canada from the continent of Europe, where I had passed nearly four years in studying my profession as a painter, I determined to devote whatever talents and proficiency I possessed to the painting of a series of pictures illustrative of the North American Indians and scenery. The subject was one in which I felt a deep interest in my boyhood. I had been accustomed to see hundreds of Indians about my native village, then Little York, muddy and dirty, just struggling into existence, now the City of Toronto, bursting forth in all its energy and commercial strength. But the face of the red man is now no longer seen. All traces of his footsteps are fast being obliterated from his once favourite haunts, and those who would see the aborigines of this country in their original state, or seek to study their native manners and customs, must travel far through the pathless forest to find them. To me the wild woods were not altogether unknown, and the Indians but recalled old friends with whom I had associated in my childhood, and though at the commencement of my travels I possessed neither influence nor means for such an undertaking, yet it was with a determined spirit and a light heart that I had made the few preparations which were in my power for my future proceedings.

The principal object in my undertaking was to sketch pictures of the principal chiefs, and their original costumes, to illustrate their manners and customs, and to represent the scenery of an almost unknown country. These paintings, however, would necessarily require explanations and notes, and I accordingly kept a diary of my journey, as being the most easy and familiar form in which I could put such information as I might collect. The following pages are the notes of my daily journey, with little alteration from the original working, as I jotted them down in pencil at the time; and although without any claim to public approbation as a literary production, still I trust they will possess not only an interest for the curious, but also an intrinsic value to the historian, as they relate not only to that vast tract of country bordering on the great chain of American lakes, the Red River settlement, the valley of Sascatchawan, and its boundless prairies, through which it is proposed to lay the great railway connecting the Atlantic and Pacific Oceans, through the British possessions; but also across the Rocky Mountains down the Columbia River to Oregon, Puget's Sound, and Vancouver's Island, where the recent gold discoveries in the vicinity have drawn thousands of hardy adventurers to those wild scenes amongst which I strayed almost alone, and scarcely meeting a white man or hearing the sound of my own language.

The illustrations—executed from my sketches, or finished paintings, for the purpose of illustrating the present work—constitute only a few specimens of the different classes of subjects which engaged my pencil during a sojourn of nearly four years among the Indians of the Northwest. In that period I executed numerous portraits of chiefs, warriors, and medicine-men of the different tribes among whom I sojourned, and also of their wives and daughters. The Indian fishing and hunting scenes, games, dances, and other characteristic customs, also occupied my pencil; while I was not forgetful of the interest which justly attaches to the scenery of a new and unexplored country, and especially to such parts of it as were either intimately associated with native legends and traditions, or otherwise specially connected with the native tribes—as their favourite fishing or hunting grounds, the locations of their villages, or the burying-places of the tribes. The whole of these sketches are now in my possession, and I have already been honoured by a commission to execute a series of paintings from them for the Legislature of the Province of Canada, which now have a place in the Library of the Provincial Parliament. A much more extensive series of oil paintings had been executed by me, from my sketches, for George W. Allan, Esq., of Moss Park, the liberal patron of Canadian art; and I would gladly indulge the hope that the present work will not prove the sole published fruits of my travels among the Indian tribes of North America, but that it will rather be a mere illustration of the novelty and interest which attach to those rarely explored regions, and enable me to publish a much more extensive series of illustrations of the characteristics, habits, and scenery of the country and its occupants. . . .

The nine boats composing the brigade had now completed their outfit, and were all prepared for their different destinations. Mr. Lewis was to command until he arrived at his own post, Colville; but we had great difficulty in collecting the men, between sixty and seventy in number; some wanted their allowance of rum, or regale, before they started, given to the Company's men only preparatory to a long voyage. Others were bidding farewell to their Indian loves, and were hard to be found; in fact, all hesitated to give up the life of idleness and plenty in which they had been luxuriating for the last two or three weeks, for the toils and privations which they well knew were before them. However, towards evening we succeeded in collecting our crews, and Mr. Lewis promised them their regale on the first fitting opportunity. The fort gave us a salute of seven guns, which was repeated by the Company's ship lying at the store-house. The occupants of the fort crowded round us; and at last, amidst cheers and hearty wishes for our safety, we pushed off. Owing to the lateness of the hour at which we started, we only got to the Company's mills, eight miles from the fort, that evening.

We started very early this morning, and the men plied their oars with unusual vigour, as they were to get their regale this evening. By 2 o'clock P.M. we had reached the Prairie de Thé, a distance of twenty-eight miles. Here we landed to let the men have their customary debauch. In the Hudson's Bay Company's service no rations of liquor are given to the men, either while they are stopping in fort or while travelling, nor are they allowed to purchase any; but when they are about commencing a long journey, the men are given what is called a regale, which consists of a pint of rum each. This, however, they are not allowed to drink until they are some distance from the post, where those who are entitled to get drunk may do so without interfering with the resident servants of the establishment.

Immediately on landing, the camp was made, fires lit, and victuals cooked; in short, every preparation for the night was completed before the liquor was given out. As soon as the men got their allowance, they commenced all sorts of athletic games; running, jumping, wrestling, &c. We had eight Sandwich Islanders amongst the crews, who afforded great amusement by a sort of pantomimic dance accompanied by singing. The whole thing was exceedingly grotesque and ridiculous, and elicited peals of laughter from the audience; gradually, as the rum began to take effect, the brigades, belonging to different posts, began to boast of their deeds of daring and endurance. This gradually led on to trying which was the best man. Numberless fights ensued; black eyes and bloody noses became plentiful, but all terminated in good humour. The next day the men were stupid from the effects of drink, but quite good-tempered and obedient; in fact, the fights of the previous evening seemed to be a sort of final settlement of all old grudges and disputes. We did not get away until 3 o'clock P.M., and only made a distance of about fourteen miles. We encamped at the foot of the Cascades, where the first portage in ascending the Columbia commences. . . .

On Christmas-day the flag was hoisted, and all appeared in their best and gaudiest style, to do honour to the holiday. Towards noon every chimney gave evidence of being in full blast, whilst savoury steams of cooking pervaded the atmosphere in all directions. About two o'clock we sat down to dinner. Our party consisted of Mr. Harriett, the chief, and three clerks, Mr Thebo, the Roman Catholic missionary from Manitou Lake, about thirty miles off, Mr. Rundell, the Wesleyan missionary, who resided within the pickets, and myself, the wanderer, who, though returning from the shores of the Pacific, was still the latest importation from civilised life.

The dining-hall in which we assembled was the largest room in the fort, probably about fifty by twenty-five feet, well warmed by large fires, which are scarcely ever allowed to go out. The walls and ceilings are boarded, as plastering is not used, there being no limestone within reach; but these boards are painted in a style of the most startling barbaric gaudiness, and the ceiling filled with centre-pieces of fantastic gilt scrolls, making altogether a saloon which no white man would enter for the first time without a start, and which the Indians always looked upon with awe and wonder.

The room was intended as a reception room for the wild chiefs who visited the fort; and the artist who designed the decorations was no doubt directed to "astonish the natives." If such were his instructions, he deserves the highest praise for having faithfully complied with them, although, were he to attempt a repetition of the same style in one of the rooms of the Vatican, it might subject him to some severe criticisms from the fastidious. No table-cloth shed its snowy whiteness over the board; no silver candelabra or gaudy china interfered with its simple magnificence. The bright tin plates and dishes reflected jolly faces, and burnished gold can give no truer zest to a feast.

Perhaps it might be interesting to some dyspeptic idler, who painfully strolls through a city park, to coax an appetite to a sufficient intensity to enable him to pick an ortolan, if I were to describe to him the fare set before us, to appease appetites nourished by constant out-door exercise in an atmosphere ranging at 40º to 50º below zero. At the head, before Mr. Harriett, was a large dish of boiled buffalo hump; at the foot smoked a boiled buffalo calf. Start not, gentle reader, the calf is very small, and is taken from the cow by the Cæsarean operation long before it attains its full growth. This, boiled whole, is one of the most esteemed dishes amongst the epicures of the interior. My pleasing duty was to help a dish of mouffle, or dried moose nose; the gentleman on my left distributed, with graceful impartiality, the white fish, delicately browned in buffalo marrow. The worthy priest helped the buffalo tongue, whilst Mr. Rundell cut up the beavers' tails. Nor was the other gentleman left unemployed, as all his spare time was occupied in dissecting a roast wild goose. The centre of the table was graced with piles of potatoes, turnips, and bread conveniently placed, so that each should help himself without interrupting the labours of his companions. Such was our jolly Christmas dinner at Edmonton; and long will it remain in my memory, although no pies, or puddings, or blanc manges, shed their fragrance over the scene.

In the evening the hall was prepared for the dance to which Mr. Harriett had invited all the inmates of the fort, and was early filled by the gaily dressed guests. Indians, whose chief ornament consisted in the paint on their faces, voyageurs with bright sashes and neatly ornamented mocassins, half-breeds glittering in every ornament they could lay their hands on; whether civilised or savage, all were laughing, and jabbering in as many different languages as there were styles of dress. English, however, was little used, as none could speak it but those who sat at the dinner-table. The dancing was most picturesque, and almost all joined in it. Occasionally I, among the rest, led out a young Cree squaw, who sported enough beads round her neck to have made a pedlar's fortune, and having led her into the centre of the room, I danced round her with all the agility I was capable of exhibiting, to some highland-reel tune which the fiddler played with great vigour, whilst my partner with grave face kept jumping up and down, both feet off the ground at once, as only an Indian can dance. I believe, however, that we elicited a great deal of applause from Indian squaws and children, who sat squatting round the room on the floor. Another lady with whom I sported the light fantastic toe, whose poetic name was Cun-ne-wa-bum, or "One that looks at the Stars," was a half-breed Cree girl; and I was so much struck by her beauty, that I prevailed upon her to promise to sit for her likeness, which she afterwards did with great patience, holding her fan, which was made of the tip end of swan's wing with an ornamental handle of porcupine's quills, in a most coquettish manner.

Samuel Chamberlain—*Sketching Monterrey* (San Jacinto Museum of History, Houston, Texas).

~

Samuel Chamberlain (1829-1908)

Hearing of plans to build a telegraph between Maine and Texas, Henry David Thoreau sniffed, "but Maine and Texas, it may be, have nothing important to communicate." Thoreau was wrong. In fact, first awareness of what would become the American Southwest electrified the staid nation to this marvelous land of fearsome deserts and exotic peoples.

Key to the excitement was the Mexican-American War of 1846-1848. The popular press served up stories of the Army's lavish heroics while illustrators depicted battles in what the Goetzmanns call "grand operatic" terms (*The West of the Imagination* 98). All of this took place against a backdrop of a never-never land occupied by never-never-land people. What the fad lacked in accuracy was well made up for by soaring fantasy.

Perhaps no fantasy soared so high as that produced by Samuel Chamberlain, a private in the ranks who, during his secret moments, was scribbling and painting away, producing a phantasmagoric rendition of his youth in the West. Perhaps because Chamberlain went on to become a distinguished Union general in the Civil War and to raise a proper Victorian family in New England, his scandalous memoir and the accompanying illustrations were not made public until 1956; nonetheless, his work embodies a national, if furtive and intense, impulse.

Chamberlain's *My Confession: Recollections of a Rogue* has the gaudiness and compulsion of a libido turned loose. At age fifteen, instantly aroused at a slight to his girlfriend, Chamberlain decked his choirmaster. Driven from Boston for the indiscretion, the teenager becomes the wandering, misunderstood Byronic hero, victim of his lusts and unbridled energies. Enlisting as a soldier in the dragoons, he slashes his way across Texas into Mexico, dripping blood, gulping whatever alcohol is at hand, and having his way with as many women as possible.

In the course of things, Chamberlain gives vent to once-popular prejudices against Catholics, Mexicans, and anyone spawned by the "mongral races"—this latter category apparently encompassing all those on the planet not of Anglo-Saxon heritage. And to say that he treats women as objects would be putting it far too nicely. Rape, as Chamberlain describes it, comes across as a sort of rude joke rather than as an act of violence. He gets his facts as skewed as his morals, mangles both Spanish and English, places giant cacti at the Grand Canyon where no such plant exists, and describes battles taking place hundreds of miles from where he was actually serving. But, no matter. All such things are but stage props he moves around to achieve his effects.

They can be striking. Both venereal and martial, the gore of his prose evokes Gothic revulsion, while his unschooled art, with its stark architectural angles and leaden, keen-edged shadows, can chill with the surreal horrors of the later Greco-Italian painter Giorgio de Chirico.

All the better, perhaps, for Victorians—Chamberlain's intended audience—titillated by a release cloaked as moralizing by story's end and offered a fantasyland West where their prurient, secret selves could romp.

Further Reading

Chamberlain, Samuel. *My Confession: Recollections of a Rogue.* William H. Goetzmann, ed. Austin: Texas State Historical Association, 1996.

_____. *Samuel E. Chamberlain's My Confession: An Extraordinary First-Person Account of a Young Man in the War with Mexico.* William H. Goetzmann, ed. Austin: Texas State Historical Association, 1999. See also http://www.tsha.utexas.edu/~chamber (This website includes Chamberlain's text and images).

Goetzmann, William H., and William N. Goetzmann. *The West of the Imagination.* New York: Norton, 1986.

∿

From *My Confession*

The Battle of Monterey

We halted under shelter of the walls of the church, and could hear the explosion of firearms and shouts on the street to our right, giving us to understand the resistance that the other column was meeting with. Our wounded were taken care of by surgeons who kept with us, the Mexican's were quietly disposed of by those humane fellows, the Texas Rangers.

Reforming, we dashed around the church, and found the street barracaded, and the same infernal fire was again poured in to us; we rushed over the breastwork, and wild yells charged up the street, men dropping every moment. It would have required Salamanders to withstand the fire that scorched us on every side. Our run came down to a walk, our walk to a general seeking of shelter in doors and passages. I stuck to Walker, who had gained my boyish esteem in speaking a kind and cheerful word to me in the terrible storming of Independence Hill. About a dozen of us with Col. Walker were hugging a door mighty close, when a volly was fired through it from the inside. Three of our party fell. By order of the Colonel, two men with axes hewed away at the stout oak plank. Another volly was fired, when one of the axemen with a deep curse dropped his axe, a ball had broke the bone of his arm. Walker took his place, and soon the barrier gave way, and we rushed in. Some eight or ten hard looking "hombras" tried to escape through a back way, but they were cut down to a man. No quarter was given. In a back room we found some women and children who were not molested. Pickaxes and Crowbars were sent to us, also some six P'dr shells. A house on the other side of the street was forced and our men were all soon under cover. Our advance was now systematized; one party composed of the best shots ascended to the roof, and now on equal terms renewed the fight. The rest tore holes in the limestone partitions that divided the blocks into houses, then a lighted shell was thrown in, an explosion would follow, when we would rush and we generaly left from two to six dead greassers. We found plenty of eatables and large quantities of wine, and one house was a "Pulque" Fonda, or liquor store. To prevent us from getting drunk, the liquor was reported as poisoned, but we were not to be beat in that way; we would make a greasser drink some of each kind, no ill effects appearing, we would imbibe, while the "assayer" would be dispatched by a sabre thrust. When Mexicans were scarce, we used a Dutch artilleryman whose imperfect knowledge of our language prevented him from understanding why we gave him the first drink! and why we watched his countenance with so much anxiety. But the only bad effect it had was to get the Dutchman dead drunk, and the glorious so-so.

How terrible war is! Here was this beautiful city of some twenty thousand inhabitants, containing some of the most beautiful women in the world, at the mercy of a band of un-disciplined, drunken and enraged stormers.

But I don't believe that one insult was given to a female during all the fearful scenes enacted in cutting our way through one mile and a half of houses to reach the Grand Plaza! On the contrary, every thing was done to sooth and quiet the alarm. From their actions, I should judge that most of them were of the happy mind of those laides of Ismail.

> Don Juan
> some voices of the buxom middle-aged
> were also heard to wonder in the din
> (Widows of forty were these birds long caged)
> "Wherefore the ravishing did not begin!"
> But, while the thirst for gore and plunder raged,
> There was small leisure for superfluous sins:
> But whether they escaped or no; lies hid
> In darkness—I can only hope they did.

Rape has always had a conspicuous position in the annals of Mexican warfare, in fact some evil minded persons have stated that this general indulgence by the victors in their un-civil wars, is the cause of most of them! Some military Tarquin addresses being rejected by some scornfull beauty, he will issue a "Pronouncenta," and raise the flag of rebellion. This will collect all the rag muffins and Ladrones in the vicinity, to storm the town in which the fair one resides, and then by force obtain that, which fair words failed to win. His followers follow his example. Other battles follow, more cities are taken, and some fine morning our amorous hero wakes up either for the "Garrote" or the Presidental chair in the capitol! How true this is, I dont know, but I am sattisfied that the women expect it as a matter of course. I had gone into a room in one of the houses, when a Senoreita in the room commenced to scream and threw herself on her back on a sheepskin bed, making a great display of a well shaped pair of legs! I tried to make her understand what I wanted was something to eat, not what she seemed to think, but she only kicked and screamed the more. I searched and found a pot of Beans (frejollis) and sat down to eat when madam raised her head and gave me a look, and if her countenance did not belie her, she was a dissapointed woman.

A Little Old Fellow Dressed in Red

Samuel Chamberlain

Lieut. Carleton received his dispatches for Gen Wool, and seeing that I was provided with a fresh mount, left the Camp at Walnut Springs on September 29th. The morning was bright and cool, as [we] moved out on the "Pesqueria Grande" road leaving Monterey and its orange groves behind us. I was far from being well, my head pained me, my wound seemed to fairly burn, and I had indulged too freely in stimulants for my own good. I was more fit for a hospital than a march, but I said nothing and, though suffering intensely, I kept my saddle. On going over a high spur of the Sierra Madre we saw a part of Ampudia's Army in column on the Saltillo road. We passed through the town of "Pesqueria Grande," and numerous Ranchos and at sundown bivouaced in the Plaza of the pretty little town of Saleanus. The inhabitants knew already of the cessation of hostilities and appeared very kind to us, providing us with an excellent supper and forage for our horses. They also got up a fandango for our espicial benifit, but Lieut Carlton declined, and from prudential reasons, forbid any one of the escort going. But I considered it would be a shame if the United States was not represented on the occasion, and though feeling quite sick, concluded to go! I was hardly in proper dress for a Ball Room, Dragoon Jacket and trousers black with blood, and the latter torn in the rear, just enough to show the stern realities of a soldiers life. My long hair was matted and the bandage dried on with incrusted blood. My appearance caused a decided sensation. I was certainly the Lion of the evening. I felt quite flattered at the reception I met with. The hombras with muttered "crajahos" and "vamos" the "casa" leaving us with three dozzen Senoras and Senoreitas, who screamed a little but remained. I had on my sabre and Pistol, and I was well made up for a "Stage villain" but when I made my politest bow, to the Belle of the Ball, accompanied with all the Spanish I knew, "Beauna Noches" "Poco Tempo" Senoritas, and that I flew a flag of truce at my base, I certainly made a decided hit. Shouts of silver toned laughter greeted me, the black eyed beauties were my friends at once. I wanted to dance, but the musicians had fled, but there was plenty of wine, muscal, and cakes, so I had a glorious time with my fair friends, sang them songs and forgot my illness and injury by drowning the pain in the wine cup.

In the morning I found myself with my comrades in the Plaza, all right but quite drunk, my offending pants had been mended, my head washed and hair combed while a delicate cambric handkercheif was bound around my head in place of the dirty rag of the evening before. The charge of my Pistol had been withdrawn, Lieut Carleton gave me a blessing for being present and happy. After breakfast, we left the glorious little place and moved out on the Monclova road as Carleton was informed that Gen. Wool occupied that city. As I rode out of town, I tried to recognize my friends of the evening before among the ladies who crowded the balconies as we passed. But as I was in rather a confused state of mind I was not successful.

All day long I was in misery and I think at times delirous. We halted at noon for two hours, and at night we stopped at a rancho, and I expected to get a good night sleep, but I was ordered on guard, and though realy sick from loss of blood, want of sleep and excessive drinking, I made no excuse, but went on post at the entrence of the Court. Then the "man with the Poker" came for me. I fancied I saw an immense rock high in the air falling directly down on me! I tried to reason with myself that it was all imagination, the effect of my nervous state, but it was still there! and coming! I could stand it no longer and prepared to run, when a little old fellow dressed in red stood before me grinning and winking with a pair of eyes that shone like candles. I hailed him three times, and then aiming between his confounded bright eyes, fired, but he only winked the harder, while horrid things came crawling towards me and the rock fell. Carleton and the men rushed up and found me sticking right and left with my carbine! I was secured, a clear case Delirium Tremens.

Unspeakable Revenge on the Yankedos

During the war, the females of the country proved firm friends of the "Los Gringos," and we was often indebted to them for valuable information regarding the movement of the enemy, their own countrymen. This treachery to their national cause was the natural effect of the physical and moral differences between the Anglo Saxon and the mongral races known as Mexicans. Our fond fair, female friends showed the utmost contempt for the weak dissolute greasers and were public in their outspoken admiration of the stalworth frames, fair skins, blue eyes, and the kind and courteous demeanor, of the "Los Barbarianos del Norta." This was not confined to the lower classes but the "Senoritas Ricos" the "Donas puros Castianos" of the "ton" of the towns shared this feeling alike with the

"Poblano" and "Margaritas" of the villages. This state of affairs as might be supposed, did not increase the love of the "hombras" for us, or render the position of the "Yankedos" (women who lived with americans) now that their protectors were leaving the country, a plesant one. Their fate was truely fearful, they suffered the worst outrages from the returned Mexican Soldierey, and the "ladrones" of the country violated them; ears cut off, branded with the U.S. brand and, in some cases, impaled by the cowardly fiends who, being afraid to face men, thus wreaked their vengenance on defenceless women. In Saltillo a number of Nuns escaped from their convent, and lived with members of the garrison and were model women of that class. When our troops evacuated the town these unfortuneates were compelled to remain behind, some of them laides of unusual beauty. After Gen. Lombardini's Division occupied the place, the authorities got up a grand celebration to commemorate the treaty of peace. As at all Mexican celabrations fireworks formed an important part of the festivity. At midnight the Grand Plaza was all ablaze and full of drunken solders, "Polkos" and "Laddrons," when a fat greasy Dominican Monk, one "Padra Olitze" (who had been a "alcohuet" or pimp to our men) got upon the fountain in the centre of the square and in the most fiery language denounced these poor "Yankedos" to the vile mob. With yells of fiends they searched out the miserable creatures, dragged them from their beds in their night clothes to the plaza where for hours they were subjected to nameless horrors, and then prompted by the Demon Monk, an unheard of atrociety was perpetrated on them by the agency of the less brutal "burros" and then in their dying agonies had their ears cut off and the finishing stroke, (a merciful one) given by cutting their throats. Twenty three young lovely and accomplished Senoritas suffered these fearful tortures and death at this time and no notice was taken of it by Gen. Lombardini, or any other one.

Next morning at sunrise a company of Texas Rangers returning from a corn expedition, passed through Saltillo and drew up to water their horses in the fountain of the Plaza. Here they came upon the horrid sight of over twenty naked bodies of females, terribly mutilated, with dogs fighting as they devoured all that was left of what was once so beautiful and charming.

II.

The Gold Rush and Aftermath, 1849-1869

News of the 1848 gold discovery lured several hundred thousand men to California, many young and single, some with sweethearts or wives back east, a few with wives by their sides. All but a few lucky men learned that gold didn't pepper the surface of the Sierra. Failing to find a fortune, many of the Forty-Niners set about earning a living by starting farms, setting up shops, or providing some of the services that any community needs. Some artists among the gold-rushers used their palettes instead of gold pans, and they soon learned they could make more money painting than panning. Whatever these California Argonauts did, they did it with gusto—or so it seems in the account of these times written by Frank Marryat, a young British artist who also wielded a pen.

Getting to the California gold fields was sometimes hazardous and almost always took weeks or months. Since railroads had already reached the Midwest by the 1840s, there was soon talk of extending a railroad all the way to the Pacific. To make such dreams a reality, the government conducted (during 1853 and 1854) surveys of four possible routes. Artists such as H. Balduin Möllhausen, hired as members of the survey teams, sketched and painted scenes along the route to provide illustrations for the survey reports. One painter, Worthington Whittredge, even managed to join an expedition as a tag-a-long. John C. Frémont, who led an independent survey, hired an artist-turned-daguerreotypist, Solomon Nunez Carvalho. Unlike a few other artists who had started using photography in the 1840s as an aid to enhance their paintings, Carvalho worked to make photography an art in its own right. His written account of Frémont's expedition, *Incidents of Travel and Adventure,* was published in 1859.

Mining rushes in Nevada and Colorado in 1859 brought another 50,000 men to the West. Two years later, the nation plunged into civil war, but in 1862 Congress passed the Homestead Act keeping alive the popular image of the West as the land where dreams come true. For the West's Indians, however, the westward movement had become a nightmare. In 1864 the Navajos were forced to take the Long Walk to Bosque Redondo and Cheyennes were massacred by "Col." John Milton Chivington and his volunteers at Sand Creek. The buffalo were already being slaughtered in increasing numbers, and cowboys were taking great herds of cattle to railheads where they could be shipped east. On May 10, 1869, when the golden spike was driven at Promontory Point, Utah, to link the Union Pacific and the Central Pacific, the West entered a new phase.

Throughout the 1850s and 1860s, artists in the West, like those who came before them, continued to be influenced by European and Eastern predecessors and contemporaries. In the Western artists' writing, too, one can see the impress of the age's styles and themes. Although the West did not have artistic subject matter that, strictly speaking, we can call unique (after all, other continents were also in the process of being explored and colonized by European peoples), it certainly had a distinctiveness that justifies the sobriquet "Wild West." Historians have established that the Old West was not as wild a place as some painters and writers made it seem. But if stretching the facts a bit (as in the western adventure dime novels that started to pour off the presses in 1865) made for a better story, not all artist and writers could resist the temptation to embellish the commonplace.

Frank Marryat—*Where the Gold Comes From* (reproduced from *Mountains and Molehills: Or, Recollections of a Burnt Journal* [London: Longman, Brown, Green, and Longmans, 1855]).

~

Frank Marryat (1826-1855)

Although people of all sorts were swept up by the pandemic gold fever that emerged from California in the middle of the nineteenth century, two characteristics shared by most victims were youthfulness and a sense of adventure. Artist and author Frank Marryat had both of these qualities. In spades. Just twenty-four when he sailed from England for California (via Panama), Marryat was already a veteran of a three-year naval surveying cruise to the South Seas. While in the South Seas, Marryat sketched the many exotic sights that met his eye and, on returning to England, published sixty of his drawings and an accompanying narrative as *Borneo and the Indian Archipelago* (1848). In 1850 Marryat headed for the gold fields of California, no doubt looking to them not only as a source for adventure and mineral riches, but also as a source for a second book of drawings and text.

Born in Norfolk in 1826, Francis "Frank" Marryat was the son of Captain Frederick Marryat, a British naval officer and the commercially successful author of a number of adventure novels, the best known of which is *Mr. Midshipman Easy* (1836). Frank Marryat grew up in a large but well-to-do family that welcomed as house guests the likes of Charles Dickens and Washington Irving. One family visitor, a man named La Salle, was the inspiration for Captain Marryat's *Travels of Monsieur Violet in California* (1843). Both the visitor and the book may have inspired Frank Marryat's later decision to see California for himself. Destined for naval service, young Frank trained as a midshipman and, in 1843, embarked on the South Sea cruise that would serve as the starting point for his career as an artist and writer.

Marryat's California experience began when he landed at San Francisco in June 1850. Accompanied by several dogs and an ex-poacher-cum-manservant, he spent almost two years among the gold fields before family matters drew him back to England. In 1853, accompanied by his new bride, Marryat returned to California. On this second trip he was suffering not so much from gold fever as from the yellow variety—an outbreak of which had killed many of the crew and passengers during the

voyage from Panama. With Frank's health broken, the Marryats soon
returned to England where, despite illness, Marryat worked on Mountains
and Molehills, a book which details in words and pictures his California
adventures. Published in 1855, Mountains and Molehills was an immediate success, but one that Marryat himself did not have much time to relish. As a result of complications from yellow fever, Marryat died at his
family home in August 1855.

In the preface to *Mountains and Molehills,* Marryat writes:

> Nothing that I can say here will blind the reader to the deficiency
> of these pages; they are in truth as their title expresses, the recol-
> lections of a "Journal burnt," and I present them here but an out-
> line of what I have seen or heard during three years of my life; and
> if I am wanting in figures and statistics and any thing of weight as
> regard the country written of, it is certainly because I recalled this
> Journal unexpectedly, and far from the scenes it once depicted.
> (iii)

However disingenuous Frank Marryat may have been in citing the
loss of his journal as the cause of any deficiencies in his work, he is truthful when he admits that his book lacks "anything of weight." Weighty subjects are not the stuff of *Mountains and Molehills,* a work that focuses on
the fun of the Gold Rush. Displaying a puckish sense of humor that often
makes the author himself the butt of the joke, Marryat treats lawsuits,
failed speculations (especially his own), and even funerals as subjects of
fun. In light of the harm unleashed on peoples and landscapes as a result
of the California Gold Rush, Marryat's gleeful take on the doings in the
diggings seems off key; on the other hand, if it is a mistake to gloss over
the violence, injustice, and racism that were a very real part of the Gold
Rush, it is equally a mistake to ignore the fact that at least some of what
went on in the gold fields was fueled, for better or worse, by spirits of fun
and adventure.

As with the text, Marryat's drawings are light-hearted, full of detail,
and tend to emphasize the artist's jolly view of life. In tone the drawings
suggest the humorous work of Dickens' illustrator Phiz (Hablot K.
Brown) just as the text suggests the brand of humor found in Mark
Twain's *Roughing It* (1872). This is not to say that Marryat the writer is any
Twain, or even that Marryat the artist is any Phiz. Yet Marryat is such an

entertaining and exuberant guide to the Gold Rush, it is only natural to wonder what the young artist and writer might have achieved had he been given more time to hone his crafts.

Further Reading

Marryat, Frank. *Borneo and the Indian Archipelago.* London: Longman, Brown, Green, and Longmans, 1848.

_____. *Mountains and Molehills: Or, Recollections of a Burnt Journal.* London: Longman, Brown, Green, and Longmans, 1855. [First British edition includes color illustrations not found in the first American edition (New York: Harper and Brothers, 1855).]

Wilbur, Marguerite Eyer. "Introduction." *Mountains and Molehills: Or, Recollections of a Burnt Journal by Frank Marryat.* Stanford: Stanford University Press, 1952.

~

From *Mountains and Molehills*

January, 1852.

RATS are very numerous in San Francisco, as also are ratting-dogs. The roughest Skyes and most ferocious bull-dogs seem to have congregated in that city; and so much interest do the people take in the destruction of the common enemy, that a crowd is instantly collected if by chance a Scotch terrier, arrested by the flavor of a rat, wags his tail over a heap of shavings. You will one day see a crowd in the street, dense and excited; you try in vain to obtain a glimpse of what is going on in the centre; from expressions that reach you, you feel certain that a horrid murder is being perpetrated, and this opinion is confirmed as you hear re-echoed the cry, "He is dead!—all over!" As the crowd disperses, there issues from it the rejoicing owner of two young prize-fighting quadrupeds, and in his hand is a large rat now all tail and teeth, "the balance," as the owner remarks, having been "considerably chawed up."

Great risk and expense attend the shipment of these little dogs to California; and I was so unfortunate as not to land one of four very useful brutes that I shipped from the London Docks for that country. A good horse or dog is a treasure to a Californian; and he will look upon one or the other as his friend, and treat it with great kindness. . . .

I again started for the mines, and arrived at Tuttle-Town without accident.

We had tolerable hunting-ground in our vicinity, but the game was wild from having been too much shot at. The deer lived in the mountains, and to reach them required much walking, as the reader will understand if he glances at the background of the sketch that forms my frontispiece. The earth on the side of the redwood hills is generally friable, and as it gives way to the pressure of the foot, the toil of ascending is very great, when the glass is at ninety. . . .

I will mention a circumstance here in connection with shooting, which has so much of the marvelous in it that I had determined to omit it.

While encamped at Santa Rosa Valley, after leaving Carrillo's house, we were visited one morning by some Sonorians (probably those who afterward stole our cattle). As they requested us to fire a few shots with our rifles at a mark, we consented willingly enough, and being in good practice and in good luck, we fired with success at dollars and other small targets.

An hour or two afterward, the three of us proceeded in search of venison; it was about mid-day, the sun was very powerful and the sky cloudless. Making for a shady thicket where we hoped to find, we unexpectedly started a doe from the long grass; she was out of shot before we could raise a gun but there still remained a fawn. Pretty innocent! there it stood gazing at us wondrously, and I warrant had there been meat in our larder at home, not one of us would have touched a trigger; but lamb is innocent, and yet you eat it, Madam, and the only difference between us is that you have a butcher to take life, and I had not.

The fawn stood motionless as I advanced a few paces and took, as I imagined, deadly aim. I missed, and still it did not move: the others fired, and missed also. From the same distance (about seventy-five yards), we fired each four bullets without success; still the fawn moved but a pace or two, and our rifle ammunition was exhausted. I then crept up to the fawn, and within twenty paces I fired twice at it with my pistol; it then, unharmed, quietly walked away in search of its mother. We looked at each other in some doubt after this, and for a long time I was puzzled to conjecture how to account for this apparently charmed life.

At last I solved the problem in this way, as I thought. The sun was intensely powerful, and had been reflected back to us from the yellow grass on which we had kept our eyes throughout a long walk; either this glare or the rarefaction of the air had, probably, caused an optical delusion, and the fawn appearing nearer to us than in reality it was, we fired under it. Had this struck me at the time, I would have searched in the long grass for the place where the bullets struck, and I have no doubt, considering the practice we were in, that they would all have been found in the same range, and short; but on account of the height of the grass, we were unable to see while firing where our balls fell. And this is the sole way I can account for this curious adventure.

This is the sole marvelous story I have to tell, and is a fact; but so capricious is reading man, that I daresay many a one who would have believed me had I related the destruction in one long shot of three buffaloes, two coyotes, and a Digger Indian, will smile incredulously at my party firing fourteen barrels within seventy paces of a motionless deer! So be it—and annotators of circulating library books will write "Gammon!" in black-lead pencil on the margin, and I must grin while I writhe under this infliction.

About three miles from our camp was the Stanislaus River; and crossing this in a ferry-boat, we would be at once in the vicinity of a famous digging, "Carson's Hill," by name. All that we read of that is bright and fairylike, in connection with reported gold discoveries, has been presented as a Gradgrind fact at Carson's Hill.

The rivers produced, the hills produced, and even the quartz (Rich deposits were discovered, but I am not aware of the value of the quartz generally at Carson's Creek) produced, having previously been rotted by nature, that man might pick the gold out with his penknife. "Rich nests," "tall pockets," "big strikes," lumps and chunks, were the reward of labor at Carson's Hill; while the miserable population elsewhere were content with ounces of gold, or, at the best, pounds.

No one knows how many fortunes have been made at Carson's Hill, nor how many bloody battles have been fought there for the rich earth— but a great many. Two small armies met once on the brow of the hill, and parleyed, weapons in hand and with savage looks, for as much quartz as you might carry away in a fish-cart.

Mr. James Carson, the discoverer of these diggings, asserts that in 1848 the man who would work could make from fifty to one hundred pounds sterling a day, and I have no doubt of the truth of this.

At the time when this digging was first yielding such immense profits, strict honesty was the characteristic of the miners; and a man need have no fear then, as he has now, relative to keeping his dust after he had found it, for all had enough, and it is astonishing how virtuous we become under such circumstances. A sailor once asked his chum if a bishop was a good man? "He ought for to be," replies the other, "for he has nothing to do but to eat, drink, and sleep, and altogether he has a deuced fine berth of it!" and Jack hit the truth in his own way.

And sailors are, perhaps, after their manner, tolerable Christians themselves; certainly they swear a little, and are said to devour in a sandwich the banknote that would serve to enrich a hospital, as from Bill Bobstay, Esq.; but whenever there is sickness or poverty among sailors, there Jack is found at the bedside the tenderest of nurses, and sharing— honest heart!—his last copper with a comrade. A sailor in the mines is at best a rough and uncomely fellow to the sight; but will you show me any thing more pleasing to contemplate than that sturdy fellow there who plies his pick-ax to the tune of "Oh, Sally Brown!" that he may take at night to his sick friend in the tent hard by the luxuries he needs? The sailors in the mines have been ever distinguished for self-denial; and whenever I see 'prim goodness' frown at the rough, careless sailor's oath that will mingle now and then with his "ye ho!" I think to myself, "Take out your heart, 'prim goodness,' and lay it by the side of Jack's, and offer me the choice of the two, and maybe it won't be yours I'll take, for all that you are faultless to the world's eye."

Liberality was so great in those days, that if a stranger came to the mines and had but the appearance of one who would work, he had no difficulty in borrowing from any one all that was required for starting him, his muscles and sinews being the sole guarantee for repayment. . . .

A gulch which branches off from Carson's, and which proved very rich, was discovered under circumstances of great solemnity, and I am indebted to Mr. Carson for the anecdote.

One of the miners died, and having been much respected, it was determined to give him a regular funeral. A digger in the vicinity, who, report said, had once been a powerful preacher in the United States, was called upon to officiate; and after "drinks all round," the party proceeded, with becoming gravity, to the grave, which had been dug at a distance of a hundred yards from the camp. When this spot was reached, the officiating minister commenced with an extempore prayer, during which all knelt round the grave. So far was well; but the prayer was unnecessarily long, and at last some of those who knelt, began, in an abstracted way, to finger the loose earth that had been thrown up from the grave. It was thick with gold; and an excitement was immediately apparent in the kneeling crowd. Upon this the preacher stopped, and inquiringly said, "Boys, what's that? Gold!" he continued, "and the richest kind of diggings—the congregation are dismissed!" The poor miner was taken from his auriferous grave and was buried elsewhere, while the funeral party, with the parson at their head, lost no time in prospecting the new digging.

The population of the diggings, in 1848, was as varied as can be well imagined; every nation and calling was represented there, from an ex-governor to a Digger Indian. But among this motley crew lawyers predominated; and, if we may judge by the fees they received, and the quality of the law they exchanged for them, they had brought their forensic knowledge to a fine market. As magistrates and other officers were required in the different mining districts, they were elected by a majority of the miners, and formed a court of law.

All mining disputes were submitted to these courts, and whatever might be the decision given, that was considered the law, which saved all trouble of appeal. The following incident will convey some idea of law in the diggings at this time.

Two Spaniards, who had amassed a large quantity of gold dust by successful digging, quarreled over the possession of an old mule that was scarcely worth her keep, and applied to the alcalde, or magistrate, to settle the dispute. Before a word was said, however, each "Greaser" had to pay three ounces of dust for expenses of the court; and then, both speaking at once, each related his own tale in Spanish, which was a language unintelligible to the court. After this, they were informed by his Honor, through an interpreter, that they had better leave the case to the decision of a jury. To this they agreed, and having paid two ounces more in advance to the sheriff, that officer summoned a jury from the adjacent diggings. After hearing their statements, which were very voluminous, the jury retired to deliberate upon their verdict. Upon their return they declared that the testimony was so contradictory that they could not award the mule to either, but that the claimants must decide the ownership by drawing straws for the animal, and that the costs should be equally divided. These amounted to twenty ounces, to which three more were added for payment of the liquor bill. Just as the disputants had paid up this bill, and were about to settle the ownership in the prescribed manner, it was announced that they might save themselves the trouble, for another "Greaser" had taken the opportunity to steal the mule, and had departed to parts unknown.

A few Digger Indians worked occasionally in our vicinity, having discovered that gold would purchase fine clothes and rum, which was all they cared for. The outfits they procured with their dust varied according to taste. One would prefer half a dozen shirts, and wear them all at once; another would be content with a gaudy Mexican hat and a pair of jack-boots; so that their partial adoption of civilized costume only served to render the uncovered parts of their bodies ridiculously conspicuous.

The Indians of California have a tradition among them which points to the days when volcanic eruptions devastated the country, and destroyed all living things but Indians. No traces of an earlier race are to be found, however, as yet, in Upper California; nor have the Indians the faintest knowledge of pictorial signs or symbols. I am inclined, therefore, to think that the present tribes have been migratory.

It is a peculiarity of California, that although it is so rich in flowers, the wild bee is never found there, nor did I ever hear a singing-bird. Digging in the mines is suspended by general accord on the Sabbath, and that day is usually spent very quietly in camp, particularly as the more boisterous characters go to the nearest town to amuse themselves. A walk over the mountains, rifle in hand, with an eye to business in the shape of "prospecting," is often the employment of the more sedate; and if the miner sometimes finds on a Sunday what serves him for an honest livelihood on week days, he is, mayhap, no worse, sir, than you whose thoughts, even in a church, are not always separate from the pounds shillings and pence you require for the engagements of the coming week.

During this time the work at the mines progressed steadily; and the new machinery being ready, we started it, fully confident of success (Our object was still only to experimentalize). Again was our engine placed under contribution for four horses, more power than it was built for, and again did our machinery turn out a signal failure: in fact, we had iron only where we should have had the hardest of steel, and in consequence, instead of our mill grinding the quartz, the quartz had the best of it, and ground the mill; and as it was gold I wanted, and not iron filings, I determined for the present to abandon my third profitless speculation.

Agriculturally, architecturally, and mineralogically, I had been sported with by fate—and the plow in the north, the steam-engine in the south, and the hotel in the middle, had each been accompanied by pecuniary loss. Yet the days I had passed had been very happy, and Philosophy said: "You have had health, and contentment, and warm friendship; and if these were purchasable, many would buy them of you for twenty times what you have lost in money!" To which I replied, "Very true, oh, Philosophy! but had I taken my steam-engine to Russian River, and there applied its power to sawing redwoods, and had I with my plow turned up the fertile hills and valleys at Vallejo, and further, had I erected my hotel at Sonora, where it was much wanted, I might have still had the unpurchasable articles you allude to, and the money too." Upon which Philosophy, seeing me thus unreasonable, retired from the contest. . . .

Frank
Marryat

A Solomon Nunes Carvalho daguerreotype—"View of an Indian Camp. . . ."
(Library of Congress, #225585, Washington, D.C.).

~

Solomon Nunes Carvalho (1815-1897)

A chief charm of Solomon Nunes Carvalho is his obscurity. As readers we have the pleasure of seeing the emergence of a man who certainly was not a genius but who was intelligent, tolerant, talented in a number of fields, and strove brightly, observed historian Elizabeth Berman, in ". . . his life-long ambition to make sense of his world" ("Solomon Nunes Carvalho" 19). In the course of things, luck threw him an unusual chance, and, seizing it, Solomon Carvalho made important, if long-forgotten, contributions not only to our perceptions of the West but also to the means of recording them.

Born into the prospering community of Sephardic Jews in Charleston, South Carolina, which valued culture and intellectual pursuits, Carvalho spent most of his life as a painter and photographer in Philadelphia, Baltimore, and other major cities on the East Coast. Although photography was in its infancy, he perfected several technical aspects of the daguerreotype, and, showing his wide interests, he eventually became an inventor of some success by improving the efficiency of the steam boiler. All this while he was a leader in Jewish communities, founding synagogues, advocating changes in the liturgy, and arguing for the compatibility of science and theology.

By 1853 Solomon Carvalho had achieved such note that Colonel John Charles Frémont invited him to be the artist/photographer on Frémont's fifth expedition to the West. Unfortunately, Frémont never published a report of this journey, thus denying Carvalho the accolades he would have enjoyed as the illustrator of the famous Pathfinder's text. In fact, much of Carvalho's work has disappeared in the oubliette of time. Yet the photographs that remain confirm Carvalho's place as one of the earliest and most skilled imagists on the frontier. Fortunately, his own account, *Incidents of Travel and Adventure,* offers reliable prose portraits of Frémont's final western expedition.

On this foray, city-dweller Carvalho was badly out of his element as the little band of explorers, freezing and weakened by near starvation, slogged through hip-deep snow in the Rocky Mountains. Despite the additional burden of struggling with the awkward and heavy photo-graphic equipment of the day, Carvalho remained levelheaded. To the best of his abilities he adjusted to rough circumstances, putting his troubles behind him to give us memorable vignettes of the raw frontier. It should be said in passing that the Jewish proscription against the "graven image" was not a factor with Carvalho. Along with fellow artists of his faith, he did not see the Second Commandment as applying to his work.

Other aspects of his heritage came very much into play. The violations of dietary restrictions necessitated by life on the trail troubled him, and he cringed in Salt Lake City when encountering polygamy among the Mormons. But he also quickly praised their chaste language, industry, and sobriety. In such ways Carvalho gives not only portraits of the frontier, but gives of himself, an earnest and flexible man hewing as best he can to his beliefs while remaining admirably tolerant of others.

Further Reading

Berman, Elizabeth Kessin. "Solomon Nunes Carvalho: Painter and Prophet." *Solomon Nunes Carvalho: Painter, Photographer, and Prophet in Nineteenth Century America.* Baltimore: The Jewish Historical Society of Maryland, 1989. Pp. 5-21.

Carvalho, Solomon Nunes. *Incidents of Travel and Adventure in the Far West. 1857.* Bertram Wallace Korn, ed. Philadelphia: The Jewish Publication Society of America, 1954.

Sturhahn, Joan. *Carvalho: Artist, Photographer, Adventurer, Patriot. Portrait of a Forgotten American.* Merrick, New York: Richwood Publishing Company, 1976.

≈

From *Incidents of Travel and Adventure in the Far West*

The preparations for my journey occupied about ten days, during which time I purchased all the necessary materials for making a panorama of the country, by daguerreotype process, over which we had to pass.

To make daguerreotypes in the open air, in a temperature varying from freezing point to thirty degrees below zero, requires different manip-ulation from the processes by which pictures are made in a warm room.

My professional friends were all of the opinion that the elements would be against my success. Buffing and coating plates, mercurializing them, on the summit of the Rocky Mountains, standing at times up to one's middle in snow, with no covering above save the arched vault of heaven, seemed to our city friends one of the impossibilities—knowing as they did that iodine will not give out its fumes except at a temperature of 70° to 80° Fahrenheit. I shall not appear egotistical if I say that I encountered many difficulties, but I was well prepared to meet them by having previously acquired a scientific and practical knowledge of the chemicals I used, as well as of the theory of light: a firm determination to succeed also aided me in producing results which, to my knowledge, have never been accomplished under similar circumstances.

While suffering from frozen feet and hands, without food for twenty-four hours, travelling on foot over mountains of snow, I have stopped on the trail, made pictures of the country, re-packed my materials, and found myself frequently with my friend Egloffstien, who generally remained with me to make barometrical observations, and a muleteer, some five or six miles behind camp, which was only reached with great expense of bodily as well as mental suffering. The great secret, however, of my untiring perseverance and continued success, was that my honor was pledged to Col. Fremont to perform certain duties, and I would rather have died than not have redeemed it. I made pictures up to the very day Col. Fremont found it necessary to bury the whole baggage of the camp, including the daguerreotype apparatus. He has since told me that my success, under the frequent occurrence of what he considered almost insuperable difficulties, merited his unqualified approbation.

I left New York on the 5th September, 1853, having in charge the daguerreotype apparatus, painting materials, and half a dozen cases of Alden's preserved coffee, eggs, cocoa, cream, and milk, which he sent out for the purpose of testing their qualities. There was in them sufficient nourishment to have sustained twenty men for a month. I purchased a ticket by the Illinois River to St. Louis, but the water was so low in the river that it was deemed advisable to cross over to Alton by stage, as I was afraid of being detained. The cases of instruments were very heavy, and the proprietor of the stage refused to take them; it being night, I remonstrated with him, telling him of the importance that they should arrive at St. Louis; he peremptorily refused to take them. I, of course, had to succumb, and remarked inadvertently how disappointed Col. Fremont would be in

Solomon
Nunes
Carvalho

105

not receiving them. At the mention of Col. Fremont's name, he asked me if those cases were Fremont's? I told him, yes. He sang out for his boy to harness up an extra team of horses, and stow away the boxes. "I will put them through for Fremont, without a cent of expense. I was with him on one of his expeditions, and a nobler specimen of mankind does not live about these parts."

Mr. Bomar, proposed to make photographs by the wax process, and several days were consumed in preparing the paper, etc. I was convinced that photographs could not be made by that process as quickly as the occasion required, and told Col. Fremont to have one made from the window of our room, to find out exactly the time. The preparations not being entirely completed, a picture could not be made that day; but on the next, when we were all in camp, Col. Fremont requested that daguerreotypes and photographs should be made. In half an hour from the time the word was given, my daguerreotype was made; but the photograph could not be seen until next day, as it had to remain in water all night, which was absolutely necessary to develop it. Query, where was water to be had on the mountains, with a temperature of 20° below zero? To be certain of a result, even if water could be procured, it was necessary by his [Bomar's] process, to wait twelve hours, consequently, every time a picture was to be made, the camp must be delayed twelve hours. Col. Fremont finding that he could not see immediate impressions, concluded not to incur the trouble and expense of transporting the apparatus, left it at Westport, together with the photographer. The whole dependence was now on me. Col. Fremont told me if I had the slightest doubts of succeeding, it were better to say so now, and he would cancel the agreement on my part, and pay me for my time, etc.

On the night of the 20th, all hands slept in camp, a heavy rain-storm drenched us completely, giving to the party an introduction to a life on the prairies. The necessity of India-rubber blankets became evident, and I was dispatched to Westport to procure them. There were none to be had. I sent a man to Independence to purchase two dozen; he travelled thirty miles that night, and by ten next morning I had them in camp. They were the most useful articles we had with us; we placed the India-rubber side on the snow, our buffalo robes on the top of that for a bed, and covered with our blankets, with an India-rubber blanket over the whole-India-rubber side up, to turn the rain. We generally slept double, which added to our comfort, as we communicated warmth to each other, and had the advantage of two sets of coverings. During the whole journey, exposed to the most furious snow-storms, I never slept cold, although when I have been called for guard I often found some difficulty in rising from the weight of snow resting on me.

The Cheyenne village, on Big Timber, consists of about two hundred and fifty lodges, containing, probably, one thousand persons, including men, women and children.

I went into the village to take daguerreotype views of their lodges, and succeeded in obtaining likenesses of an Indian princess—a very aged woman, with a papoose, in a cradle or basket, and several of the chiefs. I had great difficulty in getting them to sit still, or even to submit to have themselves daguerreotyped. I made a picture, first, of their lodges, which I showed them. I then made one of the old woman and papoose. When they saw it, they thought I was a "supernatural being;" and, before I left camp, they were satisfied I was more than human.

The squaws are very fond of ornaments; their arms are encircled with bracelets made of thick brass wire—sometimes of silver beaten out as thin as pasteboard. The princess, or daughter of the Great Chief, was a beautiful Indian girl. She attired herself in her most costly robes, ornamented with elk teeth, beads, and colored porcupine quills—expressly to have her likeness taken. I made a beautiful picture of her.

The bracelets of the princess were of brass; silver ones are considered invaluable, and but few possess them.

After I had made the likeness of the princess, I made signs to her to let me have one of her brass bracelets. She very reluctantly gave me one. I wiped it very clean, and touched it with "quicksilver." It instantly became bright and glittering as polished silver. I then presented her with it. Her delight and astonishment knew no bounds. She slipped it over her arm, and danced about in ecstacy. As for me, she thought I was a great "Magician."

My extraordinary powers of converting "brass into silver" soon became known in the village, and in an hour's time I was surrounded with squaws entreating me to make "presto, pass!" with their "armlets and brass finger-rings."

Some offered me moccasins, others venison, as payment; but I had to refuse nearly all of them, as I had only a small quantity of quicksilver for my daguerreotype operations.

At last we are drawn to the necessity of killing our brave horses for

food. The sacrifice of my own pony that had carried me so bravely in my
first buffalo hunt, was made; he had been running loose for a week unable
to bear even a bundle of blankets. It was a solemn event with me, and rendered more so by the impressive scene which followed.

Col. Fremont came out to us, and after referring to the dreadful necessity to which we were reduced, said "a detachment of men whom he had
sent for succor on a former expedition, had been guilty of eating one of
their own number." He expressed his abhorrence of the act, and proposed
that we should not under any circumstances whatever, kill our companions to prey upon them. "If we are to die, let us die together like men." He
then threatened to shoot the first man that made or hinted at such a
proposition.

It was a solemn and impressive sight to see a body of white men,
Indians, and Mexicans, on a snowy mountain, at night, some with bare
head and clasped hands entering into this solemn compact. I never until
that moment realized the awful situation in which I, one of the actors in
this scene, was placed.

I remembered the words of the sacred Psalmist, (Psalm cviii. 4-7) and
felt perfectly assured of my final deliverance.—"They wandered in the
wilderness in a solitary way: They found no city to dwell in."

Under the operation of this law, nobody but Mormons can hold property in Great Salt Lake City. There are numbers of citizens who are not
Mormons, who rent properties; but there is no property for sale—a most
politic course on the part of the Mormons—for in case of a railroad being
established between the two oceans, Great Salt Lake City must be the half
way stopping place, and the city will be kept purified from taverns and
grog shops at every corner of the street. Another city will have to be built
some distance from them, for they have determined to keep themselves
distinct from the vices of civilization. During a residence of ten weeks in
Great Salt Lake City, and my observations in all their various settlements,
amongst a homogeneous population of over seventy-five thousand inhabitants, it is worthy of record, that I never heard any obscene or improper
language; never saw a man drunk; never had my attention called to the
exhibition of vice of any sort. There are no gambling houses, grog shops,
or buildings of ill fame, in all their settlements. They preach morality in
their churches and from their stands, and what is as strange as it is true,
the people practise it, and religiously believe their salvation depends on
fulfilling the behests of the religion they have adopted.

The masses are sincere in their belief, if they are incredulous, and have been deceived by their leaders, the sin, if any, rests on them. I firmly believe the people to be honest, and imbued with true religious feelings,—and when we take into consideration their general character previously, we cannot but believe in their sincerity. Nine-tenths of this vast population are the peasantry of Scotland, England and Wales, originally brought up with religious feelings at Protestant parish churches. I observed no Catholic proselytes. They have been induced to emigrate, by the offers of the Mormon missionaries to take them free of expense, to their land flowing with milk and honey, where, they are told, the Protestant Christian religion is inculcated in all its purity, and where a farm and house are bestowed gratuitously upon each family. Seduced by this independence from the state of poverty which surrounds them at home, they take advantage of the opportunity and are baptized into the faith of the "latter day saints," and it is only after their arrival in the Valley that the spiritual wife system is even mentioned to them.

At about three o'clock, the order was given to fill up the water cans, as we were about to traverse this immense desert where water was not to be had; every vessel that could possibly be used, was immediately put in requisition—canteens, kegs, bottles, cans, etc.

At four o'clock, having harnessed up the horses, and saddled my mule, we were on the road, which led through a loose stony ravine, with much sand; it was very heavy travelling, and our animals moved through it with a great deal of difficulty.

We travelled thus for eleven miles, and then gradually ascended the table land, on a harder and better road.

We commenced our journey in the afternoon, that we might have the benefit of the night air to travel in; a cool, north wind tempered the atmosphere, and we continued the journey through this sterile, bare, and uncovered country, until midnight, when we halted and refreshed our animals with water from our reservoirs. After a rest of three hours, we resumed our journey, and at ten o'clock in the morning of the 29th, we had crossed this dreaded Jornada without any accident, and camped on a narrow stream of deliciously cool water, which distributes itself about half a mile further down, in a verdant meadow bottom, covered with good grass.

This camp ground is called by the Mexicans, Las Vegas. Once more, we had plenty of grass for our fatigued animals, and we determined to rest here, during the day and night.

Solomon
Nunes
Carvalho

We passed a number of deserted wagons on the road; chairs, tables, bedsteads, and every article of housekeeping, were strewn along our path. The emigrant party who had preceded us about ten days, from Parowan, to lighten their wagons, threw out first one article and then another, until everything they had, was left on the road. It was not difficult to follow their trail; in one hour I counted the putrid carcasses of nineteen oxen, cows, mules and horses; what a lesson to those who travel over such a country, unadvised and unprepared.

A strong north wind blew during the morning, which raised clouds of dust, completely and unresistingly filling our eyes with a fine white dust, although I used goggles to prevent it.

The delightful and refreshing water of this oasis, soon purified me, and now, having crossed the desert, bathed and breakfasted, I feel more comfortable, both mentally and physically.

Mezquite, *(alga robia)* are the only trees growing near this stream.

We remained at camp all day yesterday, and left this morning at ten o'clock.

We followed up this delicious stream for about three miles; I was curious to see from whence it flowed, the general character of the country indicating that we were not far from its source. Several of us turned from the road, and at a short distance, we found its head waters. It was a large spring, the water bubbled up as if gas were escaping, acacias in full bloom, almost entirely surrounded it—it was forty-five feet in diameter; we approached through an opening, and found it to contain the clearest and purest water I ever tasted; the bottom, which consisted of white sand, did not seem to be more than two feet from the surface.

Parley Pratt prepared himself for a bathe, while I was considering whether I should go in, I heard Mr. Pratt calling out that he could not sink, the water was so buoyant. Hardly believing it possible that a man could not sink in fresh water, I undressed and jumped in.

What were my delight and astonishment, to find all my efforts to sink were futile. I raised my body out of the water, and suddenly lowered myself, but I bounced upwards as if I had struck a springing-board. I walked about in the water up to my arm-pits, just the same as if I had been walking on dry land.

The water, instead of being two feet deep, was over fifteen, the depth of the longest tent pole we had with us. It is positively impossible for a man to sink over his head in it; the sand on its banks was fine and white. The temperature of the water was 78°, the atmosphere 85°.

I can form no idea as to the cause of this great phenomenon; Col. Fremont made observations on the spot in 1845, and marked its existence on his map as Las Vegas; but he has since told me he did not know of its buoyant qualities, as he did not bathe in it. In the absence of any other name, I have called it the Buoyant Spring.

Great Salt Lake possesses this quality in a great degree, but that water is saturated with salt; this is deliciously sweet water; probably some of the savans can explain the cause of its peculiar properties. We lingered in the spring fifteen minutes. Twenty-three men were at one time bobbing up and down in it endeavoring to sink, without success. I made drawings of this spot, and the surrounding mountains.

The California ladies are generally brunettes; some of them with whom I became acquainted were most beautiful and accomplished. Bonnets are unknown. During the morning their magnificent tresses are allowed to hang at full length down their backs. I have seen suits of hair at least three feet long, waving gracefully around a well-formed neck. In the evening a great deal of care and pains are taken to curl and plait it. When they go out, a simple mantilla of black satin or silk, sometimes of colored silk, is gracefully thrown over their heads; they invariably carry a large fan. The most costly material is used for dresses, and the richest and most expensive shawls may be seen worn by the ladies in Los Angeles. Society is very select among the better classes, although there are but few American families residing there.

Alas! for the morals of the people at large; it was the usual salutation in the morning, "Well, how many murders were committed last night?"— "Only four—three Indians and a Mexican." Sometimes three, often two, but almost every night while I was there, one murder, at least, was committed. It became dangerous to walk abroad after night. A large number of American gamblers frequented the principal hotels, and induced the Californians to risk their money at all the famous games of monte, roulette, poker, faro, etc.

When I arrived at San Francisco, I had the curiosity to enter one of the frequented "hells," to see the process of winning and losing money. The building selected by the gentleman who accompanied me, was a celebrated one in Clay street. An orchestra of thirty-five musicians, were per-

Solomon
Nunes
Carvalho

forming fashionable operatic airs; following the sound, we were introduced into the saloon, which was brilliantly illuminated; it was truly an imposing sight. There must have been over fifty tables, at which presided most beautiful women, dealing out cards, or whirling around a roulette table; at some might have been seen old gentlemen with white hair, to all appearance respectable, and whose proper place seemed to me, to be a magistrate's bench, or a judge's forum. Few or no words are spoken at the table; men silently place their gold on a card, and before a second expires, it is swept away; once out of many times, it is doubled by the player; it remains and he wins: a second time fortune favors, it doubles again; the insatiate vice of selfishness, not satisfied with eight times what he originally staked, leaves his pile, building castles in the air with the imaginary proceeds of his winnings—when in the twinkle of an eye, a gentle sweep from the smiling syren, dissipates his dreams of fortune, and he retires from the hell penniless in reality. Hundreds of men who have acquired by hard work and industry, a little fortune at the mines, and come to town to purchase a bill of exchange to send to their families, are induced to visit one of these places, and in an hour he has lost the labor of months, leaving his family anxiously awaiting remittances which they are doomed never to receive.

These native Californians have been known to borrow money at the enormous rate of six per cent. a month, compound interest, and give their ranchos as collaterals, on purpose to gamble with; many who once were rich, are now reduced to beggary from this cause; the compound interest accumulating so fast, that unable to meet it, the mortgage is foreclosed, and a valuable property sacrificed to the usurious practices of those who call themselves men, for one twentieth part of its real value.

Balduin Möllhausen's *Steamboat "Explorer"* (from Henrich Balduin Möllhausen, *Steamboat "Explorer" [Chimney Peak]*, watercolor and gouache on paper [number, 1988.1.1], Amon Carter Museum, Fort Worth, Texas).

~

Balduin Möllhausen (1825-1905)

The reason why Balduin Möllhausen traveled to the American West in the mid-nineteenth century can still be seen today along Germany's byways. There the traveler pauses, arrested at colorful tepees pitched in green fields. Lounging about them are throngs of Indians in full warrior dress and trappers decked out in fringed buckskins. The fact that these figures of the American frontier, thousands of miles away from "home," speak German only supports the point. In the minds of Germans, and of Europeans generally, America has been a glowing, exotic place where fancies are fulfilled.

The son of an artillery officer who abandoned his family, Möllhausen served briefly in the Prussian Army in 1845 and 1846 and again during the Revolution of 1848. Poor and without much chance of success in a rigid society, he joined thousands of others who crossed the sea in 1850 in hopes of improving their lot in life. Like many of them, Möllhausen wanted to experience firsthand the American frontier he had hitherto enjoyed only vicariously in the works of James Fenimore Cooper.

In 1851, after having worked in the Midwest as a sign painter, hunter, trapper, and court reporter, Möllhausen met a German nobleman, Duke Paul of Württemberg. Like other visiting European noblemen such as Sir William Drummond Stewart and Prince Maximilian of Wied-Neuwied, Duke Paul wanted an artist to help record his travels in America, so he hired Möllhausen as his assistant.

In 1852 Möllhausen traveled to Berlin. There he met Alexander von Humboldt, the famous German scientist, and fell in love with Caroline Seifert, the daughter of Humboldt's private secretary. Möllhausen returned to the United States in 1853 and, thanks to his new-found friends in Berlin, he soon landed another job. In *Wild River, Timeless Canyons: Balduin Möllhausen's Watercolors of the Colorado,* Ben W. Huseman writes that "With recommendations from Humboldt and Leo von Gerolt, the Prussian ambassador in Washington, Möllhausen found a position as 'topographer and draughtsman' with the expedition commanded by Lieutenant Amiel W. Whipple. . . ." After the expedition had explored a possible railroad route along the thirty-fifth parallel, Möllhausen again returned to Prussia, where he married Caroline Seifert and met George Catlin, whose paintings of the American West Möllhausen had already studied.

In 1857, Möllhausen's diary of the Whipple Expedition was published and he again returned to the United States with another letter of recommendation from Humboldt, this one addressed to Jefferson Davis, outgoing secretary of war. When Joseph Christmas Ives (a lieutenant who had been second-in-command of the Whipple expedition) saw the letter, he sent a favorable response to Möllhausen and hired him for the Ives expedition of 1858.

As with the report of the Whipple expedition, Möllhausen's paintings illustrated the report of the Ives survey. But Möllhausen didn't stop there. Switching easily from brush to pen, he wrote accounts of his trips and, making more of a good thing, further turned his adventures into dozens of Cooperesque novels that proved popular in his homeland. Punctuated by dramatic plots and hair's-breadth escapes, these novels are colorful fantasies spun by a writer seeking to please a believing audience.

Far more factual, Möllhausen's travel accounts are quite another matter. Here we often see, as holds true of his paintings, a growing tension created when the romanticism driving the traveler clashes with the realities of the wilderness. In the following, the European romantic, marooned, ill, and close to death in a gelid prairie landscape, faces first the horrors of his own loneliness; then, a pair of Noble Savages, much admired in Europe, step forth from their idealized version to confront him in quite a different guise.

Möllhausen probably knew that the scene he describes would fascinate readers just as similar scenes from Cooper's *The Last of the Mohicans* had fascinated readers in Europe and America. Whether Möllhausen invented, exaggerated, or portrayed accurately his encounter with the hostile Indians, he must have known that the perils of the frontier were real enough.

To his credit, however, Möllhausen refused to be overwhelmed by the dangers and savagery of life beyond the frontier. With his paintings, he saw his job as capturing the living tapestry passing before him. As was common with other enthusiastic chroniclers, his peaks and sandstone pinnacles sometimes soar a bit too high, defying the laws of physics. At his best he combines whimsy and accuracy, showing his audience both white men and natives at work and at their ease against the strange beauty of far-off landscapes.

Such composure and tolerance had earlier earned him the friendship of aging Baron Alexander von Humbolt and other renowned European scientists, and it won Möllhausen appointment as Potsdam's custodian of libraries. The lifelong position enabled him to write over fifty volumes ranging from novels through travel books to poetry.

Further Reading

Barba, Preston Albert. *Balduin Möllhausen: The German Cooper.* Philadelphia: University of Pennsylvania Press, 1914.

Huseman, Ben W. *Wild River, Timeless Canyons: Balduin Möllhausen's Watercolors of the Colorado.* Fort Worth: Amon Carter Museum, 1995.

Möllhausen, Balduin. *Diary of a Journey from the Mississippi to the Coasts of the Pacific.* Mrs. Percy Sinnett, trans. 1858. Peter A. Fritzell, intro. New York: Johnson Reprint, 1969. 2 vols.

∾

From *Diary of a Journey from the Mississippi to the Coasts of the Pacific*

With any human creature near, were it but a child, you would not feel so wholly forsaken, and there is comfort in hearing a human voice, were it only a voice of complaint. I was never so forcibly struck with this truth before this evening; and I tried talking to myself, but that did not answer,—your own voice somehow makes you shudder when it reaches no other ear. When the sun set behind masses of snow clouds, and while his last rays were still lingering on the dreary snowy waste, a concert began, which I had heard before, but never found so little to my taste. A troop of prairie wolves broke out into a loud howl, and to their long-drawn treble was soon joined the deep bass of the large grey and white wolf. The wild music was hushed sometimes for a few minutes, and then a solo performer would begin, and make his clear piercing tones heard from afar; then again the full chorus would burst in, the wind carrying the sounds far over the desert. In the ravine where the horses had fallen, and where nothing was now to be seen of them but their polished bones and the iron rings of their harness, a fierce contest arose, and by the shrill sounds of lamentation I guessed that the little prairie wolves had the worst of it, and had been obliged to decamp. I tried for hours together to make out, by their voices, the number of the animals assembled in the ravine, but I could not succeed. It was a melancholy occupation, but it helped me to get through the hours of the black stormy night. At last I fell asleep from exhaustion, and was awakened by hunger when the sun stood high in the heavens. . . .

I do not think it would be possible for me to describe the sufferings of the next eight days. I was so lame that I had to crawl on my hands and knees to the water, and back to my tent; my head seemed to whirl like that of a drunken man, and my memory was quite failing me, I believe in consequence of the severe cold. Snow storms howled round the dreary steppe, threatening to bury me and my tent together; and I did not now dare to close my eyes at night for fear of the wolves, for hunger had rendered them bolder, and they were coming nearer and nearer to me. The great white ones especially were continually describing circles round my dwelling, howling dismally the while; I heard the snow crackling under their feet, as I lay listening to every sound; and at last I one night saw the teeth of one of them make their appearance through the tent leather. I fired my revolver at random through the thin wall into the darkness, and the fierce brutes fled in terror, but it was only to return in a few hours and renew the attack.

During the daytime these creatures were not so daring, as they dread the light, and then I ventured to take a little rest. But what kind of rest was it? Among the various properties that made a kind of chaos round me in my narrow dwelling, I had discovered a bottle of laudanum, which, with a case of quinine, formed our travelling medicine chest; and in the morning, after my scanty meal was finished, I used to indulge myself with a good dose, and by that means obtained a sleep of several hours. Gay, pleasant images then surrounded me in my dreams; I felt neither cold nor pain,—I was unconscious and happy. But on awakening, the grim reality again presented itself in all its terrors. . . .

I had still only cut the sixteenth notch in my pole, when one day, after a very scanty meal, I put my buffalo robe round me, took my rifle under my arm, and set out on my old way to the neighbouring hill. Fresh snow

118

had fallen during the night, completely effacing the tracks I had previously made, and I was slow in working my way to the top, so that by the time I reached it, the sun was declining, and sending slanting rays over the boundless white plain; not a breath of air was stirring, and I felt warm in the shaggy buffalo hide, though my breath was frozen in drops like pearls on the black wool that surrounded my face.

Standing at the top of the hill, I looked round as usual on all sides, and presently discovered, to my great terror, two human forms, which, though they were still a long way off, seemed to be approaching my camp from the north. I say to my terror, for independently of a kind of savage shyness which I had contracted, they came from a region where, I believed, there were none but thievish Pawnees. I considered that if they were Pawnees, it would not be well that they should find me unprepared in my tent; I should do better to await them in the open air, and try and find out their dispositions and intentions, so that I might in the worst case sell my scalp as dearly as possible. I reckoned that I had nearly an hour to make my preparations in, but when they had once reached a point whence they could overlook my small territory, it would be too late to withdraw myself from their sharp eyes. I therefore hastened back to my tent, armed myself with as many weapons as I could carry, and hid the remainder under the bed, after taking out the percussion caps; I then put a good quantity of wood on the glimmering fire, so that a column of smoke might rise through the opening at the top of the tent, and when I left it, took care to walk backwards, and to leave the opening fastened, so as to appear as if it were done from the inside, and that the Pawnees might suppose the occupant to be within and resting by his fire.

Sandy Hill Creek was only about a hundred and fifty paces from the tent, and flowed in a semicircular direction round it; and it had high banks overgrown with shrubs and bushes; thither, therefore, I directed my steps to seek a hiding place. I placed my feet carefully and exactly in the traces that I had left when I went to fetch water in the morning, and these led me to a convenient place on the smooth, glassy surface of the ice, from which the nightly gale had swept all the snow, and drifted it to the high banks. When I got upon the ice, I pulled off what remains of shoes I had on, that the nails in them might not betray me by any scratch; and treading softly, and following the windings of the stream for some time, to diminish, as far as possible, the distance between me and the tent, and yet allow me to see from the other side what was going on, I crawled up the bank between two snow drifts, and placed myself on the edge, so that I could look through the projecting twigs and stalks, and get a clear view without being hindered in the use of my weapons. Long I lay and listened, but the fever of expectation and anxiety prevented my feeling the cold, except that the hand that lay on the barrel of my rifle was almost frozen to it. At last the heads of the two figures I had noticed, rose above the neighbouring hill, and in a few seconds they stood on its summit, and remained for some time gazing on my tent, and talking with one another. I followed with my eyes their slightest gestures, and I could not help a shiver running through me when I saw them throw back their buffalo skins, draw their full quivers before them, and string their bows. Their intentions, therefore, were no longer doubtful; and I saw what I had to expect if they should get the best of it. I was prepared, however, and I knew that if they once came within range of my rifle, their lives were mine. I could not let them escape; for if I had, I should to a certainty have had them back in a few days, with a whole troop of their companions. The two Indians soon separated, and making some signs to each other, one proceeded to the hill whence I had first caught sight of them, and began to examine the track I had made, which went straight to the tent; while the other, with his eyes fixed on the ground, made a circuit round it. He examined with great care the track to the water, but appeared satisfied when he had convinced himself that the one line of footsteps lay to, and the other from, the ice. He then noiselessly approached his comrade, who, with his bow in his left hand, and an arrow in his right, was standing before the opening of the tent. No word passed between them, but the last comer raised his finger, and put his right hand on his cheek, and his head a little on one side,—I suppose to signify sleep; he then pointed to the rising smoke, placed his bow before him on the ground, and taking the arrow between his teeth, made with his hands the motion of shooting; after which he took up his bow again, and the two fitted their arrows. Had I been in the tent, nothing could have saved me: I understood their gestures but too well. "Here lives a man, he is lying by the fire asleep, a few arrows will secure this rich booty;" these were assuredly their thoughts, and they now placed themselves so that their arrows, shot in quick succession, should meet at a right angle at the empty sleeping place. . . .

I was sitting on the bank, and peeping between the frost-covered twigs and blades of grass that stuck up out of the snow, at their treacherous tricks. The blood seemed to stand still in my veins, though I could hear my heart beat, as I saw them shoot four or five arrows, one after the other, into the tent; and at that moment I made the discovery how dear life is to man, even in the most dreary and disconsolate circumstances. Nothing stirred behind the thin leathern walls, and the Indians, after listening for a time, cautiously approached the curtained opening. One then laid his bow aside and, seizing his tomahawk, knelt down; whilst the other, with his arrow on the string, stood in readiness to shoot. At this moment the shaven skull of the kneeling man was brought into my line of sight, and I cocked my rifle. Slight as the sound was, they both started, and cast keen glances all round. The kneeling man was now the least dangerous of the two, and I therefore shifted my aim, so that the naked breast of the one with the bow became my mark, and instantly fired. The Indian's sharp eye must have discovered me at the moment, for he sprang aside; but he was hit, and fell with a cry that went through every nerve in my body. The other had sprung up, but only to receive the full discharge of buck shot in his face and neck, and to fall lifeless beside his groaning comrade. My enemies were now dead, or incapable of injuring me; but an indescribable feeling of despair seized me, as I thought of what I had done, and of what remained for me to do. I loaded my rifle again, and mechanically approached the bloody spot; and only the groans of the wounded man roused me, and recalled me to myself. It was a horrible sight! There lay prostrate before me, swimming in blood, the two men who a minute before had stood there in the full vigour of life. They had indeed treacherously plotted the destruction of a man who had never done them any injury, never even seen them; and they had fallen a sacrifice to their own greediness for plunder. The body of the younger one lay stretched out, the tomahawk had fallen from his grasp, and the murderous lead had entered his neck and one of his eyes, and frightfully distorted his bronze-coloured face. I turned him on the other side that I might not see it again, and went towards the one who was only wounded. He was an older man; his long black hair almost covered his face, but the fire of deadly hate gleamed at me from his eyes. The bullet had entered the breast below the left shoulder, though whether the wound was mortal or not, I could not say; but his bleeding, and the clenching of his teeth from pain, awakened the deepest feeling of compassion in me. I bent down over him, and endeavoured to make him understand by signs and single words, that I would drag him into my tent, wash and heal his wounds, cover him with buffalo skins, and take care of him, if I could thereby gain his goodwill.

Balduin
Möllhausen

121

At last he made out what I meant, and a wild gleam of joy lighted up his face, as he signified his assent by the Indian exclamation, "Hau! Hau!" In a moment I felt glad—almost happy again—I should save the sufferer. I should gain a companion and a friend in my dreadful solitude. As I was hastening into my tent, to make what preparation I could for the reception of my patient, his loud groans called me back. He made a sign to me to come nearer, and with a finger of the left hand, he pointed to his right, which was bent in an inconvenient position under his back, and seemed to beg me to draw it out. Without the slightest suspicion, I knelt down beside him, but I had scarcely touched his arm, when the right hand, armed with a knife, flashed like lightning from beneath his body, and seizing me with his left, he stabbed twice at my breast. The blows had been well aimed, but feebly executed. I parried both with my right arm, and snatching with my left the knife which, like the Indians, I wore at my girdle, I plunged it several times into the breast of the revengeful savage. A stream of blood gushed from his mouth; there was a slight rattling sound in his throat, he stretched himself out, and I was again alone—alone in the wide wintry waste—alone with the dead!

Worthington Whittredge's *On the Plains, Colorado* (St. Johnsbury Athenaeum, St. Johnsbury, Vermont).

Worthington Whittredge (1820-1910)

Worthington Whittredge writes a fetching prose. The farm-boy born in a log cabin on the Ohio frontier stands watching the wagon leave on the annual market trip to Cincinnati. He's full of anticipation for the cakes of brown sugar his father will bring back in a week. Years later, he has a bizarre interview with Kit Carson, the two-fisted scout, caught in a dither over whether or not he should wear pumps to a ball. Those who remember gazing on the school-room painting of *Washington Crossing the Delaware* now know that we were gazing at none other than Worthington Whittredge, dandied up to look like the general and perhaps repressing a smile while he struck his pose and fellow artist Emanuel Leutze worked away with his brushes.

Lastly, the man who seemed to have made a long romp of his life, whether in the Parisian art world or on the buffalo plains, in his later days takes a breath, chiding the excesses of artists who happily delivered the flamboyant versions of the American West craved by their buyers back East.

Not only a model for General Washington, Whittredge might serve as an exemplum of a rough-hewn democracy turning a boy wearing home-spun into a kindly sophisticate of salons. Too poor to acquire much of an education, Whittredge soon left his father's farm, striking off on his own at the age of seventeen to become an artist. He began at the bottom, as a house painter, went through periods of youthful *Sturm und Drang*, and finally, gaining his sea legs, spent the years 1849 through 1859 in Europe. There he studied assiduously in Düsseldorf, Rome, and Paris—but not so assiduously as to miss a trip hi-hoing across the Alps with fellow student Albert Bierstadt.

Despite his affinity with the Hudson River School and its emphasis on a leafy, quiet beauty, Whittredge took three trips to the region often called the "Wild West." As he tells us in his *Autobiography*, "At the close of the Civil War, I was invited by General [John] Pope to accompany him on a tour of inspection throughout the department of the Missouri." Although Whittredge does not say why he accepted Pope's invitation, we can guess from the painter's *Autobiography* that he felt the tug of adventure. The following notes, from the first trip of 1866, before warming to livelier events, begin with the painter's amazement at the visual greatness of the plains.

Further Reading

Janson, Anthony F. *Worthington Whittredge.* New York: Cambridge University Press, 1989.

Taft, Robert. *Artists and Illustrators of the Old West: 1850-1900.* New York: Charles Scribner's Sons, 1953.

Whittredge, Worthington. *The Autobiography of Worthington Whittredge, 1820-1910.* 1942. John I. H. Baur, ed. New York: Arno Press, 1969.

∼

From *The Autobiography of Worthington Whittredge,*
1820-1910

I had never seen the plains or anything like them. They impressed me deeply. I cared more for them than for the mountains, and very few of my western pictures have been produced from sketches made in the mountains, but rather from those made on the plains with the mountains in the distance. Whoever crossed the plains at that period, notwithstanding its herds of buffalo and flocks of antelope, its wild horses, deer and fleet rabbits, could hardly fail to be impressed with its vastness and silence and the appearance everywhere of an innocent, primitive existence. There was the nomad and the rattlesnake to be taken into consideration, and they both occasionally made some noise. We usually made a march of thirty-three miles a day, which was performed between daybreak and one o'clock in the afternoon. On arriving in camp I gave my horse to an orderly and went at once to the wagon for my sketch box which was usually covered deep with camp furniture, but I always got it out, and while the officers were lounging in their tents and awaiting their dinners, I went to make a sketch, seldom returning before sundown. Then I had to partake of a cold dinner, if there was anything left for me at all.

After stopping a few days, we took up the line of march towards New Mexico. The trail led along over foothills at the base of the mountains which were always to the west of us; often on reaching an elevation we had a remarkable view of the great plains. Due to the curvature of the earth, no definite horizon was visible, the whole line melting away, even in that clear atmosphere, into mere air. I had never seen any effect like it, and it was another proof of the vastness and impressiveness of the plains. Nothing could be more like an Arcadian landscape than was here presented to our view. On elevations of long sloping lines, we looked out eastward from undergrowths of large pines with scarcely any underbrush or debris of any sort, the earth covered with soft grass waving in the wind, with innumerable flowers often covering acres with a single color as if they had been planted there.

We passed on rapidly until we encamped one night near the famous Garden of the Gods. I made a sketch but it grew dark before I finished—however, I was so anxious to get a sketch of the strange red cliffs from which the name had sprung, and to have as a background the gray mountain of Pike's Peak, that I mentioned my disappointment to the General. He at once said he would leave me the next morning an ambulance and two orderlies and I might follow on in the afternoon and join the camp at nightfall. I accepted this proposition very readily. At that time the Indians were none too civil; the tribe abounding in the region were the Utes. We seldom saw any of them, but an Indian can hide where a white man cannot, and we had met all along our route plenty of ghastly evidences of murders, burning of ranches, and stealings innumerable, until I had frequently been ordered to come back to camp when the General saw my white umbrella perched on an eminence in one of the most innocent looking landscapes on earth, and not an Indian having been seen for days. With the usual slight reminder from the General that Indians might be about, and an order that I was not to go out of sight of the ambulance, I set out alone long before sunrise to find some elevation from which I could view the scene I desired. I left the ambulance in a sort of valley hidden by trees and commenced my tramp over hills of no great magnitude covered with grass without any shrubbery whatever or hiding place for even a rabbit. Distances in Colorado are very deceptive. I pursued my way along from one eminence to another, and as is often the case for a sketcher, with less and less satisfaction with the view, until finally I wandered fully four miles from our last night's camp or from sight of any human being, good or bad, and there on quite a hill I stuck up my umbrella and went to work, a very conspicuous object in such a place. I had not sat there long before my eye caught sight of a dark figure of a man far away, who seemed to be approaching me. He would be lost sometimes in the grass or hollows until I would think he had disappeared (or after all was not a human being!), and then he would suddenly appear larger than ever and nearer by. I took occasion when he was out of sight to set down my sketch box and carefully examine my revolver and buckle up my straps generally, then I sat down and resumed my work. I always regarded my umbrella pike as quite as good a weapon at close range as any revolver ever made, but I concluded to leave the umbrella standing and assume the attitude of one indifferent to what might happen for I had decided that this apparition was not an Indian, whatever else it might prove to be. The fellow at last approached me from directly behind. He stopped within three feet of me and stood stock still for a long time without uttering a word, and I was equally silent. Then he said, "Harper's Weekly?" I had no connection with "Harper's Weekly," but I said, "I suppose so," and kept on with my work, still not without a side glance at his belt which was bristling with pistols. He noticed the direction of my eyes and returned the glance with a sharp look at my own pistols. This was all that happened of a tragic nature. He was a prospector on his way to Santa Fe, and seeing my umbrella, had left the lonely trail and come to see if I were not also a prospector. We struck up an acquaintance at once, and I took him in my ambulance and gave him a lift of thirty miles.

I had all my life wanted to meet a man who had been born with some gentle instincts and who had lived a solitary life, either in the woods or somewhere where society had not affected him and where primitive nature had had full swing of his sensibilities. I had met plenty of wild characters who had lived in wild places apart from civilization, but they were not of the sort I wished to see. They were all of the bragging kind who told lies and never had anything to talk about but themselves and their exploits. I wanted to see a man of more modesty and more truthful turn of mind. The nearest approach to such a character I ever met with was Kit Carson, the famous scout. I met him in Santa Fe in New Mexico.

Carson had served with the army throughout the rebellion and had been promoted to the command of a small fort in the Sangre de Cristo Mountains, and the General had sent for him to come down and meet him at Santa Fe. He was a small man with a medium-sized head, broad shoulders and very small feet. His very early history nobody seems ever to have been able to trace, other than that he was in the Rocky Mountains when he was a boy and was a trapper, and of course a hunter as well. Somebody had written a very exaggerated account of his life, in which his fights with grizzly bears were described in blood-curdling language, but when the story was read to Carson he said they were all tall lies but one, and nobody could get him to tell which one that was. He admitted he killed the bear. It was said by some that he was born in the Sangre de Cristo Mountains or somewhere near the upper Rio Grande, a region settled by trappers long antedating the American Revolution. It was certain, however, that he had lived the greater part of his early life away from white people and had come as near living a solitary life as was possible. He was extremely reticent on all subjects, and when he spoke he used the English language in a very queer way.

I had the pleasure (a pleasure I solicited) of sleeping in the same barrack room with him for several nights. He never turned in without first examining his revolver and placing it under his pillow, and he awakened at the slightest noise. I was the subject of the most profound interest to him. He said nothing about it, but I could see I was an enigma to him which he was all the time trying to solve. He looked at my sketching apparatus and then at my pictures, until finally one day he asked if he might not go with me a little way up the mountain side where I expected to make a sketch. I readily granted him permission, and I was soon at work. He stood over my shoulder a long time in silence; when finally he seemed very uneasy and asked if I would not stop painting and go a short distance and sit down on a stone with him; he had something he wanted to tell me. I went with him. He began by describing a sunrise he had once seen high up in the Sangre de Cristo. He told how the sun rose behind their dark tops and how it began little by little to gild the snow on their heads, and finally how the full blaze of light came upon them, and the mists began to rise from out the deep canyons, and he wanted to know if I couldn't paint it for him. Nature had made a deep impression on this man's mind, and I could not but think of him standing alone on the top of a great mountain far away from all human contact, worshiping in his way a grand effect of nature until it entered into his soul and made him a silent but thoughtful human being.

His modesty was constantly apparent. He was all the time afraid that he might do something which was out of place or not in strict compliance with the usages in the "States" or of the Army, which he knew little about when it came to such things as dressing for receptions and the like. A great ball was to be given in honor of General Pope and his staff, and Carson was uneasy to know whether he should attempt to go there without a pair of pumps, an article he had heard of but didn't know what they were. He hated to ask any of the officers as to how he should dress, and finally applied to me, again asking me to step aside for a little conversation. I told him pumps were a sort of low shoe but that no army officer would think of wearing pumps at a ball, and that he must go in his boots. He was still so uncertain about it that he asked me if I would not go with him to a certain store in Santa Fe, where they kept everything, he said, and see if we could not find the desired article. I had little faith in finding pumps at any place in Santa Fe at that time, but I consented to go with him and after explaining to the store keeper what pumps were, he ransacked the store and finally brought a pair of ladies' slippers, which he said had got into his stock by mistake. They were tried on, and fitted Carson perfectly, and he bought them at a high price. That evening when we all went to the ball Carson took me aside before starting and told me that he had the pumps with him and if he found when he got there, that the officers kept their boots on, he would not use them; if they all changed boots, he would have his pumps ready to put on. The officers did not change their boots, but for a moment it was difficult for me to see where in the world in his tight fitting uniform, he had managed to secrete his slippers. On close inspection it was evident he had buttoned one on each side of his breast until his figure was not unlike the figure of many of the handsome "senoras" whirling in the waltz.

It was at Santa Fe, the second oldest town in the United States, that I met another character, while at my work, of a very different type. I was making a sketch of Santa Fe itself with its low adobe huts in the foreground and looking off over their flat grassgrown roofs to the great valley of the Rio Grande with the beautiful San Dia [Sandía] mountains in the distance. The picture was of good size and very nearly finished when an exceedingly rough-looking fellow with a broken nose and hair matted like the hair of a buffalo stepped up behind me and, with a loud voice, demanded to know what I asked for the picture. I told him it was not for sale. He broke out with a volley of cuss words and, putting his hand on his pistol, drew it forth and said he would like to know if there was anything in this world that was not for sale. I said I could not sell the picture, because it already had an owner and I was not the kind of man to go back on my word. He broke in: "You think probably that I haven't any money to buy your picture. I have got money enough to buy all the pictures you could paint in a hundred years and I made it all in sight of this ramshackle town, and I want that picture to take home with me to the 'States,' and I'm going to have it." Things were getting pretty serious, especially as he kept brandishing his pistol near my head with his finger on the trigger. I finally got on my feet, and looking him straight in the eye said: "My friend, you look pretty rough but I don't believe you are a fool. You can't have this picture. It is a sketch to make a large picture from. I live in New York, and my business is to paint big pictures and sell them at a thundering price, and if you have money enough to buy a high-priced picture I can accommodate you after I get back to New York." "Money," he ejaculated, "what will the big picture cost?" I told him about $10,000 without the frame. The frame would cost him about $2,000 more. This silenced him and I handed him my studio address. He took it, put up his pistol and marched off, and I have never seen him since.

A landscape painter is only at home when he is out of doors. It matters not whether he is an "impressionist" or one of the older school who dwelt with more rigor on form and outline. We all have different eyes and different souls, and each is affected or should be, through these mediums; that all sorts of impressions are received and all sorts of work is produced is only saying that all sorts of artists are at work. There is no denying the fact that the early landscape painters of America were too strongly affected by the prevailing idea that we had the greatest country in the world for scenery. Everybody talked of our wonderful mountains, rivers, lakes and forests, and the artists thought the only way to get along was to paint scenery. This led to much wandering of our artists. Simplicity of subject was not in demand. It must be some great display on a big canvas to suit the taste of the times. Great railroads were opened through the most magnificient scenery the world ever saw, and the brush of the landscape painter was needed immediately. Bierstadt and Church answered the need.

III.

After the Railroad, 1870-1890

Less than a month after the Lakotas defeated General George Armstrong Custer at the battle of the Little Bighorn in late June 1876, Mary Hallock Foote left New York and crossed the continent by rail to join her mining-engineer husband in California. In her memoirs, Foote does not mention Custer's defeat, nor any dangers she encountered on her journey; but once in the West, when she traveled to places not accessible by railroad, she faced some of the same hazards that had beset earlier travelers.

Nevertheless, the railroads linked the West to the East and speeded the westward migration and settlement, forces that displaced many American Indians. Black Elk and other survivors of the Indian wars would eventually tell their stories to white interpreters, but some Indians such as Kicking Bear turned to art to create visual narratives. By the end of the 1880s, however, Indians had been defeated by the U.S. Army and forced onto reservations. After the massacre of Ghost Dancers at Wounded Knee, South Dakota, in 1890, major armed conflict between Indians and whites ceased.

Artists such as Frederic Remington tried to preserve in painting and in prose a picture of life during the Indian wars, many artists believing the Indians were a "vanishing race." Far from vanishing, however, many Indians survived, some of them moving to the West's growing cities. By

1890, many western urban areas could boast of eastern amenities such as theaters, museums, and colleges and universities. In fact, in 1890 the U.S. Census Bureau announced that the frontier had closed. Although it would be many more decades before the frontier mentality in the West waned, early signs of a post-frontier vision appeared in the writings of John Muir, famous preservationist and a founder of the Sierra Club. Muir influenced many of his contemporaries, including Teddy Roosevelt and William Keith, an artist who also wrote about western adventures.

A half century after the closing of the frontier, William Keith, Mary Hallock Foote, and Kicking Bear were all but forgotten. Remington, however, had indelibly impressed the national consciousness as one of the West's premier artists. And, as Brian W. Dippie has noted, "Today, Remington and Russell still define western art" ("The Visual West" 691). Whether rediscovered or long-famous, these artists also wrote the narratives from which the following selections were excerpted.

William Keith—*Grand Forest Interior* (Hearst Art Gallery, Saint Mary's College of California).

William Keith (1838-1911)

From Thomas Moran to Maynard Dixon, artists have tended to serve up the West as a wonderland, a place existing in its own ethereal realm beyond the normal boundaries of this earth. Moran's canvasses, for instance, are stage settings for operas where something grand is about to burst forth before the viewer, while Dixon's landscapes are so clean, so noble and intellectually taut, they could be glimpses into the great cranium of some equanimitous god.

It may come as something of a surprise, then, that the work of California's foremost landscapist of a century ago reflected little of these delicious inflations. Rather, many of his outdoors scenes, eschewing the clash of cymbals, are intimate views of oak groves and meadows; they might have been painted in New England, or in the Provence for that matter, but always on special days when the clouds, the set of the trees, the stillness of the grass strike a crucial balance between calm and intimations of profundity.

Despite this, William Keith was very much a westerner, and his art, showing the West's complexities, very much a product of a peculiar feature of the region.

In 1895, after visiting Keith's studio, an English lady wrote home to her mother: "It is quite extraordinary that in the middle of corrupt money grubbing San Francisco there is an inspired genius of an artist" such as Keith (Cornelius, *Keith* [1942] 339). How little she knew about the dynamics behind art! How little she knew of the Medicis. The touch of King Midas could be sanguine.

In fact, it was the wealth from gold pouring out of the mountains into San Francisco that was creating a city lively with art, scientific investigations, music, and literature—in short, creating a cosmopolitan city even while the rest of the West roiled in the rambunctiousness of an uncouth and uncultured frontier.

It cannot be said for certain, but the idea certainly suggests itself that the equanimity of Scottish-born Keith owed much to San Francisco's sophistication. Certainly, the quality showed in his friends and acquaintances: bankers, lawyers, doctors—railroad builder Collis P. Huntington and the great conservationist John Muir. Men of keen minds and fine tastes, they were already familiar with the West and didn't need its superlatives shoved down their throats. Instead, they longed for grace and depth, and they may well have considered the grandeur produced by many artists eager to awe uninformed Easterners as so much grandiosity.

How did a painter happen to know the likes of Huntington and Muir? Keith received such great critical and popular acclaim that it comes as no surprise to learn that he knew Huntington, whose millions sufficed to buy the best available art—locally and internationally. According to Kevin Starr's *Americans and the California Dream*, Keith was seen by Californians of his day as a painter of "genteel respectability," all the more reason why a successful businessman like Huntington would welcome an acquaintance with the painter. As for Keith's friendship with Muir, Starr tells us that both Muir and Keith were members of San Francisco's Bohemian Club, and both men also spent time in Carmel.

The following, from Keith's impressions during a trip into the Sierra with Muir, show the artist's honor for the beauty of landscape and his wondering care in observing it. Nonetheless, devotees of the great conservationist may get a chuckle out of the echoes when Keith, as in his use of the word "glorious" and his swipes at domesticated sheep, reflects John o' Mountains' own style.

Further Reading

Cornelius, Brother. *Keith: Old Master of California*. New York: G. P. Putnam's Sons, 1942.

_____. *Keith: Old Master of California* [Supplement]. Fresno: Academy Library Guild, 1956.

Keith, William. "An Artist's Trip in the Sierra" (Part 1). *The Overland Monthly* 15.2 (August 1875): 198-201.

_____. "An Artist's Trip in the Sierra" (Part 2). *The Overland Monthly* 15.4 (October 1875): 389-391.

Neuhaus, Eugen. *William Keith: The Man and the Artist*. Berkeley: University of California Press, 1938.

Starr, Kevin. *Americans and the California Dream, 1850-1915*. New York: Oxford University Press, 1973.

From "An Artist's Trip in the Sierra" (PART 1)

Yosemite has yet to be painted; painters' visits of a month or so have not done it. Time is required to take it in, and digest it, or else the inevitable result will be artistic dyspepsia (in the shape of the conventional yellow and red rocks), which, perhaps is the reason for the average Californian's disgust for Yosemite pictures. The cliffs are neither red nor yellow, but an indescribable shifting gray, changing and shifting even as you look. The lightness and evanescence of the morning gray, and the burnished light of evening, can not be gotten by a lucky hit. A French painter of the first rank, like Corot or Lambinet, would rejoice in this richness of gray—but French painters do not paint mountain-pictures. We have had some cloudy foggy days, when the tops of the cliffs would be hidden in places; others would seem to be moving up and out of the fog-cloud; sometimes the wind would tear into shreds the shifting fog-masses, until they looked like torn cobwebs, and out and in the Yosemite Fall would weave in a slow and downward motion, distinguished from the clouds only by its shape and opacity in the thickest places. It all looks very deep and dark in tone, yet overall is the lightness of grayness, which you can only know by trying to mix the different tones; a hasty dash will only approximate to its truth of color. "Try, try again, and if at first you don't succeed, try, try again," is a very good motto to calm your rising agitation.

Four of us—Muir the naturalist, John Swett, Mr. McChesney, and myself—came up here, with the intention of going up higher in the mountains; and, after a detention of some days which were spent very profitably in color-study, leisurely walking we started by way of Gentry, purposing to cross Yosemite Creek, up to Lake Tenaya, past Mount Hoffman, Tuolumne Meadows, Soda Springs, past Dana and Gibbs, up over the Summit, down Bloody Cañon to Mono Lake, and skirting the eastern slope of the Sierra, exploring the head of Owen's River, etc.; all of which I propose to relate.

It looked cloudy and threatening the morning we left the valley, but trusting to luck and to keeping our provisions dry, we followed an exceedingly melancholy and heavy-laden mule. Just as we passed El Capitan it commenced to drizzle, and by the time we had half-climbed the mountain the rain came down in good earnest with gusts of wind. We slowly climbed, up and up, until the rain changed to sleet, snow, and hail—poor companions for a journey in the mountains. When we got to Gentry's, on the top of the mountain, we found a deserted cabin, and resolved to stay there for the night at least. It stormed and thundered and lightened all night, and next morning was like a winter morning—the ground covered a foot or more deep with snow. The day was half sunshine, half cloud, and the snow rapidly melted—the flowers looked curious peeping out from their beds of snow—and at evening there was a glorious sunset, with the sky perfectly clear, while below were patches of snow and snow-shadow, sunlight on distant cliff and pine, and the valley beneath filled nearly to the brim by a great heavy sodden mass of cloud, moving with a scarcely perceptible motion, slow and solemn, weird and white, except where touched by the sunlight. At the top the cloud was shaped square, and angular at the bottom, and it filled the valley with a foam-like smoke; the purple middle-ground of pine gradually receding, fainter and fainter, into this ghostly mass; the foreground in sharp and sudden relief, in color a yellow-green, the green fused into the yellow, as in a roaring night-camp fire you see the fusion of orange, sulphur, and gold. I made a quick sketch, which looked better next morning, and watched the light throbbing away, fainter and fainter, into the night. Next morning we went through magnificent groves of pines (noblest among them all, the yellow-pine), through the shifting sunshine, deeper and deeper through the thick rich forest, climbing up and down; on every side riches of color, riches of sunshine and shadow; passing two still lakes, that seem to have lost themselves in the woods and grown contented there; down steep and rocky moraines, and, after a rough scramble cross Yosemite Creek, and on the Mono trail, up and up, until the sun told us to camp, which we did by a little meadow, where there was feed for the horses, and by its side fragrant pine-boughs, which we made into springy beds for the party.

Early next morning on the trail again, still passing through rich forests, with glimpses now and then of the promised land. There was the head of South Dome, on one side shadowed by gray, purple, and blue; on the other bathed with that light-gray radiance which is neither shadow nor light, but simply radiance—with bare promontories clear and cutting against their background of purple and green woods. Higher and higher we slowly climbed until we arrived at the top of the ridge; then down, over glaciated pavements glittering and shining in the sun. As we descended we caught glimpses of Lake Tenaya—a blue-black, at the edge lighter in tone, and dashed with greenish-gray light. These mountain lakes have this peculiarity—I mean their intense depth of gray color; they look like spots in the picture, and seem to make the shadows of other things lighter; they are much darker than the top of the sky, which is an intense blue-gray, wonderfully soft and deep.

Still going down, and crossing over bare rocks—ribbed and cleft, showing the tremendous pressure to which they had been subjected—we approached the lake, through groves of pine (two-leafed), small and stunted comparatively—dwarfed by their winter flights. Some stand two and three together, as if for mutual protection; others spring from one round yellowish trunk, and then split, one half full of life and vigor, the other a silver-gray stick, sapless, dead. The green-tufted ends of their foliage (something like the yellow-pine tufts, but lacking their flexibility, grace, and silvery shine) have a certain sturdy vigor which challenges admiration. Through such groves the trail winds on to the meadow, green in spots, everywhere traversed by clear snow-fed streams, two, three and four feet wide; their beds full of pebbles, rocks, and sand; their waters, cool and transparent, tempting you all the time to drink, and the more you drink the more you want.

Crossing the stream which issues from the lake, we arrived at the lake's edge. Lake Tenaya is 8,500 feet above sea-level, and is one of the largest and finest lakes in this part of the Sierra, fed constantly by the snow-streams from the higher mountains. Strange dome-shaped rocks, round and bare, hemmed us in; no chaparral; on the sides occasionally a pine-tree. In fact, the chief characteristics of this region are its rocks, bareness, the round and burnished domes, and dwarf two-leafed pines. The deep transparent waters of the lake—on the edge great white and grim bowlders, brown under the water, and swaths of sand—seem a pale opalescent green, gradually melting into an intense blue-black, an effect which is more marked when you are on a level with the lake. Faint reflections of the dome-shaped cliffs, especially when they are in full sunshine, and the reflection of the trees, show the local color of the lake's water more fully. When ruffled it seems to partake of the extreme top of the sky, modified by a deeper purplish hue; the deep blue of the sky joining to the light-gray rounded and polished cliffs and the purpled and browned pines in the distance the green foliage and yellow-trunked trees of the foreground, together with the clear pure waters of the lake. Gaudy butterflies; bees droning and humming in the summer air; winged insects of different

William Keith

kinds—all unite to make a picture which indelibly impresses itself on the mind. Breathing in such beauty with the pure air, free from taint of every kind, no wonder that to us the echoes sounded their returns joyously on and up through the glittering sunshine, sparkling on every twig and rock and leaf, dancing back from the surface of laughing and gurgling brooks. We seemed to float on ethereal wings up and up, until, looking back, the deep dark lake appeared to have ingulfed the sunlight.

Nature takes kindly to her children, if they would but leave their swaddling-clothes of conventionality and submit themselves to her influences—leave carking cares and come to the mountains, for a little while at least. Do not fancy that June is the only month; July is good, August is better, September is yet better, and October is the blessed one of all the year.

Riding along—coming now to snow-banks, with living water, clear and pure, streaming out from every side—past Mount Hoffman, sometimes hidden, other times nodding and smiling to itself in some still secret lake; on our right strange flat-topped trees upon high cliffs, gnarled and twisted, and seemingly in inextricable confusion; over striated rocks, and loose bowlders looking just as if they had been left by nature in a hurry; up and down, getting confused with the different impressions. There are glimpses every now and then of a great valley. One climb more—and there are the Tuolumne meadows lying at our feet, green and grassy, and the main Tuolumne River flowing down to the sea. Up the valley, slowly and more slowly as the camping-place appears in view; across the ford, the strong steady stream almost carrying the horse from his feet; a slight acclivity gained—here's camp! A drink at the soda springs cheers tired nature, and on a fragrant pine-bough bed we are at rest.

"An Artist's Trip in the Sierra" (PART 2)

As the light gains in the east, faint twitters are heard, gradually gaining strength and volume, and just as the first flush of sunlight falls on distant snow-covered dome and peak, the song is loudest. You spring up, not as in the sleepy town, but with a keen sense of enjoyment. A drink at the soda spring, of clear cool champagne-like water, and you are ready for your simple breakfast, which is all the better for its simplicity. On looking about we find ourselves on a broad plateau, about 100 or 200 feet above the Tuolumne Meadows; at our right the soda springs bubbling out in half-a-dozen places, dyeing the earth around with reddish incrustations, and gradually oozing its way through rank grass to the river. Beneath spreads the Tuolumne, winding in graceful curves through the meadow; beyond, Cathedral Peak, patched with snow at its base, a noble forest growth of Williamson spruce, and mountain, yellow, and two-leafed pine-groves of the latter interspersed in the meadows, as if planted by a landscape gardener; farther to the left, a series of nameless peaks leading on up the valley toward Mount Lyell, which is hidden from sight by the lofty walls girdling the meadows; the panorama completed by an immense rounded mass of smooth-polished rock called Eagle Cliff, around whose base the river roars in rapids: all this landscape in clear gray shadow which does not give one the feeling of shadow, and only the tops of the peaks in warm-colored sunlight. I was much struck by this appearance, and found myself wishing for a little conventional studio-shadow tone in the landscape. There are, I fancy, but few painters who think for themselves, and who leave the studio behind them when studying from nature, who have not had some sense of this puzzled feeling in finding nature oblivious to their preconceived ideas. Saddling and packing our animals, we leave our camp for the next comers, and, with a glorious sense of freedom, we ride up the meadows for a mile or two, past Eagle Cliff; pass flocks of sheep that stupidly run and ba-a-h, in treble and bass. We cross the river, and after climbing a thousand feet or more of steep hill-side we come to another meadow full of white bowlders, flocked together in the green pastures; the background filled by Dana and Mount Gibbs, a reddish purple in the morning light (they being composed of metamorphic red slate). Patches of meadow, and pines—green and purplish-brown—stretch up their rounded sides, contrasting beautifully with a foreground of living green; clear water flowing stilly over sparkling beds of sand, at times over loose rocks in hurrying gurgling speed, at our right, walled in by cliffs whose feet are bathed by small lakes of melted snow, clear and cool, to which a few groups of contorta give a character both stern and wild. Slowly climbing the Mono trail, the sternness and wildness increase. Patches of snow melting in the hot sun—the grasses becoming thinner and more gray, boggy, and marshy—make walking anything but pleasing for the animals. Three hours of hard exercise bring us to the summit.

The elevation is 11,000 feet above sea-level, and at this season of the year (middle of June) the landscape looks very different from the summer appearance of things, 5,000 or 6,000 feet below. It reminds me of sketching-days in Maine in the early spring—the ground where uncovered by

William
Keith

the snow pale and dead-looking, every now and again a feeble tuft of grass trying to live in the thin and marly soil—but the distance and foreground tree-foliage was Sierra itself; the *flexilis*, hardy and vigorous, round and flesh-trunked, its sombre velvety rich foliage contrasted by dead trunks of a pale straw color, spiked and stiffened by death, in their attitudes defiant still. There is a feeling of sadness in the whole landscape, and in the blue-black sky which seems to close in upon you. Muir here told us that we were near the top of Bloody Cañon, and we all gave an extra cinch to the saddles: "For," said Muir, "the descent is dangerous." With stake-ropes in hand, leading our animals, in a short time we were cautiously placing our feet in the smoothest places; the slate (metamorphic red slate composes the top of Bloody Cañon) standing up like knife-blades, chafing and cutting the horses' feet; sliding and scrambling; now skirting a lakelet bridged by the winter's snow, and dripping softly in miniature falls through slushy sedgy mud; coming to long avalanches of snow, down which shouting and sliding we glide, followed by the plunging snorting animals; brought to a sudden stand at times by the reluctant horses refusing to budge; in places breaking through down into the torrent flowing beneath, the spice of danger adding a fierce pleasure to our efforts. By and by we are cautiously threading our way over loose rock, our left hands almost touching a perpendicular wall; close at our feet a dark cavernous-looking lake about 500 yards wide and looking as if bottomless. Careful climbing brings us to the outlet of the lake, where we find a narrow place to rest. As the excitement of motion dies away, we begin to feel the influence of the savage desolateness of the place, and impressions from Dante's *Inferno* crowd the mind. Here, right in front of you, the black lake—colorless, except at your feet, where the submerged bowlders look green and brown, abruptly fading into the blackness—suggesting unknown horrible depths; behind you the shadowed wall, sombre and terrible in its brown blackness; in front, and across the lake, long stretches of shadowed snow; reaching up among the chocolate-colored rocks, dusky olive-green patches of squatting scrubby pine. A general feeling of blackness of darkness completes the picture, leaving fearful impressions which the real danger behind and before us failed to create. Up and at it again. We pass alongside of the fall which forms the outlet of the lake, tearing and foaming its way down to the Mono plains; crossing and recrossing where practicable; stopping now and again for a few minutes' rest. At one of these resting-places we see Mono Lake, the volcanoes, the eastern flank of the Sierra peak piled on peak, flashing fields of snow glistening and shining in the sun, luminous gray rocks, fields of forest sinking to the purpled sage-brush plains below. Faint markings of greenish gray show the tracks of streams directing their course toward Mono Lake, which fades in the distance, shimmering and fainting, into the quivering sky—light and heat radiating and reflecting from lake to sky, and from plain to peak. A contrast this to the sights of an hour ago. Without accident we arrive at the bottom of Bloody Cañon, at the close of a memorable day, skirting the shores of another lake lined by willow, cotton-wood, and yellow pine, and cross a long meadow where 2,000 or 3,000 sheep are grazing. Following the stream for a mile or two, we camp on its banks for the night.

William Keith

Kicking Bear (Mato Wanahtaka)—*Battle of the Little Bighorn* (Southwest Museum, Los Angeles, California).

~

Kicking Bear (Mato Wanahtaka) (c. 1847-1904)

For much of the twentieth century, a figure dressed in buckskin shirt and leggings stood on display in the Smithsonian Museum. Though a museum label led the crowds that shuffled past to believe they were looking at the likeness of a generic "Sioux Warrior," they were in fact looking at the likeness of Kicking Bear—Sioux warrior, holy man, and artist.

Born an Ogalala shortly before mid-century, Kicking Bear grew up to become a notable warrior, taking part in fights against both rival tribes and the United States Army. His career as a warrior reached its climax in June 1876 when he fought alongside Crazy Horse, his first cousin, at the Battle of the Little Big Horn. Despite the great victory, Kicking Bear soon enough found himself stuck on the reservation, enduring the misery of a diminished life there. It was this misery that, in 1890, sent Kicking Bear and a handful of his fellow tribesmen to Nevada to hear a Paiute messiah named Wovoka preach the Ghost Dance religion. An enthusiastic convert, Kicking Bear was instrumental in introducing the new religion, called *Wanagi Wacipi* by the Sioux, to the reservation. Soon Sioux men, women, and children were abandoning farm and school house to dance the Ghost Dance and sing the holy songs that would bring back the buffalo and send the white man packing. One of the Ghost Dance songs was composed by Kicking Bear:

> Over the glad new earth they are coming,
> Our dead come driving the elk and the deer.
> See them hurrying the herds of buffalo!
> This the Father has promised.
> This the Father has given.
> (Duncan, "The Object at Hand" 24)

The Ghost Dance did not bring the buffalo. Instead, it brought the boom of Hotchkiss guns at Wounded Knee and yet more death and misery for the Sioux. For his part leading the fleeting, futile Sioux resistance mounted in the wake of the Wounded Knee massacre of December 1890,

Kicking Bear was, for a few months, imprisoned at Fort Sheridan, Illinois. He was then paroled to Buffalo Bill Cody's Wild West show, with which he toured for a year before returning to the Pine Ridge Reservation. In 1896, Kicking Bear traveled to Washington to petition the government for better conditions on the reservation, and it was at this time that anthropologists at the Smithsonian made the life mask from which the face of the warrior figure would be cast. Two years after his trip to Washington, at the urging of fellow artist Frederic Remington, Kicking Bear painted his *Battle of the Little Big Horn.* He spent the last years of his life as a preacher at Pine Ridge, at first spreading the Christian gospel but eventually returning to the Ghost Dance religion.

Unlike the other artists in this volume, Kicking Bear did not leave behind a written narrative detailing any events in his life. This is not surprising. Like virtually all Indians of his time and place, Kicking Bear was not literate. In spite of this, Kicking Bear's pictographic *Battle of the Little Big Horn* can be read as an autobiographical text as well as appreciated as art. It is presented here as both.

There is no arguing that Kicking Bear's watercolor-on-muslin *Battle of the Little Big Horn* is a work of art. A striking example of ledger drawing—a genre of American Indian art that encompassed the transition from traditional hide painting to painting with media adopted from white culture—*Battle of the Little Big Horn* today hangs in the Southwest Museum in Los Angeles. Whether or not *Battle of the Little Big Horn* is a text as well as a work of art is more debatable. Certainly the people of Kicking Bear's culture used pictographs to record history and to transmit news in the same way that literate cultures use text. To give one remarkable example of the textuality of pictographs, there is the story of a group of Cheyenne warriors imprisoned at Fort Marion, Florida, who, in 1876, received a pencil drawing sent by their tribesmen in the West. Rendered—significantly—on U.S. Army muster roll paper, the pictograph gave the sequestered Cheyenne their first news of the defeat of the U.S. Army at the Little Big Horn (Werner, "Captive Warriors' Eloquent Sketches" 29).

One quality that makes Kicking Bear's *Battle of the Little Big Horn* more like a text than a painting is the fact that it does not portray a single, frozen moment in time. Instead, in typical ledger-drawing fashion, nonsynchronous events are laid out on the canvas in an attempt to narrate a story that unfolds over time. In the lower right-hand corner of *Battle of the Little Big Horn* are the tepees of the Indian encampment. Among the tepees is a woman on the run, presumably fleeing the charging soldiers who are shown reaching only the edge of the encampment before being driven back. Many dead soldiers and fewer dead Indians are strewn across the battlefield. Custer, dressed in buckskins and surrounded by dead troopers, is shown left center. The line of soldiers across the top of the painting depicts their departing souls. On the left-hand side of the painting are clusters of angled black lines representing the large number of gunshots fired by the Indians; other gunshots are depicted coming from the barrels of individual weapons. The hoof prints in the upper right and center of *Battle of the Little Big Horn* depict Kicking Bear's movements. Nearly encircled by hoof prints is a dead Arikara scout, slain by Kicking Bear before he rides on to join Crazy Horse, standing among the group of Indians near the center of the painting.

As a work of art, *Battle of the Little Big Horn* lacks the depth and realism of paintings that adhere to the European tradition; yet, in its way, Kicking Bear's rendering is as thrilling and realistic as the many paintings of the battle executed by white artists. As a text, *Battle of the Little Big Horn* is a reasonably accurate eye-witness account of the battle. Readers and viewers of *Battle of the Little Big Horn* should, however, consider Mick McAllister's caution:

> The . . . life story in vogue in the first half of the twentieth century often was not written for self-expression, self-examination, vindication, or validation. It was, instead, "coerced," written for hire and detailed according to the interests of the employer, sometimes even shaped in defiance of the subject's desires. ("Native Sources" 134)

So is Kicking Bear's *Battle of the Little Big Horn* an example of artistic self-expression or an example of coercion? Did he choose to depict himself killing an Arikara scout because it was the truth or because he dared not depict himself killing a white soldier? Did Kicking Bear give Custer a prominent place in his rendering because he considered Custer an important figure or because he knew that a white audience would not be receptive to any painting of the battle that omitted the famous leader? Is Kicking Bear's work of art a heartfelt account, or does it inhabit the same fantastic territory as F. Otto Becker's *Custer's Last Fight*—a patently phony depiction of the battle that the Anheuser-Busch brewing company distributed (as a chromolithograph) to virtually every saloon in the United States? We can no more satisfactorily answer these questions than we can, in this single volume, satisfactorily do justice to all the Indian artists—many of them anonymous—who painted the American West during the frontier period.

Why include Kicking Bear in this volume without including such artists as Red Horse, White Elk, and Crazy Wolf, all of whom painted eyewitness accounts of the fight at the Little Big Horn? Is to include only Kicking Bear an act of tokenism, a disservice as great as displaying a great man's image in the Smithsonian without identifying him by name? Perhaps. On the other hand, by presenting Kicking Bear's *Battle of the Little Big Horn* as a text we hope to suggest how much richer both our literature and our history would be had more narratives by nineteenth-century Native Americans been preserved in formats more durable than a story told around some long-dead fire.

Further Reading

Duncan, David Ewing. "The Object at Hand." *Smithsonian Magazine.* 22.6: 22-30.

McAllister, Mick. "Native Sources: American Indian Autobiography." *Updating the Literary West.* Fort Worth: Texas Christian University Press, 1997. 132-149.

Werner, Louis. "Captive Warriors' Eloquent Sketches." *Americas.* 50.3 (May 1998): 28-35.

A drawing by Mary Hallock Foote (reproduced from *Century* magazine, vol. 38, no 2, June 1889).

Mary Hallock Foote (1847-1938)

"Contrary to the myth, the West was not made entirely by pioneers who had thrown everything away but an ax and a gun," says the narrator of Wallace Stegner's Pulitzer Prize winning novel *Angle of Repose* (1971). Stegner's narrator is speaking of his grandmother, a character modeled, in part, on Mary Hallock Foote, a real-life artist and author who came West armed only with a sketch pad and a pen.

Foote came from a genteel Eastern background. Born in 1847 on a farm near Milton, New York, she went to New York City in 1864 to study at what is now the Cooper Union. There she met Helena de Kay, who became a lifelong friend and who married Richard Watson Gilder, a poet destined to become the editor of *Century* magazine. Foote's own marriage to Arthur De Wint Foote, a mining engineer, took place in 1876, almost a decade after she had begun a career as a professional illustrator.

For the next fifty-six years, the Footes lived in the West, with occasional trips and a few long stays in the East and one memorable journey to Mexico. Arthur began work as a mining engineer and then switched to irrigation, his jobs taking the family from New Almaden and Santa Cruz in California to Leadville, Colorado; Boise, Idaho; then back to California where he served as manager of the North Star mine in Grass Valley. Mary not only raised their three children (two daughters and a son) but also wrote travel sketches, stories, and novels and drew the illustrations for her own work. In 1932, the Footes moved to Hingham, Massachusetts, to be with their daughter Betty. Arthur died in 1933; Mary in 1938.

As a writer Mary Hallock Foote is "By no means a major figure"; yet, as Wallace Stegner adds, "she is too honest to be totally lost" (*Selected American Prose* xi). In referring to her achievements as an illustrator, Lee Ann Johnson writes that Foote's "black-and-white drawings were among the very best of those produced when American illustration enjoyed its heyday" (*Mary Hallock Foote* 155).

The first of the selections that follow is taken from Foote's reminiscences, begun in 1922 and published posthumously in 1972 under the title *A Victorian Gentlewoman in the Far West*. In it, she tells about her first trip to Leadville, a journey that would have been terrifying for anyone, let alone a genteel young lady from a quiet Quaker farm along the Hudson. *A Victorian Gentlewoman* was superbly edited by the late Rodman Paul, a distinguished historian who wrote about mining in the West. He included lengthy detailed footnotes in his edition of Foote's reminiscences. Since our emphasis is on Foote's work as narrative—not as historical document—we have chosen to take the footnotes out of the text. Here, however, we will summarize the information that Paul gives us in his notes.

Paul refers readers to his *Mining Frontiers* for more information about the Iron Mine that Foote mentions. He notes that Charles S. Thomas (1849-1934) was born on a Georgia plantation and later became a governor of Colorado as well as a United States senator. The Clarendon Hotel mentioned in Foote's narrative was, Paul says, "the best hotel in Leadville," with eighty bedrooms and a number of "public rooms." The elevation of Mosquito Pass is 13,600 feet. "Border Ruffians" is a term from the pre-Civil War era, "when men from western Missouri 'invaded' Kansas in order to force slavery upon that region." Paul also explains that many of the early mountain railroads were narrow gauge, "because it was so much less costly to build, equip, and operate them under mountain conditions." Finally, Paul reveals that Foote's letters to her friend Helena de Kay Gilder give an account of the Footes' journey that is sometimes different from the account we find in Mary's reminiscences.

This anthology also includes one of Foote's illustrations, a reminiscence, and two brief selections from her work published in one of the leading journals of the time. Foote's illustration, "The Irrigating Ditch" (*Century*, June 1889), shows the view that greeted her husband after building irragation canals in Idaho. The next selections consist of a passage from the memoirs and two brief essays that accompanied "The Irrigating Ditch" and "The Last Trip In," illustrations in the "Far West" series published by *Century* in 1888-89. The illustrations and essays convey the sense that, although settlers must contend with the West's natural forces, domestic comfort and security will reward those who brave the mountains and the "desert."

Further Reading

Foote, Mary Hallock. "The Irrigating Ditch." *Century* 38.3 (July 1889): 298-300.

_____. "The Last Trip In." *Century* 38.3 (July 1889): 341-343.

_____. *A Victorian Gentlewoman in the Far West: The Reminiscences of Mary Hallock Foote.* Ed. with an introduction by Rodman W. Paul. San Marino, California: Huntington Library, 1972.

Johnson, Lee Ann. *Mary Hallock Foote.* Twayne's United States Authors Series 369. Boston: Hall, 1980.

Ljungquist, Kent P. "Mary Hallock Foote." *Nineteenth-Century American Fiction Writers.* Kent P. Ljungquist, ed. *Dictionary of Literary Biography,* vol. 202. Detroit: Gale Research, 1999.

Maguire, James H. *Mary Hallock Foote.* Boise State College Western Writers Series 2. Boise: Boise State College, 1972.

_____. "Mary Hallock Foote." *Fifty Western Writers.* Fred Erisman and Richard W. Etulain, eds. Westport, Connecticut: Greenwood, 1982.

Marsh, Carrie L. "Mary Hallock Foote." *American Book and Magazine Illustrators to 1920.* Steven E. Smith, et al, eds. *Dictionary of Literary Biography,* vol. 188. Detroit: Gale Research, 1998.

Smith, Christine Hill. "Mary Hallock Foote." *Nineteenth-Century American Western Writers.* Robert L. Gale, ed. *Dictionary of Literary Biography,* vol. 186. Detroit: Gale Research, 1997.

Stegner, Wallace. *Angle of Repose.* Garden City: Doubleday, 1971.

_____. *Selected American Prose: The Realistic Movement, 1841-1900.* New York: Holt, 1958.

Taft, Robert. *Artists and Illustrators of the Old West: 1850-1900.* New York: Charles Scribner's Sons, 1953.

≈

From *Victorian Gentlewoman,* BOOK II: *An Engineer's Capital*

The mining interests were unsettled that year [1878] like a swarm of bees excited and undecided where to alight. The fame of Leadville silver had eclipsed Deadwood's promises in gold and the new camp was booming at an altitude of ten thousand feet, close to the ridgepole of the continent; the men who went up there liked to speak of it as the Camp above the Clouds. A. was bound there and at Denver he encountered capital again, this time in the person of a queer old tightwad whose metier might have been that of a successful country storekeeper, hardly of a mine operator with a fortune reckoned in millions. The Iron Mine was said to be worth four millions; its product was not iron but silver, in the peculiar Leadville formation which was attracting all the foremost geologists as well as practical miners to the camp. One need not mention the owner's name; he and his mine had a story of their own which has long been forgotten. The incident we remember him by was more characteristic of my husband's way of making a bargain than it was of capital in whatever guise.

The Iron Mine was in litigation, as good mines are apt to be; no one covets a poor mine. The defendant was in Denver when Arthur arrived and he asked him to go on the case for him and to name his price. A. was not quite a novice, but he had never testified before on so important a suit, with such large interests at stake. Charles F. Thomas, who conducted it for the defense, was a man of high character and a lawyer of distinctions. The trial would come off in Denver with the whole state, or territory perhaps it was then, looking on; in short he was keen for the job, and not knowing the extent of the work required, he merely stipulated for his expenses and the usual fee for expert testimony based on a personal examination. If a man's testimony was worth anything at all on such a case it was worth a good deal, but it was a "gentleman's agreement."

He spent two months at the mine, and in it, making his own surveys and maps, large and small—large, to show on the courtroom walls, and small for the judge and counsel to examine in detail. His glass model of the vein scored a hit with the jury who admired it like a toy; for awhile it became a quite celebrated little toy. The new expert worked away in his room at the hotel in Denver which was crowded all day with mining men discussing the suit. He went into court knowing his part rather better than the opposing lawyer knew his, and his cross examination was "fun" for the defense. The Iron Mine won the suit and lawyer Thomas very generously (though he had laurels to spare) gave Foote's testimony, and the way he presented it, the honors of the case. The gentleman's agreement was settled by the owner of the $4 million mine handing his expert a cheque for $100. A good dishwasher could have made more at a pantry sink in the Clarendon Hotel, or washing tumblers behind a bar, as wages went (not to speak of fees) in Leadville then.

A. could not of course keep the story to himself. It added to the gaiety of the camp for a brief while; and he had his chance to get even later; but getting-even stories are hardly worth telling. My husband could never sell anything; I didn't mind his being "sold" so long as he had done the work and earned the respect of his ranking officer. It was always a pleasure to remember his relations with Charles F. Thomas.

Work flowed in. He was making money, he wrote me, hand over fist. I shall not attempt to describe a man's winter in Leadville that year [1878-1879] when men were pouring in faster than the stages could bring them and many had not where to lay their heads. The road over Mosquito Pass from the end of the track began to look like the route of a demoralized army; there was no road—there were wheel-ploughed tracks upon tracks and sloughs of mud, dead horses and cattle by hundreds scattered along wherever they dropped, and human wreckage in proportion. Many of the derelicts, men or cattle, would not have been worth fetching in where the climate selected the fit very surely and promptly; a man had to live right or he could not live long at that altitude, it was said.

Of those winter rides over the mountains to examine outlying claims, caught in blinding blizzards, often on precipitous trails where a horse's misstep would mean a lonely death in the snow, I heard little at the time; such tales were kept for the long safe talks to come. But the man did brag of his horse Dick, and of his other faithful assistant, Sam Clark, a tall Vermonter, son of a farmer and graduate of Dartmouth, who was as true at his job in the office as Dick on the high trails. As to where and how they ate and slept, that was one of the huge boyish jokes shared by thousands in the camp and passed back east where wives and sweet hearts were waiting and mothers were holding their breath. The fruit of our discussions in letters had been that Leadville at present was not a place for babies, but A. proposed that the baby's mother should come out for a summer's visit [1879] and leave his nibs in that "safest place in the world," with his grandmother and Aunt Bessie and the family doctor in Poughkeepsie. All the wives and mothers at home united in saying it was "the right thing to do." I wish to call attention to the unusualness of such advice from a set of conservative women at that time. American mothers did not do then as the English have done for generations, stay by their men and leave the children or send them home. It was considered unnatural to part a woman from her child, selfish on the husband's side and rather fond and feverish of her to consent to the sacrifice. I needed upholding and I got it, from my own people who were neither feverish nor selfish; they said it would be selfish of me not to go. I have always found those simple women in the right when it came to any unsimple choice in conduct.

Arthur had heard of a young couple who were setting out from New York for Leadville early in March and he desired me to come on the same train. He would meet me in Denver. He had never seen Mr. and Mrs. Dawes; he had merely heard of their plans and that they were "nice folks." There was not a wife in Leadville at that time—yes; I think there was one, the wife of a German miner who had walked in with her man over the pass and helped him carry their goods. It would be a German wife when it came to carrying goods.

On the morning of the day fixed for my starting, Boykin looked so ill, after a bad night, that we sent at once for the doctor. He pronounced his symptoms serious—the beginning of a long fever, it proved to be. There was no question now of his mother's leaving him. I was to have taken the westbound train at Poughkeepsie; the Daweses were on board expecting me to join them. John Sherman went up to explain my change of plan and to send my telegram to Arthur. For some reason he could not send it himself that night. He gave it to Mr. Dawes to forward at the first stop next morning, "collect"—we did not know the rates beyond Denver. Mr. Dawes decided, in the interests of economy, to wait a day and send it from farther west. That day cost Arthur the message which was to prevent his starting for Denver. He had given himself ample time, allowing for accidents on the road, and the dispatch came a day too late. There was no one for him to meet but the Daweses. I rather think he damned the well-meant thrift which had saved him a dollar perhaps, at the cost of $200 and the drive back, a cheated man. The Daweses had a comfortable ride, however, instead of going by stage as they had expected—the ill wind blew them some good. But that was the man's side of it: to have a piece of news like that handed him by strangers and walk out to the cabin and sit with it alone.

This was the first case of sickness I had ever nursed. I had never done anything for anybody—I was the "baby" of the family; everyone did things for me. And now my sister, leaving her own children to the care of others, watched with me day and night. Our orders were: every two hours a table-spoonful of milk forced between the fever-crusted lips, every four hours the shuddering dose of raw quinine dissolved in water. We took the watch by turns, but if this ordeal came during my watch I woke her, for my nerve failed. She had the quiet strength and gentleness to overcome quickly, and with the least possible excitement, the resistance of a half-unconscious child. And she never betrayed the impatience she must have felt with my helplessness and panic.

It was a white fever—deep-seated, and no one who knows fever cases need be told how critical was the convalescence. If it had been hard to leave him before, when his spine was like a willow withe and his sturdy legs bore him about the house on a steady trot, it may be guessed that it was no easier to leave my little two-year-old after that disintegrating fever. I marvel still at the nerve of those women who undertook the care of him and the responsibility of telling his mother when it was right and time for her to go. His father would not have asked me to leave him then; the decision lay with me. It was one of those invisible divides from which little streams of circumstance part which may turn into tides of fate.

On the run out from New York to Chicago something went wrong and we lost hours and I missed my connection. But the one person I knew in the city was at the station to meet me, Walter Vail, son of a family much esteemed and loved by us all, and a friend of my New York winters. His mother had written him the date of my journey and he was there to see me safe across the city. But as it turned out, there was much more than that for him to do. I wrote out a long telegram to A., which he reworded to save expense. He combated my idea of keeping on in a day train and taking the Overland next morning at Kansas City. But I could see that he considered himself my host for the time and he had no time—a young businessman with engagements he could not break off hand. So I persisted, and he helped me to carry out what he called a mad plan, to ramble through Missouri on the "Hannibal and St. Jo" [railroad] and spend the night in Kansas City. I confessed my childhood's impressions of Missouri as a state with a lost soul, inhabited chiefly by slave catchers and Border Ruffians. He was much amused and said I might trust myself without hesitation to the Border Ruffian who might be in charge of that train, and take his advice as to my affairs. Which I did—and was treated like an official guest! There was nothing he could think of that he did not do for me, even to asking me to come forward and ride in the cab of his engine. No one had ever asked me to ride on an engine before, nor has anyone since; still I allowed this opportunity of a lifetime to escape me. I felt quite sporting enough going alone on the giddy Hannibal and St. Jo to spend the night in Kansas City. My conducting friend did not forget me next day; being at the end of his run he found time to call for me at my hotel and see me aboard my right and proper train, connected up with all the other overlanders.

Walter Vail I never saw again—nor any of his lovable family. That was one of the losses of going west. Families have their own histories to make, and there were six young histories in that family just beginning to shape their courses. It was Mrs. Vail, by the way, who secured us our first year of comfortable housekeeping, in finding for us Lizzie Griffen.

All down the years of change and journeys, looking back, I see those long continental trains coming in at their last stations, the dust of state after state upon them, and the waiting crowds in sight. Others jump off first, nor am I among those who are tall enough to be seen at a distance; but I see another person who stands in the crowd on the platform, a pair of attentive eyes that pass from face to face expressionless, till suddenly they change; it comforts one who has lost one's self for days among strangers to be recognized, to be waited for, as we hope to be recognized and waited for by one or two, when we come to the last terminus. . . .

It had begun to seem like a dream that anyone could be waiting for me at Denver; I became half panic-stricken as the train pulled in, lest he should not be there. But of course he was there—for the second time he was waiting. He looked thinner than I had ever seen him; the high altitudes are not fattening. He did not look older precisely, but the year and more since I had seen him had done its work; I thought he looked like a man one might go to Leadville with. The absurdity of our going to a place like Leadville at all struck me, yet it seemed the next thing to do, and I had resolved never to lay a finger in the way of hindrance on my husband's "legitimate work."

We left Denver by the narrow-gauge that afternoon and started out from the end of the track just at dusk; it was then a provisional sort of place called "Slacks." Trotting along with our light loads we very soon overtook the Leadville stage, packed with passengers and piled with baggage, and A. pulled out to pass when a voice from the driver's seat hailed him quite humanly: "Hello, hello! That you, Mr. Foote? How's the Old Woman's Fork tonight!" It was the ex-driver of the Deadwood stage on that record journey from Cheyenne—moved on like the rest of the mining population to the new camp. With the eyes those men have for faces and the memory they have for comradeship, he had recognized his passenger of the year before who rode his off-swing through high water at the ford. The Leadville stage with six fresh horses, making time while the night is young, does not haul up for idle conversation: he had a valuable piece of information to give us as to a bad place on the road ahead where we were liable to plunge on in the dark and be mired in a slough where a team had perished by a day or two before. Owing to this encounter we did not spend the night disastrously on the road to Fairplay, but reached it about midnight and slept there before climbing the pass.

The mountains of the Great Divide are not, as everyone knows, born treeless, though we always think of them as far above timberline with the eternal snow on their heads. They wade up through ancient forests and plunge into canons tangled up with watercourses and pause in little gem-like valleys and march attended by loud winds across high plateaus, but all such incidents of the lower world they leave behind them when they begin to strip for the skies: like the Holy Ones of old, they go up alone and barren of all circumstance, to meet their transfiguration.

We spent the early part of the day steadily climbing; our horses had no load to speak of, yet before noon one of them was hanging back and beginning to show signs of that rapid lung fever which if a horse has taken cold in those altitudes has but one end. A. thought he might hold out till we reached English George's, but from that on, the drive was spoiled by seeing the gasping creature kept up to his work. On the last and steepest grade, before you got to English George's, a sharp turn with a precipice on one side narrowed the road suddenly. The view was cut off ahead, and here we met the stage coming down, all six horses at full speed—they had the precipice on their right, we had the bank and we had to go up the side of it if only on two wheels, for there was no room to pass. I felt that moment I would just as soon die myself as see my husband force that dying horse up the bank, but it had to be done. He stood out on the buggy step, throwing his weight on the upper wheels, and laid on the lash; we did not turn over and we did get by, with a few inches to spare. The two men driving exchanged a queer smile—they understood each other; and I am glad I have forgotten what I said to my husband in that moment when he saved our lives, and I hope he has too! The horse died after we got to English George's and there we hired another, or the remains of one, and he died the day after we reached Leadville. A. paid for both—and how much more the trip cost him (both trips) I never knew, but that is the price of Romance: to have allowed his wife to come in by stage in company with drunkenness and vice, or anything else that might happen, would have been realism.

We knew that we were nearly "in" when corrals and drinking places and repair shops began to multiply, and rude, jocose signs appeared on doors closed to the besieging mob of strangers: "No chickens, no eggs, no keep folks—dam!" was one that A. pointed out to me. . . .

Mary
Hallock
Foote

"Shall we drive out or walk?—there is a trail?" he asked. . . . "Let's walk, of course!"

We left behind us that disorganized thoroughfare called Harrison Avenue, with its blaring bands of music and ceaseless tramp of homeless feet on board sidewalks; if I remember, there was a moon to show us our way along the hydraulic ditch—which came to be in a year or two the fashionable promenade and was known as the Ditch Walk. Our cabin then was the first and only one on the ditch; there were woods behind us and on one side, and the lights of the town in Carbonate Gulch lay below and climbed and scattered on the flanks of Fryer and Carbonate Hills. And Sam Clark had made a good fire in the cabin, and no one was there.

Of the many details of that summer that come back to me there is no end—the foolish nothings that make "all the difference!" If I were to let myself go I should be writing a book soon which no one . . .

[In his edition of Foote's reminiscences, Rodman Paul says that this is one of the few points in the narrative where there are pages missing. See Paul's edition for his speculation about the reasons for the gap in the text.]

. . . were married, that he had a "devil of a temper" (exercised in disputing the authority of five older brothers). I shouldn't be surprised if he had; yet the day he lashed that dying horse up the bank he was cool, and when I screamed at him, he was too big or too busy to notice it. Perhaps it takes a devil of a temper to do things like that when they have to be done; he never wasted any of it sputtering around. All things he saw largely and men the same way, but if anyone handled him in a mean and petty way, he became what he would have called "ugly" and he was slow, when once deeply angry, to forgive. It was part of my content, wherever we went, to see him shoulder his job and take whatever blame went with it, and blame there is sure to be. Men in the Far West working for men in the cities of the East are exposed on a wide area of possible misunderstanding; they have to decide and decide quickly—they make mistakes, but they do not, if they are men, whine or sidestep when the blame follows the failure. And I particularly liked his way of choosing his subordinates and standing by them. His boys all loved him; almost every one of them who is not dead is counted a lifelong friend. I speak as if we were all dead—and in effect we are. No one could see in us now what we were then, or what we fancy that we were. All the above is merely to explain what I mean by the sort of man it was safe to go to Leadville with; it would have been a regrettable experience to have gone there, that summer, with some men.

Mary Hallock Foote

"The Irrigating Ditch"

The word "desert" is used, in the West, to describe alike lands in which the principle of life, if it ever existed, is totally extinct, and those other lands which are merely "thirsty."

West of the Missouri there are immense, sad provinces devoted to drought. They lie beneath skies that are pitilessly clear. The great snow-fields, the treasury of waters, are far away, and the streams which should convey the treasure are often many days' journeys apart. These wild water-courses are Nature's commissaries sent from the mountains to the relief of the plains; but they scamper like pickpockets. They make away with the stores they were charged to distribute. They hurry along, making the only sound to be heard for miles in those vacant lands which they have defrauded. Year by year, or century by century, they plow out their barren channels: gradually they sink, beyond any possibility of fulfilling their mission. Now and then one will dig for itself a grave in the desert, bury its mouth in the sand, and be known as a "lost" river.

Meantime the long-repressed soil vents itself in extravagant, contorted growths of sage-brush. Where the sage grows rank and covers the ground like a dwarfed forest the settler chooses his location. But the prospector usually comes before the settler; he takes the greater risks which go with the higher chances. He has found, or fought, his way into the mountains, whence rumors of rich strikes quickly breed the mining fever. Hard upon the news of the first "boom" comes the settler, sure of his market. He ventures into the nearest valley, taps the runaway river, makes a hole in its pocket, and a little of the wrested treasure leaks out and fertilizes his wild acres. The new crops are miracles of abundance: mining-camp markets, while they last, are the romance of farming; very soon the primitive irrigator can afford to enlarge his ditches and improve his "system." New locators crowd into the narrow valley; the ranches lock fences side by side. Small ventures in stock are cast, like bread upon the waters, far forth into the hills, which are the granaries of the arid belt.

The river and its green dependencies strike a new and shriller color-note, which quavers through the dun landscape like the note of a willow-whistle on warm spring days—clear, sweet, but languid with the oppression of the bare, unshaded fields around. It is the human note, familiar in its crudeness, but dearly welcome to the traveler after days of nothing but sky and sage-brush, sun and silence.

The new settlement is but an outpost of the frontier: if the mines hold out, if the railroads presently remember that it is there, its young fields need not wither nor its ditches be choked with dust. Twenty years, if it should survive, will have brought it beauty as well as comfort and security. The older ranches will show signs of prosperous tenantage in their tree-defended barns and long lines of ditches, dividing, with a still sheen, the varied greens of the springing crops. Each freshly plowed field that encroaches upon the aboriginal sage-brush is a new stitch taken in the pattern of civilization which runs, a slender, bright border, along the skirt of the desert's dusty garment.

Faces, too, will soften, and forms grow more lovely as the conditions of life improve. The men and women who took the brunt of the siege and capture of those first square miles of desert will carry in their countenances something of the record of that achievement. The second generation may seek to forget that its fathers and mothers "walked in" behind a plains' wagon; but in the third, the story will be proudly revived, with all the honors of tradition; and in the fourth generation from the sage-brush the ancestral irrigator will be no less a personage, in the eyes of his descendants, than the Pilgrim Father, the Dutch Patroon, or the Virginia Cavalier.

"The Last Trip In"

The teamster, as one of the types of the frontier, is seldom introduced in print without allusions to his ingenious and picturesque profanity; whereas it is his silence, rather than his utterances, that gives him among his brethren of the way almost the distinction of a species.

The sailor has his "chanty," the negro boat-man his rude refrain; we read of the Cossack's wild marching chorus, of the "begging song" of the Russian exiles on the great Siberian road, of the Persian minstrel in the midst of the caravan, reciting, in a high, singing voice, tales of battle and love and magic to beguile the way. For years the parlor vocalist has rung the changes upon barcarolles and Canadian boat-songs, but not the most fanciful of popular composers has ventured to dedicate a note to the dusty-throated voyageur of the overland trail.

He is not unpicturesque; he has every claim that hardship can give to popular sympathy; yet, even to the most inexperienced imagination, he pursues his way in silence along those fateful roads, the names of which will soon be legendary. As a type he was evolved by these roads to meet their exigencies. He was known on the great Santa Fe trail, on the old Oregon trail, on all the historic pathways that have carried westward the story of a restless and a determined people. The railroads have driven him from the main lines of travel; he is now merely the link between them and scattered settlements difficult of access. When the systems of "feeders" to the main track are completed, his work will be done. He will have left no record among songs of the people or lyrics of the way, and in fiction, oddly enough, this most enduring and silent of beings will survive— through the immortal rhetoric of his biographers—as one whose breath is heavy with curses.

The teamster is usually a man of varied experience, acquainted with life through its misfortunes. His philosophy easily condenses itself into the phrase, "It's dogged that does it." He is a fatalist, but he has not ceased to plan. In this, whatever his nationality, he is always American. It is a big country, and though he gets over it but slowly, he has all the more time to collect his faculties, and his chance is as good as another's, should luck take a turn.

As he plods along he nurses a passive discontent. The future does not press him. It is the season of summer travel; the sun is hot upon the road; from two to three miles an hour is his average rate of progress. The monotonous shuffle of feet, the clanking of bits and chain-traces, the creak and roll of the heavy wagons as they trundle along, the wind that bellies the wagon-sheet and carries the dust before him, are opiates that might dull a livelier fancy than his. But the cadence in his brain does not make itself audible in musical phrases; his is the silence of solitude and latent resistance.

The teamster either has or affects a great contempt for his calling— unlike the stage-driver, who is always, figuratively speaking, on the box. He calls himself, and submits to be called, by derogatory epithets allusive to the animals he is driving. He will tell you that he is a "bull-puncher" or a "mule-skinner," but he says it with more of ostentation than humility. It is part of that ironical acceptance of fortune's latest freak so characteristic of the Western man, who never apologizes for his circumstances but by making sport of them.

The teamster is a man of simple habits. In a life of rough passages he has "lightened ship" by dispensing with all useless wants and conventions that tend to complicate existence. He has forgotten the use of a bed. When he arrives he sleeps in his blankets in the corral, which is his hotel. On the journey he spreads his bedding in the dust or the mud or the snow, at the hind wheels of his wagon. When he makes camp for the night he barely "hauls out" of the road, his inertia being equal to that of "Brer Tarrypin" when the man set the field on fire, and his philosophy much the same. The harness belonging to each mule of the string, 14, 16, or 20, as the case may be, is dropped in the animal's tracks on the spot where he came to a halt. When that proud society man and aristocrat of the road, the stage-driver, comes spanking along about nightfall, six-in-hand, and the pick of his passengers on the box beside him, he encounters the freighter's outfit distributed in heaps along the road. If he be a placable man he will submit to swing his team out, contenting himself with cursing the slumbering teamster in his blankets; but should he have wrongs in the past to avenge, or happen to be in a grim, joking humor, he will, as likely as not, drive straight on, smashing hames and grinding collars into the dust. On his return trip next day he meets the freighter where he has crawled, scarcely a mile from his last camp, his crippled harness tied up with "balin' rope," and the two men will pass each other without a word; but a counter-grudge is saving up in the heart of the teamster, to be worked out by degrees on the road.

Relatively the teamster is but a small figure in that imposing procession of the forces of civilization on its march westward. But upon his humble chances of one sort or another, his luck as regards the weather, his personal influence with his team,—perhaps upon some incantation of sounds with which he conjures those mysterious brute natures in their spellbound moments,—as well as upon his endurance and dogged resolution, the fate of many of the bravest experiments has rested. And as the season advances and the question presses, in some doubtful foothold of men in the wilderness, "Can we hold out till spring?" the arrival of the last freighter "in" is looked for as, on the verge of winter, on the Atlantic coast the colonists watched for the promised shipload of supplies from the mother country.

Fredrick Remington—*The Sign Language* (reproduced from *Century* magazine, vol. 36, no 6, April 1889).

~

Frederic Remington (1861-1909)

Arizona. 1888. Frederic Remington—civilian, easterner, artist—tags along on a cavalry patrol through the mountains and blistering deserts of the San Carlos Reservation. He is uniquely out of place. Well over 200 pounds, he is half again the size of the typical cavalryman and uncomfortable in the saddle. A patriotic admirer of all things military, he nonetheless harbors a growing sympathy for Indians who were, just months before, at war with the very soldiers with whom he shares campfires. Yale-educated and already something of a national celebrity, his charmed life stands in black-and-white contrast to the lives of his Buffalo Soldier companions—the sons of slaves if not themselves born into slavery. The artist's fair skin fries under the desert sun, challenging his belief in the superiority of the white race almost as much as does the courage and competence of the black troopers. That so unlikely a person as Frederic Remington would come to be remembered—and frequently resented—as the great artistic chronicler of America's westward expansion is an irony that the contradictory and complicated Remington would have appreciated.

The son of an upstate New York newspaper editor turned Union Army officer, Remington grew up with a profound respect for the United States military. He also grew up with a love of the outdoors, passing the days of his youth hunting, fishing, and camping along the St. Lawrence River. The budding artist enjoyed sketching both horses and outdoor scenes, the latter reflecting his reading of such western writers as Lewis and Clark, James Fenimore Cooper, and Washington Irving. In 1881, after a two-year stint as a Yale fine-arts student, boxer, and football player, Remington made his first trip out West.

During the summer of 1885, Remington was sketching Indians and soldiers in Arizona. As the United States and Mexico intensified their wars against Geronimo and his followers, Remington's drawings became hot properties. Sales to *Outing* magazine and *Harper's Weekly* soon established his reputation as a leading illustrator of western life. Remington's career as a writer began in 1889, the year he published four western-themed articles (including "A Scout with the Buffalo-Soldiers") in *Century* magazine. December 1890 found Remington on the Sioux Reservation, South Dakota. Having sketched his fill of Sioux Indians and soldiers, he boarded a train for his home in the East one day before the Wounded Knee massacre left 200 Sioux—mostly unarmed women and children—dead at the hands of U.S. soldiers.

After 1890, with his youthful fantasies of the West in tatters, Remington focused his attention on Europe, Africa, and the events of the Spanish-American War. Even so, he would go on to publish two western novels, four volumes of collected short stories (most of them on western themes), and numerous uncollected essays and news reports. He would continue to paint and sculpt western subjects, remaining prolific until his death from appendicitis in December 1909.

Ninety years after Remington's death, the artist's admirers still tend to think of him much as Harold McCracken did when he wrote in 1960, "The name of Frederic Remington has become synonymous with the realistic portrayal of our Old West" (7). To most of his fans, Remington is above all a realist and a documentarian; his paintings, the closest things we have to color photographs of the Old West. On the opposite pole, Remington's detractors see the artist as the personification of all the worst characteristics of nineteenth-century America: manifest destiny, racism, jingoism, exploitation, and the genocide of the American Indian. Thus the artist who helped shape popular stereotypes of the West has himself been stereotyped in two very different ways, both of which fail to consider the true complexity of Remington and his work.

Writing off Remington the human being as the "evil white male" incarnate is too easy. It is certainly true that Remington subscribed to pseudo-scientific ideas of white superiority and could be paternalistic or outright hostile towards non-whites. This same man gained during the course of his life, however, an understanding of non-white peoples and cultures that few persons of his background would ever achieve. Remington's clear-eyed insight into Indian life is perhaps best expressed in *Sundown LeFlare*, a collection of short stories based on a métis storyteller Remington befriended. Remington also knew Buffalo Soldiers firsthand and in writing about them goes out of his way to praise the troopers' courage and self reliance—characteristics that most whites of the day would not have ascribed to blacks under any circumstances.

Categorizing Remington the artist and writer as a realist and documentarian is too easy a generalization. Remington abandoned artistic realism early in his career, with his artwork becoming highly impressionistic after 1890—a change that critic Ben Merchant Vorpahl attributes to Remington's disgust over the treatment of Indians in general and to the Wounded Knee massacre in particular ("Frederic Remington" 423). Much as Remington's art shifted from realism to impressionism, his writing shifted from journalistic reportage to naturalistic fiction. In most of his fiction (which he did not begin to publish until 1894), Remington writes of a West in which human beings are buffeted by forces of nature, history, and racial identity that they cannot control; in fact, Remington's fiction is more akin to the naturalism of authors like Theodore Dreiser, Stephen Crane, and Frank Norris than to the romanticism of Remington's close friend Owen Wister.

"A Scout with the Buffalo-Soldiers" is a non-fiction essay in the mold of Remington's early journalistic work, though in the description of Lieutenant Jim—a Conradian figure who has clearly gone native after years among the Apaches—there is a strong suggestion of the naturalist writer that Remington would become. Also present in this essay is the sardonic humor that is typical of Remington, a writer not too proud to make himself the butt of several jokes as he tries to keep up with the hard-riding troopers. At the same time, he absorbs the land and people around him for later expression in works of art and literature that are still worthy of the attention of an age that will never know, firsthand, Buffalo Soldiers, unconquered Indians, or Western vistas unmarked by the scars of progress.

Further Reading

Buckland, Roscoe L. *Frederic Remington*. Twayne's United States Authors Series 716. New York: Twayne, 2000.

Erisman, Fred. *Frederic Remington*. Western Writer Series 16. Boise, Idaho: Boise State University, 1975.

McCracken, Harold. *Frederic Remington's Own West*. New York: Dial Press, 1960.

Remington, Frederic. "A Scout with the Buffalo-Soldiers." *Century,* 37 (April 1889): 899-911.

_____. *Sundown LeFlare*. New York and London: Harper & Brothers, 1899.

Samuels, Peggy and Harold Samuels. *Frederic Remington: A Biography.* Garden City: Doubleday, 1982.

Vorpahl, Ben Merchant. "Frederic Remington." *Dictionary of Literary Biography* 12. Detroit: Gale. 1982.

~

From "A Scout with the Buffalo-Soldiers"

I sat smoking in the quarters of an Army friend at Fort Grant, and through a green latticework I was watching the dusty parade and congratulating myself on the possession of this spot of comfort in such a disagreeably hot climate as Arizona Territory offers in the summer, when in strode my friend the lieutenant, who threw his cap on the table and began to roll a cigarette.

"Well," he said, "the C.O. has ordered me out for a two-weeks' scouting up the San Carlos way, and I'm off in the morning. Would you like to go with me?" He lighted the cigarette and paused for my reply.

I was very comfortable at that moment, and knew from some past experiences that marching under the summer sun of Arizona was real suffering and not to be considered by one on pleasure bent. I was also aware that my friend the lieutenant had a reputation as a hard rider and would in this case select a few picked and seasoned cavalrymen and rush over the worst possible country in the least possible time. I had no reputation as a hard rider to sustain, and, moreover, had not backed a horse for the year past. I knew, too, that Uncle Sam's beans, black coffee, and the bacon which every old soldier will tell you about would fall to the lot of anyone who scouted with the Tenth Dragoons. Still, I very much desired to travel through the country to the north, and in a rash moment said, "I'll go."

"You quite understand that you are amenable to discipline," continued the lieutenant, with mock seriousness, as he regarded me with that soldier's contempt for a citizen which is not openly expressed but is tacitly felt.

"I do," I answered meekly.

"Put you afoot, citizen; put you afoot, sir, at the slightest provocation, understand," pursued the officer, in his sharp manner of giving commands.

I suggested that after I had chafed a Government saddle for a day or two, I should undoubtedly beg to be put afoot, and, far from being a punishment, it might be a real mercy.

"That being settled, will you go down to stable call and pick out a mount? You are one of the heavies, but I think we can outfit you," he said; and together we strolled down to where the bugle was blaring.

At the adobe corral the faded coats of the horses were being groomed by the black troopers in white frocks; for the Tenth United States Cavalry is composed of colored men. The fine alkaline dust of that country is continually sifting over all exposed objects, so that grooming becomes almost as hopeless a task as sweeping back the sea with a house broom. A fine old veteran cavalry horse, detailed for a sergeant of the troop, was selected to bear me on the trip. He was a large horse of a pony build, both strong and sound, except that he bore a healed-up saddle gall, gotten, probably, during some old march upon an endless Apache trail. His temper had been ruined, and a grinning soldier said as he stood at a respectful distance, "Leouk out, sah. Dat ole hoss shore kick youh head off, sah."

The lieutenant assured me that if I could ride that animal through and not start the old gall, I should be covered with glory; and as to the rest, "What you don't know about cross-country riding in these parts, that horse does."

Well satisfied with my mount, I departed. That evening numbers of rubber-muscled cavalry officers called me and drew all sorts of horrible pictures for my fancy, which greatly amused them and duly filled me with dismal forebodings. "A man from New York comes out here to trifle with the dragoons," said one facetious chap, addressing my lieutenant; "so now, old boy, you don't want to let him get away with the impression that the cavalry don't ride." I caught the suggestion that it was the purpose of those fellows to see that I was "ridden down" on that trip; and though I got my resolution to the sticking point, I knew that "a pillory can outpreach a parson," and that my resolutions might not avail against the hard saddle.

On the following morning I was awakened by the lieutenant's dog-robber and got up to array myself in my field costume. My old troop horse was at the door, and he eyed his citizen rider with malevolent gaze. Even the dumb beasts of the Army share that quiet contempt for the citizen which is one manifestation of the military spirit, born of strength, and as old as when the first man went forth with purpose to conquer his neighbor man.

Down in front of the post trader's was gathered the scouting party. A tall sergeant, grown old in the service, scarred on battlefields, hardened by long marches—in short, a product of the camp—stood by his horse's head. Four enlisted men, picturesquely clad in the cavalry soldier's field costume, and two packers, mounted on diminutive bronco mules, were in charge of four pack mules loaded with *apperajos* and packs. This was our party. Presently the lieutenant issued from the headquarters' office and joined us. An orderly led up his horse. "Mount," said the lieutenant; and swinging himself into his saddle, he started off up the road.

Out past the groups of adobe houses which constitute a frontier military village, or post, we rode, stopping to water our horses at the little creek, now nearly dry—the last water for many miles on our trail—and presently emerged upon the great desert. Together, at the head of the little cavalcade, rode the lieutenant and I, while behind, in single file, came the five troopers, sitting loosely in their saddles with the long stirrup of the United States cavalry seat, forage hats set well over their eyes, and carbines, slickers, canteens, saddle pockets, and lariats rattling at their sides. Strung out behind were the four pack mules, now trotting demurely along, now stopping to feed, and occasionally making a solemn and evidently well-considered attempt to get out of line and regain the post which we were leaving behind. The packers brought up the rear, swinging their "blinds" and shouting at the lagging mules in a manner which evinced a close acquaintance with the character and peculiarities of each beast.

The sun was getting higher in the heavens and began to assert its full strength. The yellow dust rose about our horses' hoofs and settled again over the dry grass and mesquite bush. Stretching away on our right was the purple line of the Sierra Bonitas, growing bluer and bluer until lost in the hot scintillating atmosphere of the desert horizon. Overhead stretched the deep blue of the cloudless sky. Presently we halted and dismounted to tighten the packs, which work loose after the first hour. One by one the packers caught the little mules, threw a blind over their eyes, and, "Now, Whitey! Ready! eve-e-e-e- gimme that loop," came from the men as they heaved and tossed the circling ropes in the mystic movements of the diamond hitch. "All fast, Lieutenant," cries a packer, and mounting, we move on up the long slope of the mesa toward the Sierras. We enter a break in the foothills and the grade becomes steeper and steeper, until at last it rises at an astonishing angle.

The lieutenant shouts the command to dismount and we obey. The bridle reins are tossed over the horses' heads, the carbines thrown butt upward over the backs of the troopers, a long drink is taken from the canteens, and I observe that each man pulls a plug of tobacco about a foot long from one of the capacious legs of his troop boots and wrenches off a chew. This greatly amused me, and as I laughed, I pondered over the fertility of the soldier mind; and while I do not think that the original official military board which evolved the United States troop boot had this idea in mind, the adaptation of means to an end reflects great credit on the intelligence of someone.

Up the ascent of the mountain we toiled, now winding among trees and brush, scrambling up precipitous slopes, picking a way across a field of shattered rock, or steadying our horses over the smooth surface of some boulder, till it seemed to my uninitiated mind that cavalry was not equal to the emergencies of such a country. In the light of subsequent experiences, however, I feel confident that any cavalry officer who has ever chased Apaches would not hesitate a moment to lead a command up the Bunker Hill Monument. The slopes of the Sierra Bonitas are very steep, and since the air became more rarefied as we toiled upward, I found that I was panting for breath. My horse—a veteran mountaineer—grunted in his efforts and drew his breath in a long and labored blowing; consequently I felt as though I was not doing anything unusual in puffing and blowing myself. The resolutions of the previous night needed considerable nursing, and though they were kept alive, at times I reviled myself for being such a fool as to do this sort of thing under the delusion that it was an enjoyable experience. On the trail ahead I saw the lieutenant throw himself on the ground. I followed his example, for I was nearly "done for." I never had felt a rock that was as soft as the one I sat on. It was literally downy. The old troop horse heaved a great sigh, and dropping his head, went fast asleep, as every good soldier should do when he finds the opportunity. The lieutenant and I discussed the climb, and my voice was rather loud in pronouncing it "beastly." My companion gave me no comfort, for he was "a soldier, and unapt to weep," though I thought he might have used his official prerogative to grumble. The Negro troopers sat about, their black skins shining with perspiration, and took no interest in the matter in hand. They occupied such time in joking and in merriment as seemed fitted for growling. They may be tired and they may be hungry, but they do not see fit to augment their misery by finding fault with everybody and everything. In this particular they are charming men with whom to serve. Officers have often confessed to me that when they are on long and monotonous field service and are troubled with a depression of spirits, they have only to go about the campfires of the Negro soldier in order to be amused and cheered by the clever absurdities of the men. Personal relations can be much closer between white officers and colored soldiers than in the white regiments without breaking the barriers which are necessary to Army discipline. The men look up to a good officer, rely on him in trouble, and even seek him for advice in their small personal affairs. In barracks, no soldier is allowed by his fellows to "cuss out" a just and respected superior. As to their bravery: "Will they fight?" That is easily answered. They have fought many, many times. The old sergeant sitting near me, as calm of feature as a bronze statue, once deliberately walked over a Cheyenne rifle pit and killed his man. One little fellow near him once took charge of a lot of stampeded cavalry horses when Apache bullets were flying loose and no one knew from what point to expect them next. These little episodes prove the sometimes doubted self-reliance of the Negro.

After a most frugal lunch we resumed our journey toward the clouds. Climbing many weary hours, we at last stood on the sharp ridge of the Sierra. Behind us we could see the great yellow plain of the Sulphur Spring Valley, and in front, stretching away, was that of the Gila, looking like the bed of a sea with the water gone. Here the lieutenant took observations and busied himself in making an itinerary of the trail. In obedience to an order of the Department commander, General Miles, scouting parties like ours are constantly being sent out from the chain of forts which surround the great San Carlos reservation. The purpose is to make provision against Apache outbreaks which are momentarily expected, by familiarizing officers and soldiers with the vast solitude of mountain and desert. New trails for the movement of cavalry columns across the mountains are threaded out, water holes of which the soldiers have no previous knowledge are discovered, and an Apache band is at all times liable to meet a cavalry command in out-of-the-way places. A salutary effect on the savage mind is then produced.

Here we had a needed rest, and then began the descent on the other side. This was a new experience. The prospect of being suddenly overwhelmed by an avalanche of horseflesh as the result of some unlucky stumble makes the recruit constantly apprehensive. But the trained horses are sure of foot, understand the business, and seldom stumble except when treacherous ground gives way. On the crest, the prospect was very pleasant, as the pines there obscured the hot sun; but we suddenly left them for the scrub mesquite which bars your passage and reaches forth for you with its thorns when you attempt to go around.

We wound downward among the masses of rock for some time, when we suddenly found ourselves on a shelf of rock. We sought to avoid it by going up and around, but after a tiresome march we were still confronted by a drop of about a hundred feet. I gave up in despair; but the lieutenant, after gazing at the unknown depths which were masked at the bottom by a thick growth of brush, said, "This is a good place to go down." I agreed that it was if you once got started; but personally I did not care to take the tumble.

Taking his horse by the bits, the young officer began the descent. The slope was at an angle of at least sixty degrees and was covered with loose dirt and boulders, with the mask of brush at the bottom concealing awful possibilities of what might be beneath. The horse hesitated a moment, then cautiously put his head down and his leg forward and started. The loose earth crumbled, a great stone was precipitated to the bottom with a crash, the horse slid and floundered along. Had the situation not been so serious, it would have been funny, because the angle of the incline was so great that the horse actually sat on his haunches like a dog.

"Come on!" shouted the redoubtable man of war; and as I was next on the ledge and could not go back or let anyone pass me, I remembered my resolutions. They prevailed against my better judgment, and I started. My old horse took it unconcernedly, and we came down all right, bringing our share of dirt and stones and plunging through the wall of brush at the bottom to find our friend safe on the lower side. The men came along without so much as a look of interest in the proceeding, and then I watched the mules. I had confidence in the reasoning powers of a pack mule, and thought that he might show some trepidation when he calculated the chances; but not so. Down came the mules without turning an ear, and then followed the packers, who, to my astonishment, rode down. I watched them do it, and know not whether I was more lost in admiration or eager in the hope that they would meet with enough difficulty to verify my predictions.

We then continued our journey down the mountains through a box canyon. Suffice it to say that, as it is a cavalry axiom that a horse can go wherever a man can if the man will not use his hands, we made a safe transit.

Our camp was pitched by a little mountain stream near a grassy hill-side. The saddles, packs, and *apperajos* were laid on the ground, and the horses and mules herded on the side of the hill by a trooper, who sat perched on a rock above them, carbine in hand. I was thoroughly tired and hungry, and did my share in creating the famine which it was clearly seen would reign in that camp ere long. We sat about the fire and talked. The genial glow seems to possess an occult quality; it warms the self-confidence of a man; it lulls his moral nature; and the stories which circulate about a campfire are always more interesting than authentic. One old packer possessed a wild imagination, backed by a fund of experiences gathered in a life spent in knocking about everywhere between the Yukon River and the City of Mexico, and he rehearsed tales which would have staggered Baron Munchausen.

The men got out a pack of Mexican cards and gambled at a game called "Coon-can" for a few nickels and dimes and that other soldier "currency"—tobacco. Quaint expressions came from the card party. "Now I'se agoin' to scare de life outen you when I show down dis hand," said one man after a deal.

The player addressed looked at his hand carefully and quietly rejoined, "You might scare *me*, pard, but you can't scare de cards I'se got yere."

The utmost good-nature seemed to prevail. They discussed the little things which make their lives. One man suggested that "De big jack mule, he behavin' hisself pretty well dis trip; he hain't done kick nobody yet." Pipes were filled, smoked, and returned to that cavalry man's gripsack, the bootleg, and the game progressed until the fire no longer gave sufficient light.

Soldiers have no tents in that country, and we rolled ourselves in our blankets, and gazing up, saw the weird figure of the sentinel against the last red gleam of the sunset, and beyond that, the great dome of the sky, set with stars. Then we fell asleep.

When I awoke the next morning, the hill across the canyon wall was flooded with a golden light, while the gray tints of our camp were steadily warming up. The soldiers had the two black camp pails over the fire and were grooming the horses. Everyone was good-natured, as befits the beginning of the day. The tall sergeant was meditatively combing his hair with a currycomb; such delightful little unconventionalities are constantly observed about the camp. The coffee steamed up in our nostrils, and after a rub in the brook, I pulled myself together and declared to my comrade that I felt as good as new. This was a palpable falsehood, as my labored movements revealed to the hard-sided cavalryman the sad evidence of the effeminacy of the studio. But our respite was brief, for almost before I knew it, I was again on my horse, following down the canyon after the black charger bestrided by the junior lieutenant of K Troop. Over piles of rocks fit only for the touch and go of a goat, through the thick mesquite which threatened to wipe our hats off or to swish us from the saddle, with the air warming up and growing denser, we rode along. A great stretch of sandy desert could be seen, and I foresaw hot work.

In about an hour we were clear of the descent and could ride along together, so that conversation made the way more interesting. We dismounted to go down a steep drop from the high mesa into the valley of the Gila, and then began a day warmer even than imagination had anticipated. The awful glare of the sun on the desert, the clouds of white alkaline dust which drifted up until lost above, seemingly too fine to settle again, and the great heat cooking the ambition out of us, made the conversation lag and finally drop altogether. The water in my canteen was hot and tasteless, and the barrel of my carbine, which I touched with my ungloved hand, was so heated that I quickly withdrew it. Across the hot-air waves which made the horizon rise and fall like the bosom of the ocean we could see a whirlwind or sandstorm winding up in a tall spiral until it was lost in the deep blue of the sky above. Lizards started here and there; a snake hissed a moment beside the trail, then sought the cover of a dry bush; the horses moved along with downcast heads and drooping ears. The men wore a solemn look as they rode along, and now and then one would nod as though giving over to sleep. The pack mules no longer sought fresh feed along the way, but attended strictly to business.

A short halt was made, and I alighted. Upon remounting, I threw myself violently from the saddle, and upon examination found that I had brushed up against a cactus and gotten my corduroys filled with thorns. The soldiers were overcome with great glee at this episode, but they volunteered to help me pick them from my dress. Thus we marched all day, and with canteens empty, we pulled into Fort Thomas that afternoon.

At the fort we enjoyed that hospitality which is a kind of freemasonry among Army officers. The colonel made a delicious concoction of I know not what, and provided a hammock in a cool place while we drank it. Lieutenant F—got cigars that were past praise, and another officer had provided a bath. Captain B—turned himself out-of-doors to give us quarters, which graciousness we accepted while our consciences pricked. But for all that, Fort Thomas is an awful spot, hotter than any other place on the crust of the earth. The siroccos continually chase each other over the desert, the convalescent wait upon the sick, and the thermometer persistently reposes at the figure of 125 degrees F. Soldiers are kept in the Gila Valley posts for only six months at a time before they are relieved, and they count the days.

On the following morning at an early hour we waved adieus to our kind friends and took our way down the valley. I feel enough interested in the discomforts of that march to tell about it, but I find that there are not resources in any vocabulary. If the impression is abroad that a cavalry soldier's life in the Southwest has any of the lawn-party element in it, I think the impression could be effaced by doing a march like that. The great clouds of dust choke you and settle over horse, soldier, and accouterments until all local color is lost and black man and white man wear a common hue. The *"chug, chug, chug"* of your tired horse as he marches along becomes infinitely tiresome, and cavalry soldiers never ease themselves in the saddle. That is an Army axiom. I do not know what would happen to a man who "hitched" in his saddle, but it is carefully instilled into their minds that they must "ride the horse" at all times and not lounge on his back. No pains are spared to prolong the usefulness of an Army horse, and every old soldier knows that his good care will tell when the long forced march comes someday, and when to be put afoot by a poor mount means great danger in Indian warfare. The soldier will steal for his horse, will share his camp bread, and will moisten the horse's nostrils and lips with the precious water in the canteen. In garrison, the troop horses lead a life of ease and plenty; but it is varied at times by a pursuit of hostiles, when they are forced over the hot sands and up over the perilous mountains all day long, only to see the sun go down with the rider still spurring them on amid the quiet of the long night.

Through a little opening in the trees we see a camp and stop in front of it. A few mesquite trees, two tents, and some sheds made of boughs beside an *acequia* make up the background. By the cooking fire lounge two or three rough frontiersmen, veritable pirates in appearance, with rough flannel shirts, slouch hats, brown canvas overalls, and an unkempt air; but suddenly, to my intense astonishment, they rise, stand in their tracks as immovable as graven images, and salute the lieutenant in the most approved manner. Shades of that sacred book the *Army Regulations,* then these men were soldiers! It was a camp of instruction for Indians and a post of observation. They were nice fellows, and did everything in their power to entertain the cavalry. We were given a tent, and one man cooked the Army rations in such strange shapes and mysterious ways that we marveled as we ate.

After dinner we lay on our blankets, watching the groups of San Carlos Apaches who came to look at us. Some of them knew the lieutenant, with whom they had served and whom they now addressed as "Young Chief." They would point him out to others with great zest, and babble in their own language. Great excitement prevailed when it was discovered that I was using a sketchbook, and I was forced to disclose the half-finished visage of one villainous face to their gaze. It was straightway torn up, and I was requested, with many scowls and grunts, to discontinue that pastime, for Apaches more than any other Indians dislike to have portraits made. That night the "hi-ya-ya-hi-ya-hi-yo-o-o-o-o" and the beating of the tom-toms came from all parts of the hills, and we sank to sleep with this gruesome lullaby.

The following day as we rode we were never out of sight of the brush huts of the Indians. We observed the simple domestic processes of their lives. One naked savage got up suddenly from behind a mesquite bush, which so startled the horses that quicker than thought every animal made a violent plunge to one side. No one of the trained riders seemed to mind this unlooked-for movement in the least, beyond displaying a gleam of grinning ivories. I am inclined to think that it would have let daylight upon some of the "English hunting seats" one sees in Central Park.

All along the Gila Valley can be seen the courses of stone which were the foundations of the houses of a dense population long since passed away. The lines of old irrigating ditches were easily traced, and one is forced to wonder at the changes in nature, for at the present time there is not water sufficient to irrigate land necessary for the support of as large a population as probably existed at some remote period. We "raised" some foothills, and could see in the far distance the great flat plain, the buildings of the San Carlos agency, and the white canvas of the cantonment. At the ford of the Gila we saw a company of doughboys wade through the stream as our own troop horses splashed across. Nearer and nearer shone the white lines of tents until we drew rein in the square, where officers crowded around to greet us. The jolly post commander, the senior captain of the Tenth, insisted upon my accepting the hospitalities of his "large hotel," as he called his field rent. Right glad have I been ever since that I accepted his courtesy, for he entertained me in the true frontier style.

Being now out of the range of country known to our command, a lieutenant in the same regiment was detailed to accompany us beyond. This gentlemen was a character. The best part of his life had been spent in this rough country, and he had so long associated with Apache scouts that his habits while on a trail were exactly those of an Indian. He had acquired their methods and also that instinct of locality so peculiar to red men. I jocosely insisted that Lieutenant Jim only needed breechclout and long hair in order to draw rations at the agency. In the morning, as we started under his guidance, he was a spectacle. He wore shoes and a white shirt, and carried absolutely nothing in the shape of canteens and other "plunder" which usually constitute a cavalryman's kit. He was mounted on a little runt of a pony so thin and woebegone as to be remarkable among his kind.

It was insufferably hot as we followed our queer guide up a dry canyon, which cut off the breeze from all sides and was a veritable human frying pan. I marched next behind our leader, and all day long the patter, patter of that Indian pony, bearing his tireless rider, made an aggravating display of insensibility to fatigue, heat, dust, and climbing. On we marched over the rolling hills, dry, parched, desolate, covered with cactus and loose stones. It was nature in one of her cruel moods, and the great silence over all the land displayed her mastery over man.

When we reached water and camp that night, our ascetic leader had his first drink. It was a long one and a strong one, but at last he arose from the pool and with a smile remarked that his "canteens were full." Officers in the regiment say that no one will give Lieutenant Jim a drink from his canteen, but this does not change his habit of not carrying one; nevertheless, by the exercise of self-denial which is at times heroic, he manages to pull through. They say that he sometimes fills an old meat tin with water in anticipation of a long march, and stories which try credulity are told of the amount of water he has drunk at times.

Yuma Apaches, miserable wretches, come into camp, shake hands gravely with everyone, and then, in their Indian way, begin the inevitable inquiries as to how the coffee and flour are holding out. The campfire darts and crackles, the soldiers gather around it, eat, joke, and bring out the greasy pack of cards. The officers gossip of Army affairs, while I lie on my blankets, smoking and trying to establish relations with a very small and very dirty little Yuma Apache, who sits near me and gazes with sparkling eyes at the strange object which I undoubtedly seem to him. That "patroness of rogues," the full moon, rises slowly over the great hill while I look into her honest face and lose myself in reflections.

It seems but an instant before a glare of sun strikes my eyes and I am awake for another day. I am mentally quarreling with that insane desire to march which I know possesses Lieutenant Jim; but it is useless to expostulate, and before many hours the little pony constantly moving along ahead of me becomes a part of my life. There he goes. I can see him now—always moving briskly along, pattering over the level, trotting up the dry bed of a stream, disappearing into the dense chaparral thicket that covers a steep hillside, jumping rocks, and doing everything but halt.

We are now in the high hills, and the air is cooler. The chaparral is thicker, the ground is broken into a succession of ridges, and the volcanic boulders pile up in formidable shapes. My girth loosens and I dismount to fix it, remembering that old saddle gall. The command moves on and is lost to sight in a deep ravine. Presently I resume my journey, and in the meshwork of ravines I find that I no longer see the trail of the column. I retrace and climb and slide downhill, forcing my way through chaparral, and after a long time I see the pack mules go out of sight far away on a mountain slope. The blue peaks of the Pinals tower away on my left, and I begin to indulge in mean thoughts concerning the indomitable spirit of Lieutenant Jim, for I know he will take us clear over the top of that pale blue line of far-distant mountains. I presume I have it in my power to place myself in a more heroic light, but this kind of candor is good for the soul.

In course of time I came up with the command, which had stopped at a ledge so steep that it had daunted even these mountaineers. It was only a hundred-foot drop, and they presently found a place to go down where, as one soldier suggested, "there isn't footing for a lizard." On, on we go, when suddenly, with a great crash, some sandy ground gives way, and a collection of hoofs, troop boots, ropes, canteens, and flying stirrups goes rolling over in a cloud of dust and finds a lodgment in the bottom of a dry watercourse. The dust settles and discloses a soldier and his horse. They rise to their feet and appear astonished, but as the soldier mounts and follows on, we know he is unhurt. Now a coyote, surprised by our cavalcade and unable to get up the ledge, runs along the opposite side of the canyon wall. *"Pop, pop, pop, pop,"* go the six-shooters, and then follow explanations by each marksman of the particular thing which made him miss.

That night we were forced to make a "dry camp," that is, one where no water is to be found. There is such an amount of misery locked up in the thought of a dry camp that I refuse to dwell upon it. We were glad enough to get upon the trail in the morning, and in time found a nice running mountain brook. The command wallowed in it. We drank as much as we could hold and then sat down. We arose and drank some more, and yet we drank again, and still once more, until we were literally waterlogged. Lieutenant Jim became uneasy, so we took up our march. We were always resuming the march when all nature called aloud for rest. We climbed straight up impossible places. The air grew chill, and in a gorge a cold wind blew briskly down to supply the hot air rising from sands of the mesa far below. That night we made a camp, and the only place where I could make my bed was on a great flat rock. We were now among the pines, which towered above us. The horses were constantly losing one another in the timber in their search for grass, in consequence of which they whinnied while the mules brayed and made the mountain hideous with sound.

By another long climb we reached the extreme peaks of the Pinal range, and there before us was spread a view which was grand enough to compensate us for the labor. Beginning in "gray reds," range after range of mountains, overlapping each other, grow purple and finally lose themselves in pale blues. We sat on a ledge and gazed. The soldiers were interested, though their remarks about the scenery somehow did not seem to express an appreciation of the grandeur or the view, which impressed itself strongly upon us. Finally one fellow, less aesthetic than his mates, broke the spell by a request for chewing tobacco, so we left off dreaming and started on.

That day Lieutenant Jim lost his bearings and called upon that instinct which he had acquired in his life among the Indians. He "cut the signs" of old Indian trails and felt the course to be in a certain direction—which was undoubtedly correct, but it took us over the highest points of the Mescal range. My shoes were beginning to give out, and the troop boots of several soldiers threatened to disintegrate. One soldier, more ingenious than the rest, took out some horseshoe nails and cleverly mended his boot-gear. At times we wound around great slopes where a loose stone or the giving way of bad ground would have precipitated horse and rider a thousand feet below. Only the courage of the horses brings one safely through. The mules suffered badly, and our weary horses punched very hard with their foreparts as they went downhill.

We made the descent of the Mescals through a long canyon where the sun gets one in chancery, as it were. At last we reached the Gila, and nearly drowned a pack mule and two troopers in a quicksand. We began to pass Indian huts, and saw them gathering wheat in the river bottoms, while they paused to gaze at us and doubtless wondered for what purpose the buffalo-soldiers were abroad in the land. The cantonment appeared, and I was duly gratified when we reached it.

I hobbled up to the "Grand Hotel" of my host, the captain, who laughed heartily at my floundering movements and observed my nose and cheeks, from which the sun had peeled the skin, with evident relish at the thought of how I had been used by his lieutenant. At his suggestion I was made an honorary member of the cavalry, and duly admonished "not to trifle again with the Tenth Nubian Horse if I expected any mercy."

In due time the march continued without particular incident, and at last the scout "pulled in" to the home post, and I again sat in my easy chair behind the latticework, firm in the conviction that soldiers, like other men, find more hard work than glory in their calling.

Frederic
Remington

IV.

After the Closing of the Frontier, 1891-1920

When the post-frontier stage of western history began in the 1890s, most western states had colleges and universities (and those that didn't would soon begin some). Railroad companies continued to build lines that opened speedier transportation to all but the most inaccessible areas of the region. Although many Native Americans approached starvation on reservations, the Indian wars had ended. In the face of this increased settlement and urbanization, many Americans, including some artists, could not cease dwelling on what they saw as the glories of the era that had just passed. Of Charles M. Russell, for example, Brian W. Dippie has observed: "His work was consistently commemorative, his heart in the past, not the present. He never changed."

That fixation on the past gripped even artists who had a firsthand knowledge of the latest styles and techniques of European art. As had happened decades earlier in the East, once Indians ceased to be seen as a threat, they became subjects for whites hoping to make a record of a "vanishing race." And artists and writers who could see that Indians weren't vanishing nevertheless expressed some understandable nostalgia for the departed glory-days of the native peoples.

In the art of Emily Carr, Maynard Dixon, and Edward S. Curtis, the

Indian world is depicted as dignified and noble, with an aura of wisdom and mystery about it. If this view of Indians seems a bit romanticized, it counterbalances earlier depictions of Indians as nothing but bloodthirsty savages. Some artists who came west around the turn of the century to paint landscapes and Indians stayed to become the Indians' neighbors. Ernest L. Blumenschein, for example, arrived in Taos in 1898 and decided to make the place his home, thereby becoming one of the first artists in the famous Taos art colony.

By 1910, the West, along with the rest of the nation, was entering an age of automobiles and movies. Soon, no art colony, no reservation, no ranch, no national park or forest would be beyond the reach of the ubiquitous Model T. Although western customs still retained a distinctive regional quality, attempts to act as if the Old West still existed came to seem more and more factitious. What was left of that by-gone West existed only in remaining wilderness and in what had been written by those who had seen the West when it was "new." Among those memoirists were the artists who wrote the selections in this anthology, and we turn to their writings, just as we read *The Autobiography of Benvenuto Cellini,* because they help us to see feelingly not only the horrors and atrocities but also the glory and the dream of a past that no eyes—not even the "different eyes" of artists—will ever gaze upon again.

Thomas Moran's *Cliffs of the Upper Colorado River, Wyoming Territory*
(Smithsonian American Art Museum [Bequest of Henry Ward Ranger through
the National Academy of Design], Wahsington, D.C.).

~

Thomas Moran (1837-1926)

After John Colter left the Lewis and Clark expedition as it was returning from its epic journey to the Pacific Coast, his travels took him to that region of the Rocky Mountains now known as Yellowstone National Park. Thanks to Colter's description of the area, Americans started calling the area "Colter's Hell." It retained that unflattering name until the government expedition led in 1871 by Ferdinand V. Hayden brought back watercolors, sketches, woodblock designs, and photographs that stunned the public with the beauty and wonders of the place we now call Yellowstone. William H. Jackson took the photographs, and their effect helped make a national heaven of Colter's Hell; but the artist whose watercolors, sketches, and paintings moved the United States to create our first national park in 1872 was Thomas Moran, called, at the time of his death in 1926, "the dean of American painters," and known, both during and after his career, as "the American Turner."

Although he was born in England in 1837, Moran had little chance in early life to see works by the famous English artist J. M. W. Turner. Moran's father moved to Baltimore in 1843 and sent for his family to follow him in 1844. After a short time in Baltimore, the Morans moved to Philadelphia, one of the centers of American art, a fact that might explain why four of the sons of English weaver Thomas Moran, Sr., became artists. The young Thomas, Jr., took art lessons and apprenticed himself to an engraver in 1853.

While serving as an apprentice and simultaneously embarking upon the first stages of his career as an artist, Moran decided he had to see first-hand the work of Turner. In 1861, with the Civil War already beginning, Moran and his brother Edward took ship for England, where Thomas spent a year transfixed before every Turner watercolor and painting he could find. He might have been content to gaze at Turner's work ad infinitum except for his strong sense that as an American he must return to America to paint and sketch its landscapes. Moran had also fallen in love with Mary Nimmo, a native of Scotland who lived in a small town near Philadelphia and who would become his bride in 1863.

Return to America the young artist did, yet Turner's influence on Moran continued throughout his long life, as one can surmise from the following comment that he made about the English artist:

> Turner is a great artist, but he is not understood, because both painters and the public look upon his pictures as transcriptions of Nature. He certainly did not so regard them. All that he asked of a scene was simply how good a medium it was for making a picture; he cared nothing for the scene itself. Literally speaking, his landscapes are false; but they contain his impressions of Nature, and so many natural characteristics as were necessary adequately to convey that impression to others. The public does not estimate the quality of his works by his best paintings, but by his latest and crazier ones, in which realism is entirely thrown overboard (*Thomas Moran: Watercolors of the American West* 9).

Ironically, art critics would later fail to understand Moran for some of the same reasons given above: Moran, like Turner, was mistakenly considered nothing but a literalist.

However misunderstood, Moran's painting *The Grand Canyon of the Yellowstone* inspired Americans to create the national park system, and it also made the artist a famous and wealthy man. Much in the manner of Albert Bierstadt, Moran continued to live in the East, journeying to the West periodically to replenish his stock of western scenes. All told, between 1871 and 1892, Moran served as an artist on three government expeditions and made five other trips to the West. What drew him west again and again went beyond just the aesthetic effect of the scenery. He said of his 1871 trip to Yellowstone that "the impression then made upon me by the stupendous & remarkable manifestations of nature's forces will remain with me as long as memory lasts" (*Thomas Moran: Watercolors of the American West* 11).

Moran believed, however, that he could not adequately convey his impressions in words:

> I have decided that my literary capacity is "Nil." I tried it once before, & resolved not to again take pen in hand for publication . . . while I wish that I had literary capacity to give others what I see in the Grand Cañon, I am convinced that I can only paint it,

which I expect to continue to do until my hand ceases to work
(*Home-Thoughts, from Afar* 8).

The selection that follows is his one effort at writing for publication. Although one might agree that his writing fails to convey the detail, color, and form that one finds in his watercolors and paintings, he clearly undervalued his ability to tell a story, for his narrative of his journey to Devil's Tower succeeds in giving a sense of the challenges of such a trip.

Further Reading

Clark, Carol. *Thomas Moran: Watercolors of the American West.* Austin: University of Texas Press, 1980.

Fryxell, Fritiof M. "Thomas Moran's Journey to the Tetons in 1879." *Augustana Historical Society Publications* no. 2 (1932): 3-12.

_____, ed. *Thomas Moran: Explorer in Search of Beauty.* East Hampton, New York: East Hampton Free Library, 1958.

Moran, Thomas. *Home-Thoughts, from Afar: Letters of Thomas Moran to Mary Nimmo Moran.* Amy O. Bassford, ed. Introduction and notes by Fritiof Fryxell. East Hampton, New York: East Hampton Free Library, 1967.

_____. "A Journey to the Devil's Tower in Wyoming," *Century,* vol. 47, no. 3 (January 1894): 450-455.

Morand, Anne R., Joni L. Kinsey, and Mary Panzer. *Splendors of the American West: Thomas Moran's Art of the Grand Canyon and Yellowstone.* Birmingham, Alabama: Birmingham Museum of Art (in association with University of Washington Press), 1990.

Wilkins, Thurman. *Thomas Moran: Artist of the Mountains.* Norman: University of Oklahoma Press, 1966.

~

From *Century,* vol. 47, no. 3 (January 1894).

"A Journey to the Devil's Tower in Wyoming"

We were on our way to the Yellowstone and the Tetons, by way of Gillette and the Big Horn Mountains, intending to enter the park by the

East Fork of the Yellowstone. Our party consisted of Jackson, the photographer, of Denver; young Millet, his assistant; and myself. We were to meet our outfit at Sheridan. Our plan also included a trip to the Devil's Tower on the Belle Fourche River. Moorcroft was the nearest point to the tower on the railroad; but as no outfit for the trip was to be had there, we were compelled to go to Gillette, twenty-eight miles farther, a declining town of the character usually found at the end of a railroad section during construction. The night before our departure we engaged a light wagon and team, and were assured that we could make the journey in a day, spend one day at the tower, and return the next. We were told that we should find ranches along the way, where we could either stop at night or get what was needful. We carried nothing but Jackson's photographic apparatus, my sketching-outfit, and our blankets. Our inquiries as to the distance of the tower were variously answered by estimates of sixty, sixty-five, and seventy-five miles.

After twenty miles of travel we noticed that our team seemed to have a tired air and a startling indifference to the whip, and that our plans had been too hastily made. However, we were too far on the road to turn back; even had we done so, there was no other team to be had in Gillette, so we pushed on. A map is a sorry guide to follow in a country devoted to cattle-raising, where roads branch out everywhere and seem to end nowhere. Our way, however, was supposed to be clear to Ranch 101, said to be twenty-eight miles distant from Gillette, and there we would refresh ourselves and feed the horses. All Gillette had said we could not miss our way.

About noon "101," as we supposed, came in sight; but we forded the Belle Fourche only to find what we supposed to be "101" deserted. This rather dampened our ardor: no deserted place had been spoken of by our Gillette guides. At some distance off we saw a herder lying in the shade of a tree, and we asked him about "101." He said it was a little farther on over the hill. The hill proved to be really about 1000 feet up. We mounted it with joy, only to find another equally high beyond it, and another and two others beyond these. It was hot, and we had had nothing to eat since five in the morning, and were feeling in need of a little rest.

From the top of our last hill we could see the Belle Fourche winding away for miles in its fringe of cottonwoods before it entered its cañon, cut in a sandstone ridge heavily timbered. Far beyond rose the Black Hills of Dakota; and away to the southeast lay the great "Inyan Kara" (mountain within a mountain). It was a magnificent panorama. Beneath us lay Ranch

101, about a mile away, embowered in a lovely grove of cottonwood trees, with an air of comfort about it that reminded me of a well-kept and prosperous farmer's house in the East.

It was now two o'clock in the afternoon, and instead of twenty-eight miles to "101," we had come about thirty-five. However, we had made about half our journey, and if we pushed on hard we could reach some ranch on the Belle Fourche near the tower before night came on. Going down to "101," we found a neatly painted frame dwelling-house surrounded by log houses for the various needs of the ranch. All ranches in this region are known by their cattle-brand—as the Currycomb, the Crown, the Anchor, etc.; and "101" was the brand of this one. It was a corporation ranch with a superintendent.

Finding the superintendent in, we inquired if we could get something for ourselves and horses. We stated that we were strangers to the country, on our way to the tower, and that we needed some directions. His reply was rather chilling. He said that he did not keep a road-house, and he had no horse-feed; but he kindly informed us that there was plenty of grass outside. He did not offer to give us any directions. As we left the house, we were followed out by one of the young men, who seemed to feel that our reception had been uncivil. He asked us where we were going, and although unable to direct us himself, he said we could get directions from the man at the next ranch across the Belle Fourche, at the same time pointing out about where it lay.

After crossing the stream, we had no difficulty in finding the log house, where we were greeted by a young woman. The front room was very poorly furnished even for that part of the country; and on our requesting information as to our route, she said she did not know, but would ask the man of the house. He did not come out of the back room, but we could hear them talking there. When she returned she said we were to follow the wire fence through the swamp until we came to the road about a mile away, and keep right on past the old derrick until we reached the second creek, where we would see the road that led down to the Belle Fourche; she could not say how far it was to the tower.

When we reached the road we found it excellent, passing over gently sloping hills, with occasional arroyos. Descending into a broad valley, we passed the derrick, which was situated on the edge of a small stream, and we also passed many ranch houses, all of logs, but in every instance deserted. These were the ranches where we had calculated to refresh ourselves and our horses! They were plentiful enough to have given the name of Cabin Creek (the creek we were to follow down to the Belle Fourche) to the stream that in the wet season flowed through the valley.

The woman had said nothing of diverging roads, and we now became uncertain which we ought to take of the many that branched off from the one on which we were traveling. She had said we were to cross the divide and go down to Cabin Creek, where the road would be clear down the creek to the Belle Fourche. We saw a divide some miles away, at the head of the valley; but the other roads that led from ours also crossed divides. We concluded to take the one at the head of the valley, because that seemed most traveled and trended in the direction of the tower. When we reached the top, we could look far down into the valley below us to a fringe of cottonwoods that indicated the windings of a running stream. This must be Cabin Creek. We started down the slope with rising spirits, believing that there must be a ranch house there; and we tried to put some of our own buoyancy into the tired animals, but in vain. When about half-way down we caught a glimpse of the tower through a rift in the mountains about twenty-five miles away, rising pale and immense against a clear sky. Presently we noticed a dark mass of cumulus clouds rising in the west, which increased so rapidly in size and blackness that the sun was soon obscured. When the sun had disappeared behind the great cloud, its edges were fringed with a sharply defined band of light, of a most extraordinary and dazzling brightness that I can compare only to a fringe of stationary lightning. Higher and higher it rose and spread until it covered the sky. Ominous shafts of lightning began to shoot from it, and the distant mutterings of thunder indicated that a storm was at hand. We were about to stop and arrange our affairs with that in view, when the cattle that had been grazing on the hillsides came tearing into the valley in a perfect stampede, making for the shelter of the pinegroves on the other side of a deep arroyo that separated us from the woods.

The wind had now risen to a gale, when we noticed a few small white objects driven along toward us, and bounding as they came. A ghostly grayness began to obscure the previously dark-plum-purple-colored hills to the west. The sun must have gone below the horizon, for a sudden darkness came on. Our horses refused to move a step. We were entirely unprepared for the suddenness and severity with which there broke upon us a storm of hail. The hills disappeared entirely, and we could see only a few feet from us. Everything that might have served as protection for us had been securely packed and strapped before starting; and with this fierce storm raging it was impossible to do anything for our defense. Light summer clothing and thin felt hats were our only protection against this awful fusillade of ice-balls that struck us with a force as if coming from a sling.

The horses, smarting under the blows, suddenly made an attempt to turn about so as not to face the storm, and in doing so they nearly overturned the outfit. We feared they might stampede; but, fortunately for us, they were too used up to do so, and simply winced under the blows, as we did ourselves. How long would it last? How long could we stand it? Our hands were beginning to show purple lumps where they had been struck, and our heads were aching, and sore, and lumpy, from the pelting ice-balls. Night was coming on. Our wagon was loaded with ice-balls, which were rather flat in form and from two to three inches in diameter, and the landscape was covered with them to the depth of four inches.

Soon after the hail began to fall, the wind became a cold, chilling blast that greatly increased our discomfort. We shivered and shook as though seized with an ague. Now rain intermingled with the hail, and soon it was a drenching downpour of water; but it was comforting to know that the storm of ice was over. Then the hills began to reappear, and the glow through the rain indicated that the storm had about spent its force, and that clear skies lay beyond.

Do you know what gumbo is? Well, it is the clay of northern Wyoming. When wet it is the blackest, stickiest, most India-rubber-like mud that exists on earth. Like the gathering snowball, it accumulates on whatever comes in contact with it, and is so adhesive that it never falls away of its own weight, as any well-regulated mud will do, but must be laboriously removed when you or your wagon-wheels become clogged with it. Up to the breaking of the storm, gumbo had not troubled us, for the weather had been fine and dry for weeks, and gumbo roads are good when dry. It is of such fine texture that it will receive an impression as clean as wax. During this short storm the gumbo had softened to the depth of an inch or two, and our trials with it were about to begin. The sun had been down about half an hour, and the darkness of night was beginning to settle about us in the valley, while the twilight glow still illumined the higher mountain-tops, as we made a start to reach the creek. The horses really seemed to have had some new life infused into them by the storm, for they started off cheerfully; but the terrible gumbo soon began to discourage them. We tried walking them to relieve them of our weight, but soon found that the friendly gumbo had us in its embrace, making our feet like lead. After repeated stoppages to clear the wheels, we at last reached the creek. Searching for the road was out of the question. It was dark now, with several inches of hail covering the ground, and completely hiding all traces of a road, if there were any. We could not make camp where we were, in water and soft gumbo.

About two miles farther, across the creek, was a great clump of pines on the top of a gently sloping hill; and it seemed that if we could reach that we would be all right for the night, as it would be drier, and we could have a fire, if our matches had not been spoiled by the rain. But to cross the creek was a serious matter. The bank upon which we were was about fifteen feet high; the road made a very precipitous descent to the water, but was easy on the other side. The gumbo had been softened to the depth of about an inch on the slope, but was hard underneath. A dangerous matter by daylight, to make such a descent was doubly so under the present conditions. Yet there was nothing for it but to make the attempt. Jackson took the reins, while we remained on the bank. The horses shied at first, the darkness making it seem deeper and steeper than it really was. They finally made the plunge, but instantly found they had no foothold, and wagon and horses simply slid down into the creek—without accident. We followed them, and, getting into the wagon, reached the other bank without further trouble.

Slowly, wearily, we made our way to the pine clump on the hillside, but it took us two hours to cover those two miles. It was ten o'clock when we reached the pines, wet, hungry, and worn out. We found it had been the camping-place of herders, whose pine-bough beds were there, dry underneath, and ready to be used for lighting our fire. The used-up horses were turned loose to find food for themselves, as we knew they were too tired to wander far away, and grass was plentiful. Our matches proved to be in good condition, and we soon had a fire fit to roast an ox. Our wet blankets were brought out and dried, and we turned our steaming selves before the fire until we were dry enough to take to our blankets. Our pine-bough beds were as welcome as the softest down.

Early next morning we retraced our way to the creek to find the road that was to lead us down to the Belle Fourche. Arriving at the gumbo slide of the previous night, we emptied the wagon of everything to make it as light as possible. Jackson undertook to get it up the slide, and was successful. The great camera, the boxes of plates, and the bedding we managed to get over on a bridge made of the legs of the camera. Having safely reached the other side, we wandered in all directions to find the road, but no trace of a road leading down the creek could be found. After an hour's fruitless search we gave it up. Were we on Cabin Creek, or had we passed it at the derrick? We concluded to retrace our way to the derrick, and to follow the road down to the cañon. This meant twenty or twenty-five miles to reach the river; but we knew there were ranches and farms on the Belle Fourche, and that we could reach the tower by that way.

We reached the cañon early in the afternoon, but did not know which side of the river to take, as there was a road on both sides. We chose the side we were on, but soon found that it led away from the river and up a side ravine. There we saw smoke rising in the air some distance ahead of us, and soon reached a house, where we were well received. We were very grateful indeed to get something to eat, as we had had no food for thirty-eight hours. The ranchman told us we were on the wrong side of the river, but by going over the hill opposite and descending to the river, we could cross it just above where we descended. And such a descent we made! A narrow trail over a series of sandstone terraces so steep and rocky that I never expected to see our wagon whole at the bottom! But by great care and good luck we managed to get to the river all right. Knowing that we were at last on the right road for the Devil's Tower, and within reach of habitations, we almost forgot the sufferings of the previous day.

The scenery along the river to the tower was fine: a very wide cañon in sandstone worn into castellated forms, inclosing a fertile valley studded with the houses and fields of prosperous farmers and ranchers. It was evident that we could not reach the tower that day; and when we inquired in regard to accommodation for the night, everybody told us to go to Johnson's. We concluded that Johnson's was a place of entertainment for travelers. When we arrived there, early in the evening, we found that it was the home of an English gentleman who was given to horse-raising. He and his wife welcomed us heartily, and did everything to make our sojourn pleasant. His house was a neatly built frame, and luxuriously furnished, even to a grand piano. From there the great tower loomed up grandly some twelve miles away. In the morning our host had the herder bring in about a hundred of his horses to show us, after which we regretfully left his hospitable home and made our way on to the tower, which we reached about noon.

This wonderful mass of columnar basalt rises about 2000 feet above the Belle Fourche. It is somewhat of a geological puzzle, standing alone as it does, and rising directly out of a country entirely made up of sedimentary rock. One theory is that it is the core of a great volcano, crystallized into its present form, and that the mountain of which it was the core has been carried off by erosion. Be that as it may, it is a grand and imposing sight, and one of the remarkable physical features of this country. We sketched and photographed it during the remainder of the day. In the evening we were hospitably received at the ranch of Burke and Mackenzie, two Englishmen also engaged in horse-raising; and the next morning, under their direction, we started on our return to Gillette by way of Cabin Creek. On the way we passed over the old camping-ground and the scene of the hail-storm, to find that we had been on the right road after all, and that our camp that night had been only twenty miles from the Devil's Tower!

Emily Carr—*Guyasdoms D'Sonoqua*, 1928-1930
(Art Gallery of Ontario, Toronto).

Emily Carr (1871-1945)

After leaving his native England in 1837 and spending the next twelve years at various occupations in America, Richard Carr joined the gold rush to California in 1849. In less than a year, his prospecting gained him $3,000, which he invested in general stores. By 1854 he was worth $25,000, a sum more than sufficient to pay for his return to England, where he married Emily Saunders. After the deaths of two infant sons, the Carrs moved in 1863 to Victoria, British Columbia, where more of their children were born, including Emily in 1871.

Orphaned before she was eighteen, in 1891 Emily convinced her guardian to send her to San Francisco to study art. After she returned to Victoria in 1893, she began visiting Indian villages along Vancouver Island and the Northwest Coast, sketching and painting her favorite subjects—the forests and the totem poles. She writes about these trips in her first book, *Klee Wyck* (1941), which can be found in *The Emily Carr Omnibus*.

Eager to learn more about art, in 1899 she journeyed to England. There she suffered a physical collapse and a "nervous breakdown" (she was diagnosed as having "hysteria"). In 1904, after eighteen months in a sanatorium, she returned to Vancouver. As she tells us in her autobiographical sketches, her English experience did not change what Doris Shadbolt says was Carr's "admirable eccentricity." A stay in France from 1910 to 1911 gave her a knowledge of new developments in art, some of which began to influence her own work, much to the dismay of art critics in Vancouver and Victoria.

Most of the local critics failed to appreciate Carr's art because they lacked an understanding of modern art, and Carr was one of the artists who created modern art, although she produced different styles during different phases of her career. As Doris Shadbolt explains:

During one phase of her career, Carr painted in a post-impressionist manner and at times revealed a distinctly Fauvist influence; during another period, her work showed stylistic links with Cubism. Late in her life, her passionate search for identification with universal primal energies produced occasional paintings that evoke van Gogh or suggest spiritual affinities with German Expressionism. Closer to home, her relationship to Canadian art and to the work of Lauren Harris and other members of the Group of Seven can be more readily observed. Yet she remained a highly individualistic artist, never truly part of larger world movements or their Canadian expressions, even though from time to time she borrowed their mannerisms (*The Art of Emily Carr* 11).

Because of the provincial stodginess of those local critics, Carr remained relatively unknown until 1927, when the director of Canada's National Gallery learned about her work and arranged for an exhibition. About a decade later Carr began writing the many narratives that, when gathered into book form, would bring her more popularity than had her paintings. She enjoyed that popularity for only four years before her death in 1945.

Interest in Carr, her art, and her writing has continued to grow since her death, so much so that the bibliography in Stephanie Kirkwood Walker's *This Woman in Particular: Contexts for the Biographical Image of Emily Carr* (1996) lists almost eighty books and essays about Carr and her work. Walker says, "In the case of Emily Carr the nexus of personal, social and metaphysical matters has generated deliberations on the status of women as artists, in language, as political creatures, and as mediators between this world and another accessible through nature" (*This Woman* 4). *The Emily Carr Omnibus* (published jointly in 1993 by Douglas and McIntyre in Canada and by the University of Washington Press in the United States) collects in one volume all of Carr's published writings. *Klee Wyck* is still her best-known book (the title comes from what the Indians called Carr; it means "laughing one"). The following selection, "D'Sonoqua," describes a totem that she also made a painting of. Together, Carr's painting and essay convey some of the power of myth. "Cariboo Gold," from her autobiography, *Growing Pains* (1946), tells us in no uncertain terms that Carr thought of herself as a westerner and was glad to be one.

Further Reading

Carr, Emily. *The Emily Carr Omnibus.* Introduction by Doris Shadbolt. Vancouver: Douglas & McIntyre, 1993. Seattle: University of Washington Press, 1993.

Shadbolt, Doris. *The Art of Emily Carr*. Seattle: University of Washington Press, 1979.

Tippett, Maria. *Emily Carr: A Biography*. New York: Oxford University Press, 1979.

Walker, Stephanie Kirkwood. *This Woman in Particular: Contexts for the Biographical Image of Emily Carr*. Waterloo, Ontario: Wilfrid Laurier University Press, 1996.

~

From *Klee Wyck*

"D'Sonoqua"

I was sketching in a remote Indian village when I first saw her. The village was one of those that the Indians use only for a few months in each year; the rest of the time it stands empty and desolate. I went there in one of its empty times, in a drizzling dusk.

When the Indian agent dumped me on the beach in front of the village, he said, "There is not a soul here. I will come back for you in two days." Then he went away.

I had a small griffon dog with me, and also a little Indian girl, who, when she saw the boat go away, clung to my sleeve and wailed, "I'm 'fraid."

We went up to the old deserted Mission House. At the sound of the key in the rusty lock, rats scuttled away. The stove was broken, the wood wet. I had forgotten to bring candles. We spread our blankets on the floor, and spent a poor night. Perhaps my lack of sleep played its part in the shock that I got, when I saw her for the first time.

Water was in the air, half mist, half rain. The stinging nettles, higher than my head, left their nervy smart on my ears and forehead, as I beat my way through them, trying all the while to keep my feet on the plank walk which they hid. Big yellow slugs crawled on the walk and slimed it. My feet slipped and I shot headlong to her very base, for she had no feet. The nettles that were above my head reached only to her knee.

It was not the fall alone that jerked the "Oh's" out of me, for the great wooden image towering above me was indeed terrifying.

The nettle bed ended a few yards beyond her, and then a rocky bluff jutted out, with waves battering it below. I scrambled up and went out on the bluff, so that I could see the creature above the nettles. The forest was behind her, the sea in front.

Her head and trunk were carved out of, or rather into, the bole of a great red cedar. She seemed to be part of the tree itself, as if she had grown there at its heart, and the carver had only chipped away the outer wood so that you could see her. Her arms were spliced and socketed to the trunk, and were flung wide in a circling, compelling movement. Her breasts were two eagle-heads, fiercely carved. That much, and the column of her great neck, and her strong chin, I had seen when I slithered to the ground beneath her. Now I saw her face.

The eyes were two rounds of black, set in wider rounds of white, and placed in deep sockets under wide, black eyebrows. Their fixed stare bored into me as if the very life of the old cedar looked out, and it seemed that the voice of the tree itself might have burst from that great round cavity, with projecting lips, that was her mouth. Her ears were round, and stuck out to catch all sounds. The salt air had not dimmed the heavy red of her trunk and arms and thighs. Her hands were black, with blunt finger-tips painted a dazzling white. I stood looking at her for a long, long time.

The rain stopped, and white mist came up from the sea, gradually paling her back into the forest. It was as if she belonged there, and the mist were carrying her home. Presently the mist took the forest too, and, wrapping them both together, hid them away.

"Who is that image?" I asked the little Indian girl, when I got back to the house.

She knew which one I meant, but to gain time, she said, "What image?"

"The terrible one, out there on the bluff."

"I dunno," she lied.

I never went to that village again, but the fierce wooden image often came to me, both in my waking and in my sleeping.

Several years passed, and I was once more sketching in an Indian village. There were Indians in this village, and in a mild backward way it was "going modern." That is, the Indians had pushed the forest back a little to let the sun touch the new buildings that were replacing the old community houses. Small houses, primitive enough to a white man's thinking, pushed here and there between the old. Where some of the big community houses had been torn down, for the sake of the lumber, the great corner posts and massive roof-beams of the old structure were often left, standing naked against the sky, and the new little house was built inside, on the spot where the old one had been.

It was in one of these empty skeletons that I found her again. She had once been a supporting post for the great centre beam. Her pole-mate, representing the Raven, stood opposite her, but the beam that had rested on their heads was gone. The two poles faced in, and one judged the great size of the house by the distance between them. The corner posts were still in place, and the earth floor, once beaten to the hardness of rock by naked feet, was carpeted now with rich lush grass.

I knew her by the stuck-out ears, shouting mouth, and deep eye-sockets. These sockets had no eye-balls, but were empty holes, filled with stare. The stare, though not so fierce as that of the former image, was more intense. The whole figure expressed power, weight, domination, rather than ferocity. Her feet were planted heavily on the head of the squatting bear, carved beneath them. A man could have sat on either huge shoulder. She was unpainted, weather-worn, sun-cracked and the arms and hands seemed to hang loosely. The fingers were thrust into the carven mouths of two human heads, held crowns down. From behind, the sun made unfathomable shadows in eye, cheek and mouth. Horror tumbled out of them.

I saw Indian Tom on the beach, and went to him.

"Who is she?"

The Indian's eyes, coming slowly from across the sea, followed my pointing finger. Resentment showed in his face, greeny-brown and wrinkled like a baked apple,—resentment that white folks should pry into matters wholly Indian.

"Who is that big carved woman?" I repeated.

"D'Sonoqua." No white tongue could have fondled the name as he did.

"Who is D'Sonoqua?"

"She is the wild woman of the woods."

"What does she do?"

"She steals children."

"To eat them?"

"No, she carries them to her caves; that," pointing to a purple scar on the mountain across the bay, "is one of her caves. When she cries 'oo-oo-oo-oeo,' Indian mothers are too frightened to move. They stand like trees, and the children go with D'Sonoqua."

"Then she is bad?"

"Sometimes bad . . . sometimes good," Tom replied, glancing furtively at those stuck-out ears. Then he got up and walked away.

I went back, and sitting in front of the image, gave stare for stare. But her stare so over-powered mine, that I could scarcely wrench my eyes away from the clutch of those empty sockets. The power that I felt was not in the thing itself, but in some tremendous force behind it, that the carver had believed in.

A shadow passed across her hands and their gruesome holdings. A little bird, with its beak full of nesting material, flew into the cavity of her mouth, right in the pathway of that terrible oo-oo-oo-oeo. Then my eye caught something that I had missed—a tabby cat asleep between her feet.

This was D'Sonoqua, and she was a supernatural being, who belonged to these Indians.

"Of course," I said to myself, "I do not believe in supernatural beings. Still—who understands the mysteries behind the forest? What would one do if one did meet a supernatural being?" Half of me wished that I could meet her, and half of me hoped I would not.

Chug-chug—the little boat had come into the bay to take me to another village, more lonely and deserted than this. Who knew what I should see there? But soon supernatural beings went clean out of my mind, because I was wholly absorbed in being naturally seasick.

When you have been tossed and wracked and chilled, any wharf looks good, even a rickety one, with its crooked legs stockinged in barnacles. Our boat nosed under its clammy darkness, and I crawled up the straight slimy ladder, wondering which was worse, natural seasickness, or supernatural "creeps." The trees crowded to the very edge of the water, and the outer ones, hanging over it, shadowed the shoreline into a velvet smudge. D'Sonoqua might walk in places like this. I sat for a long time on the damp, dusky beach, waiting for the stage. One by one dots of light popped from the scattered cabins, and made the dark seem darker. Finally the stage came.

We drove through the forest over a long straight road, with black pine trees marching on both sides. When we came to the wharf the little gas mail-boat was waiting for us. Smell and blurred light oozed thickly out of the engine room, and except for one lantern on the wharf everything else was dark. Clutching my little dog, I sat on the mail sacks which had been tossed on to the deck.

The ropes were loosed, and we slid out into the oily black water. The moon that had gone with us through the forest was away now. Black pine-covered mountains jagged up on both sides of the inlet like teeth. Every gasp of the engine shook us like a great sob. There was no rail round the deck, and the edge of the boat lay level with the black slithering horror below. It was like being swallowed again and again by some terrible monster, but never going down. As we slid through the water, hour after hour, I found myself listening for the oo-oo-oo-oeo.

Midnight brought us to a knob of land, lapped by the water on three sides, with the forest threatening to gobble it up on the fourth. There was a rude landing, a rooming-house, an eating-place, and a store, all for the convenience of fishermen and loggers. I was given a room, but after I had blown out my candle, the stillness and the darkness would not let me sleep.

In the brilliant sparkle of the morning when everything that was not superlatively blue was superlatively green, I dickered with a man who was taking a party up the inlet that he should drop me off at the village I was headed for.

"But," he protested, "there is nobody there."

To myself I said, "There is D'Sonoqua."

From the shore, as we rowed to it, came a thin feminine cry—the mewing of a cat. The keel of the boat had barely grated in the pebbles, when the cat sprang aboard, passed the man shipping his oars, and crouched for a spring into my lap. Leaning forward, the man seized the creature roughly, and with a cry of "Dirty Indian vermin!" flung her out into the sea.

I jumped ashore, refusing his help, and with a curt "Call for me at sundown," strode up the beach; the cat followed me.

When we had crossed the beach and come to a steep bank, the cat ran ahead. Then I saw that she was no lean, ill-favoured Indian cat, but a sleek aristocratic Persian. My snobbish little griffon dog, who usually refused to let an Indian cat come near me, surprised me by trudging beside her in comradely fashion.

The village was typical of the villages of these Indians. It had only one street, and that had only one side, because all the houses faced the beach. The two community houses were very old, dilapidated and bleached, and the handful of other shanties seemed never to have been young; they had grown so old before they were finished, that it was then not worth while finishing them.

Rusty padlocks carefully protected the gaping walls. There was the usual broad plank in front of the houses, the general sitting and sunning place for Indians. Little streams ran under it, and weeds poked up through every crack, half hiding the companies of tins, kettles, and rags, which patiently waited for the next gale and their next move.

In front of the Chief's house was a high, carved totem pole, surmounted by a large wooden eagle. Storms had robbed him of both wings, and his head had a resentful twist, as if he blamed somebody. The heavy wooden heads of two squatting bears peered over the nettle-tops. The windows were too high for peeping in or out. "But, save D'Sonoqua, who is there to peep?" I said aloud, just to break the silence. A fierce sun burned down as if it wanted to expose every ugliness and forlornness. It drew the noxious smell out of the skunk cabbages, growing in the rich black ooze of the stream, scummed the water-barrels with green slime, and branded the desolation into my very soul.

The cat kept very close, rubbing and bumping itself and purring ecstatically; and although I had not seen them come, two more cats had joined us. When I sat down they curled into my lap, and then the strangeness of the place did not bite into me so deeply. I got up, determined to look behind the houses.

Nettles grew in the narrow spaces between the houses. I beat them down, and made my way over the bruised dark-smelling mass into a space of low jungle.

Long ago the trees had been felled and left lying. Young forest had burst through the slash, making an impregnable barrier, and sealing up the secrets which lay behind it. An eagle flew out of the forest, circled the village, and flew back again.

Once again I broke silence, calling after him, "Tell D'Sonoqua" and turning, saw her close, towering above me in the jungle.

Like the D'Sonoqua of the other villages she was carved into the bole of a red cedar tree. Sun and storm had bleached the wood, moss here and there softened the crudeness of the modelling; sincerity underlay every stroke.

She appeared to be neither wooden nor stationary, but a singing spirit, young and fresh, passing through the jungle. No violence coarsened her; no power domineered to wither her. She was graciously feminine. Across her forehead her creator had fashioned the Sistheutl, or mythical two-headed sea-serpent. One of its heads fell to either shoulder, hiding the stuck-out ears, and framing her face from a central parting on her forehead which seemed to increase its womanliness.

She caught your breath, this D'Sonoqua, alive in the dead bole of the cedar. She summed up the depth and charm of the whole forest, driving away its menace.

I sat down to sketch. What was the noise of purring and rubbing going on about my feet? Cats. I rubbed my eyes to make sure I was seeing right, and counted a dozen of them. They jumped into my lap and sprang to my shoulders. They were real—and very feminine.

There we were D'Sonoqua, the cats and the woman who only a few moments ago had forced herself to come behind the houses in trembling fear of the "wild woman of the woods," wild in the sense that forest-creatures are wild, shy untouchable.

From *Growing Pains*

"Cariboo Gold"

Just before I left England a letter came from Cariboo, out in British Columbia. It said, "Visit us at our Cariboo Ranch on your way west. The inviters were intimate friends of my girlhood. They had married while I was in England. Much of their love-making had been done in my old barn studio. The husband seconded his wife's invitation, saying in a P.S., "Make it a long visit. Leave the C.P.R. train at Ashcroft. You will then travel by horse-coach to the One Hundred and Fifty Mile House up the Cariboo Road, a pretty bumpy road too. . . . I will make arrangements."

I had always wanted to see the Cariboo country. It is different from the coast, less heavily wooded, a grain and cattle-raising country. Coming as the invitation did, a break between the beating London had given me and the humiliation of going home to face the people of my own town, a failure, the Cariboo visit would be a flash of joy between two sombres. I got happier and happier every mile as we pushed west.

I loved Cariboo from the moment the C.P.R. train spat me out of its bouncy coach. It was all fresh and new and yet it contained the breath and westernness that was born in me, the thing I could not find in the Old World.

I will admit that I did suffer two days of violence at the mercy of the six-horse stage-coach which bumped me over the Cariboo Road and

211

finally deposited me at the door of One Hundred and Fifty Mile House where my friend lived, her husband being manager of the Cariboo Trading Company there. It had been a strange, rough journey yet full of interest. No possible springs could endure such pitch and toss as the bumps and holes in the old Cariboo road-bed played. The coach was slung on tremendous leather straps and, for all that it was so ponderous, it swayed and bounced like a swing.

A lady school-teacher, very unenthusiastic at being assigned a rural school in the Cariboo, shared the front top seat with the driver and me. She did not speak, only sighed. The three of us were buckled into our seats by a great leather apron. It caught driver round the middle and teacher and me under our chins. We might have been infant triplets strapped abreast into the seat of a mammoth pram. If we had not been strapped we would have flown off the top of the stage. At the extra-worst bumps the heads of the inside passengers hit the roof of the coach. We heard them.

We changed horses every ten miles and wished we could change ourselves, holding onto yourself mile after mile got so tiresome. The horses saved all their prance for final show-off clashings as they neared the changing barns; here they galloped full pelt. Driver shouted and the whip cracked in the clear air. Fresh horses pranced out to change places with tired ones, lively and gay, full of show-off. When blinkers were adjusted on the fresh horses so as not to tell tales, the weary ones sagged into the barn, their show-off done. The whole change only took a minute, scarcely halting our journey. Sometimes the driver let us climb a short hill on foot to ease the load and to uncramp us.

It was beautiful country we passed through, open and rolling, vast cattle ranges, zig-zag snake-fences and beast-dotted pasturage with little groves of cotton-poplars spread here and there. There were great wide tracts of wild grazing too.

The cotton-poplars and the grain-fields were turning every shade of yellow. The foliage of the trees were threaded with the cotton-wood's silver-white sterns. Long, level sweeps of rippling gold grain were made richer and more luscious by contrast with the dun, already harvested stubble fields. Men had called this land "Golden Cariboo" because of the metal they took from her soil and her creeks, but Cariboo's crust was of far more exquisite gold than the ore underneath—liquid, ethereal, living gold. Everything in Cariboo was touched with gold, even the chipmunks had golden stripes running down their brown coats. They were tiny creatures, only mouse-big. They scampered, beyond belief quick, in single-file processions of twinkling hurry over the top rail of the snake-fences, racing our stage-coach.

At dark we stopped at a road-house to eat and sleep. Cariboo provides lavishly. We ate a huge meal and were then hustled off to bed only to be torn from sleep again at two A.M. and re-mealed—a terrible spread, neither breakfast, dinner, nor supper, but a "three-in-one" meal starting with porridge, bacon and eggs, and coffee, continuing with beef-steak, roast potatoes, and boiled cabbage, culminating in pudding, pie, and strong tea. The meal climaxed finally on its centre-piece, an immense, frosted jelly-cake mounted on a pedestal platter. Its gleaming frosting shimmered under a coal-oil lamp, suspended over the table's centre. At first I thought it was a wedding-cake but as every meal in every roadhouse in Cariboo had just such a cake I concluded it was just Cariboo. The teacher's stomach and mine were taken aback at such a meal at such an hour. We shrank, but our hostess and the driver urged, "Eat, eat; it's a long, hard ride and no stop till noon." The bumps would digest us. We did what we could.

At three A.M. we trembled out into the cold stillness of starry not-yet-day. A slow, long hill was before us. The altitude made my head woozey. It wobbled over the edge of the leather apron buckled under our chins. Between teacher and driver I slept, cosy as jam in a "roly-poly."

The One Hundred and Fifty Mile trading post consisted of a store, a roadhouse where travellers could stop or could pause between stages to get a meal, and a huge cattle barn. These wooden structures stood on a little rise and, tucked below, very primitive and beyond our seeing and hearing (because the tiny village lay under the bluff on which sat the Cariboo Trading Company) were a few little houses. These homes housed employees of the Company. On all sides, beyond the village, lay a rolling sea of land, vast cattle ranges, snake-fenced grain-fields—space, space. Wild creatures, big and little, were more astonished than frightened at us; all they knew was space.

My friend met the coach.

"Same old Millie!" she laughed. Following her point and her grin, I saw at my feet a small black cat rubbing ecstatically round my shoes.

"Did you bring her all the way uncrated?"

"I did not bring her at all; does she not belong here?"

"Not a cat in the village."

Wherever she belonged, the cat claimed me. It was as if she had expected me all her life and was beyond glad to find me. She followed my every step. We combed the district later trying to discover her owner. No one had seen the creature before. At the end of my two months' visit in the Cariboo I gave her to a kind man in the store, very eager to have her. Man and cat watched the stage lumber away. The man stooped to pick up his cat, she was gone—no one ever saw her again.

I can never love Cariboo enough for all she gave to me. Mounted on a cow-pony I roamed the land, not knowing where I went—to be alive, going, that was enough. I absorbed the trackless, rolling space, its cattle, its wild life, its shy creatures who wondered why their solitudes should be plagued by men and guns.

Up to this time I had always decorously used a side-saddle and had ridden in a stiff hat and the long, flapping habit proper for the date. There was only one old, old horse, bony and with a rough, hard gait that would take side-saddle in the Cariboo barns. My friend always rode this ancient beast and used an orthodox riding-habit. I took my cue from a half-breed girl in the district, jumped into a Mexican cow-boy saddle and rode astride, loping over the whole country, riding, riding to nowhere. Oh goodness! how happy I was. Though far from strong yet, in this freedom and fine air I was gaining every week. When tired, I threw the reins over the pommel and sat back in the saddle leaving direction to the pony, trusting him to take me home unguided. He never failed.

I tamed squirrels and chipmunks, taking them back to Victoria with me later. I helped my host round up cattle, I trailed breaks in fences when our cattle strayed. A young coyote and I met face to face in a field once. He had not seen nor winded me. We nearly collided. We sat down a few feet apart to consider each other. He was pretty, this strong young prairie-wolf.

The most thrilling sight I saw in the Cariboo was a great company of wild geese feeding in a field. Wild geese are very wary. An old gander is always posted to warn the flock of the slightest hint of danger. The flock were feeding at sundown. The field looked like an immense animated page of "pothooks" as the looped necks of the feeding birds rose and fell, rose and fell. The sentinel honked! With a whirr of wings, a straightening of necks and a tucking back of legs, the flock rose instantly—they fell into formation, a wedge cutting clean, high air, the irregular monotony of their honking tumbling back to earth, falling in a flurry through the air, helter-skelter, falling incessant as the flakes in a snow storm. Long after the sky had taken the geese into its hiding their honks came back to earth and us.

Bands of coyotes came to the creek below our windows and made night hideous by agonized howlings. No one had warned me and the first night I thought some fearfulness had overtaken the world. Their cries expressed woe, cruelty, anger, utter despair! Torn from sleep I sat up in my bed shaking, my room reeking with horror! Old miners say the coyote is a ventriloquist, that from a far ridge he can throw his voice right beside you, while from close he can make himself sound very far. I certainly thought that night my room was stuffed with coyotes.

In Cariboo I did not paint. I pushed paint away from me together with the failure and disappointment of the last five years.

There was an Indian settlement a mile or two away. I used to ride there to barter my clothing for the Indians' beautiful baskets. At last I had nothing left but the clothes I stood in but I owned some nice baskets.

My friend was puzzled and disappointed. We had known each other since early childhood. She had anticipated my companionship with pleasure—but here I was! "Millie!" she said disgustedly, "you are as immature and unsophisticated as when you left home. You must have gone through London with your eyes shut!" and, taking her gun, she went out.

She seldom rode, preferring to walk with gun and dog. She came home in exasperated pets of disgust.

"Never saw a living creature—did you?"

"All kinds; the critters know the difference between a sketching easel and a gun," I laughed.

We never agreed on the subject of shooting. She practiced on any living thing. It provoked her that creatures would not sit still to be shot.

"London has not sophisticated you at all," she complained. "I have quite outgrown you since I married."

Perhaps, but maybe London had had less to do with retarding my development than disappointment had. She was bored by this country as I had been bored by London. Quite right, we were now far apart as the poles—no one's fault. Surfacely we were very good friends, down deep we were not friends at all, not even acquaintances.

Winter began to nip Cariboo. The coast called and Vancouver Island, that one step more Western than the West. I went to her, longing yet dreading. Never had her forests looked so solemn, never her mountains so high, never her drift-laden beaches so vast. Oh, the gladness of my West again! Immense Canada! Oh, her Pacific edge, her Western limit! I blessed my luck in being born Western as I climbed the stair of my old barn studio.

During my absence my sister had lent the studio to a parson to use for a study. He had papered the walls with the Daily Colonist, sealed the windows. There were no cobwebs, perhaps he had concocted them into sermons. As I ran across the floor to fling the window wide everything preached at me.

Creak of rusty hinge, the clean air rushed in! The cherry tree was gone, only the memory of its glory left. Was everything gone or dead or broken? No! Hurrying to me came Peacock, my Peacock! Who had told him I was come? He had not been up on the studio roof this last five years. Glorious, exultant, he spread himself.

Victoria had driven the woods back. My sister owned a beautiful mare which she permitted me to ride. On the mare, astride as I had ridden in Cariboo, my sheep-dog following, I went into the woods. No woman had ridden cross-saddle before in Victoria! Victoria was shocked! My family sighed. Carrs had always conformed; they believed in what always has been continuing always to be. Cross-saddle! Why, everyone disapproved! Too bad, instead of England gentling me into an English Miss with nice ways I was more me than ever, just pure me.

One thing England had taught me which my friends and relatives would not tolerate—smoking! Canadians thought smoking women fast, bad. There was a scene in which my eldest sister gave her ultimatum. "If smoke you must, go to the barn and smoke with the cow. Smoke in my house you shall not."

So I smoked with the cow. Neither she nor I were heavy smokers but we enjoyed each other's company.

And so I came back to British Columbia not with "know-it-all" fanfare, not a successful student prepared to carry on art in the New World, just a broken-in-health girl that had taken rather a hard whipping, and was disgruntled with the world.

Of my three intimate school friends two were married and living in other places, the third was nursing in San Francisco. I made no new friends; one does not after school-days, unless there are others who are going your way or who have interests in common. Nobody was going my way, and their way did not interest me. I took my sheep-dog and rode out to the woods. There I sat, dumb as a plate, staring, absorbing tremendously, though I did not realize it at the time. Again I was struck by that vague similarity between London crowds and Canadian forests; each having its own sense of terrific power, density and intensity, but similarity ceased there. The clamorous racing of hot human blood confused, per-haps revolted me a little sometimes. The woods standing, standing, hold-ing the cool sap of vegetation were healing, restful after seeing the boil of humanity.

It did me no harm to sit idle, still pondering in the vastness of the West where every spilled sound came tumbling back to me in echo. After the mellow sweetness of England with its perpetual undertone of human-ity it was good to stand in space.

Emily
Carr

Ernest L. Blumenschein's *Sangre de Cristo Mountains* (Anschutz Collection, Denver, Colorado).

Ernest L. Blumenschein (1874-1960)

This is the way legends begin. In September of 1898, two young and footloose but mechanically inept artists hit a rough spot in the road. On the rebound, their wagon lurched, then stopped, teetering over a precipice high in the mountain wilderness of northern New Mexico. The two perplexed painters managed to wrestle the broken wheel from its axle; then, after losing the coin flip, Ernest L. Blumenschein rode away on a draught horse, awkwardly lugging the wheel to the nearest village, twenty miles away.

The village, Taos, contrasts strikingly with Paris, where Blumenschein had studied at the Academie Julien from 1894 to 1896. What he saw in that New Mexico valley in 1898 struck him as "the first great unforgettable inspiration of my life." Nevertheless, he left Taos and, except for a brief return visit in 1901, he spent the next decade in Paris. He couldn't forget Taos, however, and in 1910 he began spending his summers there, joining with five fellow artists to form the Taos Society of Artists in 1913. When his wife received an inheritance, Blumenschein moved the whole family permanently to Taos in 1919. He achieved success there, being elected to the National Academy in 1927. He died in Albuquerque at the age of eighty-six.

What was it about northern New Mexico that made such a strong impression on Blumenschein? Surely it had much to do with the natural setting: great, god-like clouds soaring over toward important destinations; deep mountain forests seeming to harbor messages in their interminable depths; the sharp-edged, revivifying air itself. And much to do with the arresting cultures, far different than those known by Easterners: Hispanics steeped in centuries-old traditions; Indians in colorful blankets, gazing down without expression from the roofs of their pueblo and keeping their own set of secrets cast up from an unknowable past but alive, right there. Everywhere in New Mexico the incoming artists saw the richness of the primitive haunting the present.

Yet, in realistic terms, all was not well in Taos and nearby Santa Fe.

The cultures, now joined by the intruding Anglo element, had sharp edges, and—as they do today—they rubbed against one another, occasionally drawing blood and hatred. And in old age, Blumenschein, along with many of the old-timers, suffered from modernity's vast changes for the worse. In an interview with Katy Marview a few years before his death, the founding artist groaned at the tawdriness of popular culture flooding into New Mexico. For him the addictive glitz of television, movies, and advertising—new fixations in New Mexico as well as for the whole nation—lacked "the depth of centuries," his life's food.

Such things were not within the gaze of the early, yearning souls, however. With their creative vision, the newcomers reveled in a rich ensemble of man and nature blessing their lives. The result was a matrix of wholeness and harmony presented on the canvases before us, in the places where we can never go except through art.

We begin Blumenschein's legend where we should, at the beginning of his encounter with his first great inspiration.

Further Reading

Bickerstaff, Laura M. *Pioneer Artists of Taos.* 1955. Denver: Old West, 1983.

Blumenschein, Ernest L. "The Broken Wagon Wheel: Symbol of Taos Art Colony." *The Santa Fe New Mexican.* June 26, 1940.

Broder, Patricia Janis. *Taos: A Painter's Dream.* Boston: New York Graphic Society. 1980.

Coke, Van Deren. *Taos and Santa Fe: The Artist's Environment, 1882-1942.* Albuquerque: University of New Mexico Press, 1963.

Grant, Blanche C. *When Old Trails Were New: The Story of Taos.* 1934. Glorieta, New Mexico: The Rio Grande Press, 1983.

Lawrence, D. H. "New Mexico." *The Survey* 66.3 (May 1, 1931): 153.

Marview, Katy. "City's Intellectual Growth Lags, Says Blumenschein." *Albuquerque Tribune.* February 27, 1952.

*Ernest
L.
Blumenschein*

~

From "The Broken Wagon Wheel:
Symbol of Taos Art Colony"

In the parade of the Taos Fiesta of 1939 was a striking float, sponsored by the Taos Association of Artists. A huge wagon wheel with broken spoke, in vermilion and silver, was mounted on a long wagon, and flanked by the two oldish painters who are connected with this tale.

Exactly 41 years before this parade, the original broken wagon wheel made its entry into the Taos Plaza. Its story is the beginning of the art group which made fame for itself and drew much attention to New Mexico by paintings exhibited all over the United States and in Canada, South America, France, Italy, England, Sweden, Germany, Hungary, Australia and New Zealand.

I want to record the "official beginning," so will slip back a long time when I was an art student in Paris. There I met Henry Sharp, who, learning of my interest in the American Indian told me of the village of Taos, where for a couple of weeks he had sketched. It was located at the foot of a mountain in northern New Mexico. I recall being impressed, as I pigeon-holed that curious name in my memory with the hope that some day I might pass that way.

Returning soon after to America, *McClure's Magazine,* destined to become famous, and die, assigned me a job of illustrating that obliged me to visit New Mexico and Arizona. It was a short trip, but a thrilling one, in mid-winter. A story of its own, which I will skip. When I got back from this journey, my first west of the Mississippi, I was so enthusiastic over the possibilities of a sketching trip in the plateau country, that I induced Bert Phillips to save his money and accompany me the following summer.

Phil and I decided to outfit at Denver. We purchased a light wagon, to be delivered, with harness, at a corral where we had negotiated for two broncos. We loaded the vehicle to its capacity with our camping and painting apparatus. Without betraying our woeful ignorance, we carefully observed the cowboys hitch the horses to our wagon, crawled into the driver's seat and were off on our way to New Mexico. When night overtook us, we camped by the roadside, cooked supper on a frying pan, staked out the animals and slept on the folded tent under the wagon. Thus we lived, sketching in Colorado when we pleased, during the months of June, July and August.

Early in September we crossed La Veta Pass into New Mexico. A decided change came in the scenery—and also, in the roads. The heavy thunderstorms of summer had ruined the mountain roads. We soon found that our light wagon was no match for New Mexico. We broke double-trees and single-trees before we had gone far. A disaster occurred each day. The final one happened at the top of a steep climb on a bad curve, when we slid into a deep rut and broke a rear wheel. It was a serious predicament, with the wagon tilted over the edge of a canyon and just about ready to roll into oblivion! So we sat down and had refreshments—a cold can of baked beans and a pickle.

We decided, without much wisdom, to take the broken member to the nearest blacksmith shop. That would be Taos, 20 miles away. One of us must remain with the wagon. It was my lot to win the toss of a coin, and the job of carrying the wheel horseback, to Taos. At 4 p.m. on the third of September, 1898, I started down the mountain, on what resulted in the most impressive journey of my life. It took me until dark to reach the foot of this long hill. There I spent the night with a hospitable Spanish-American farmer—one dollar for frijoles, bed, and frijoles again for breakfast. It was early in the morning when I resumed the 40-mile horse-back ride. My muscles soon ached from carrying the broken wheel. What had seemed a simple job when we tossed the coin, had become a painful task. The wheel grew larger and heavier as I shifted it to all conceivable positions, from arm to arm, then around my neck or on my back, or balanced on a foot. Even the horse resented the unwieldy load on his saddle and grunted his displeasure at every step. Vividly I recall the discomfort with no relief in sight on the road, no wagon going my way, no hope to ease sore muscles until I reached Taos, a dim picture of which I had made from Sharp's slight description.

But Sharp had not painted for me the mountains or plains or clouds. No artist had ever recorded the superb New Mexico I was now seeing. No writer had, to my knowledge, ever written down the smell of this sage-brush air, or the feel of the morning sky. I was receiving, under rather painful circumstances, the first great unforgettable inspiration of my life. My destiny was being decided as I squirmed and cursed while urging the bronco through those many miles of waves of sage-brush. The morning was sparkling and stimulating. The beautiful Sangre de Cristo range to my left was different in character from the Colorado mountains. Stretching away from the foot of this range was a vast plateau, cut by the Rio Grande and by lesser gorges in which were located small villages of flat roofed adobe houses built around a church and plaza, all fitting into the color scheme of the tawny surroundings. The sky above was clear clean blue with sharp moving clouds. The color, the reflective character of the land scape, the drama of the vast spaces, the superb beauty and severity of the hills, stirred me deeply. I realized I was getting my own impressions from nature, seeing it for the first time probably with my own eyes, uninflu-enced by the art of any man. Notwithstanding the painful handicap of that broken wheel I was carrying, New Mexico inspired me to a profound degree. My grunting horse carried me down and across the gorges, around the foothills over long flat spaces that were like great lakes of sage-brush, through 20 slow miles of thrilling sensations.

It had to end in the Taos valley, green with trees and fields of alfalfa, populated by dark-skinned people who greeted me pleasantly. There I saw my first Taos Indians, blankets artistically draped. New Mexico had gripped me—and I was not long in deciding that if Phillips would agree with me, if he felt as inspired to work as I, the Taos valley and its sur-rounding magnificent country would be the end of our wagon trip.

The Broken Wheel was mended by the blacksmith, and I returned the next day to Phil.

Soon after reaching Taos in the wagon, we sold that much abused vehicle, the harness, the horses, and pitched into work with an unknown enthusiasm. There were no other artists in New Mexico at that time, but soon they came to join Bert, who from the day we arrived made his home in that adobe village. I went abroad to study more, married, and returned to the land of my inspiration. Artists came from all parts of the United States and foreign countries. Today about 50 painters have permanent homes at Taos, and three times that number spend their summers work-ing about the village. A dozen writers, some of national fame, are also established here.

Recent years of automobiles and good roads, education and hygiene—and increased taxes—have slightly altered the native Spanish people. The Taos Indians are but slightly changed. The aggressive Anglo businessman, despite his collossal ignorance of the fine qualities in the culture about him is improving in breadth of view. Artists, writers and archaeologists have combined to convince the population that this state has something unique

Ernest
L.
Blumenschein

worth preserving. Instead of modernizing our dwellings, the general sentiment now is to preserve the charm of the adobe village with its folk lore, the fiestas and dances of the Spanish and Indians.

If I could picture in words the superb mountains, the moving grandeur of great plains, the sunshine that makes people happy, the storms that inspire paintings and books, the grand forests of pine and spruce and juniper, the beautiful streams, the out-door life of work and sports, it would be New Mexico, the land where my great adventure was started as I sat in agony carrying the broken wheel, and where it has long continued, as I shouldered the other burdens of a happy industrious artist's life.

Maynard Dixon's *Desert Journey* (the Anschutz Collection, Denver, Colorado, photo by William J. O'Connor).

Maynard Dixon (1875-1946)

Like Robert Frost, artist Maynard Dixon had a lover's quarrel—a most productive one—with the world. As a boy in Fresno, California, where his father was a lawyer-rancher, young Dixon tasted the lingering wildness of rural California—the vaqueros with great rowel spurs and the allure of a Mexican culture at ease among vast spaces. That bright world flashed the colors of an older California fast fading even as Dixon matured. This was for him, however, the authentic West to which his mind clung, and throughout his adult life he chafed, having to produce a synthetic, shoot-'em-up West in the magazine drawings that provided much of his living, just as he did during an especially painful early period in New York City, working as an illustrator for *Century, Scribner's,* and other popular magazines of the day. By 1912, however, he was back in California. Settling in San Francisco, whose Bohemian life Dixon enjoyed, he found enough commercial work to keep him afloat and support periodic forays into the land of his imagination, the American Southwest.

The yearning for the older, more authentic ways and the lingering sadness that they never can be regained has been a major theme in Western art, indeed, in the romanticization of the American West generally. There may be a certain adolescence at work here, the Rousseauean craving for a wild land, a stage on which the ego has free play to romp at will. Often missed in such powerful longings is the unreality at their root—the failure to recognize that "untainted" Indians and Mexicans and wildernesses possess entities other than those imagined, that they come with their own sets of miring complexities as well as heady potentials. It is an old and perhaps excusable fallacy: We perceive peoples and landscapes in terms of our own needs.

In craving the exotic, Dixon substituted one cliché for another. The West of his serious art is not of the bar brawls and delectable frontier maidens illustrating the dime novels of the day but of a god-like spirit pulsing behind the scenes he painted—there, but always just beyond reach, the ". . . something I cannot name, yet more than half believe . . ." longed for in the artist's following essay about Arizona in days gone by.

Yet, on a further level, all clichés are not the same. If the one Dixon rejected smacks of the tawdriness of a Phineas T. Barnum, the one he adopted, by comparison, is far more convincing, and it has enriching possibilities. He expressed his view of the West in paintings that avoided sensational frontier melodrama and that brought to Western subjects modern techniques. For example, after Dixon saw paintings by the Impressionists at the Panama-Pacific Exposition of 1915, he used his revised ideas about color to paint *Apache Land,* one of his best-known works. We can also see how the photographs taken by his second wife, Dorothea Lange, influenced his art after their marriage in 1920. Art begins, as Oscar Wilde said, where imitation ends, and if one finds Dixon's prose and poetry dominated by fairly standard sentiments, that only shows how what is weighted with dross in one art form may become superb alchemy when transformed into another.

Further Reading

Burnside, Wesley M. *Maynard Dixon, Artist of the West.* Provo: Brigham Young University Press, 1973.

Dixon, Maynard. "Arizona in 1900." *Arizona Highways* 18.2 (February 1942): 17-19, 40.

_____. *Rim-Rock and Sage: The Collected Poems of Maynard Dixon.* Introduction by Kevin Starr. San Francisco: California Historical Society, 1977.

Hagerty, Donald J. *Desert Dreams: The Art and Life of Maynard Dixon.* Layton, Utah: Gibbs Smith, 1993.

Samuels, Peggy and Harold, Joan Samuels, and Daniel Fabian. *Techniques of the Artists of the American West.* Secaucus, New Jersey: Wellfleet Press, 1990.

Starr, Kevin. "Introduction." *Rim-Rock and Sage: The Collected Poems of Maynard Dixon.* San Francisco: California Historical Society, 1977. ix-xxix.

≈

From *Rim-Rock and Sage*

January

The fir stands waist-deep in the bedded snow;
The storm-birds twitter, and in dark array
The broken peaks in shadow stand—when slow
The sun makes for a space all-blinding day,
While brown deer shyly track their silent way,
Hoof-patterning the snow-drifts as they go.

World's End

I stand upon the shore of my release;—
Out into the immeasurable west,
Far over, down into eternal Space,
Is spread the great blue shining sea of Peace,—
Far-glimmering in deep unshaken rest;—
A shimmering sleep upon her sunlit face.
The brown and fierce-browed hills stand bare and bar
The sky's bright rim along the silent east;
And here the yearning land outreaches far
To take the glad sea in his shining arms;
A thousand thousand ages these wan sands
Have shone where men have dared to build few hopes,—
Bent like a bow of death between God's hands.

Among the humble hills sly savages
With keen-cut eyes go wandering in the thorn;
With thirst-and-hunger-sharpened sense they steal
Their victual of despair 'tween night and morn,—
And men of stronger hearts appeared.—Forlorn
They came,—who knows through what unspoken pains?—
Gauntly they saw with desert-saddened eyes
This sea that reached to Nothing. . . . Others built
And taught and tilled, and passed; but This remains. . . .

And over all the vast and hollow skies
Of infinite tenderness from their deep mouth
Vibrate the Song of Silence; and the drouth
Bears hard upon the land and mummifies
These death-contorted ranges of the south.

I am a city's wan unwilling guest;
With three good friends,—a dog, a horse, a gun,—
Would I might wander where the great Southwest
Lies throbbing with the pulses of the sun,
And waiting silent with her warm brown breast
Turned up to him; where gray Time for a span
Has dropped the seasons. . . . She awaits the best
Soul-singing thought of some great silent man.

From "Arizona in 1900"

Arizona—the magic name of a land bright and mysterious, of sun and sand, of tragedy and stark endeavor. So long had I dreamed of it that when I came there it was not strange to me. Its sun was my sun, its ground my ground.

That was in 1900—only thirteen years after Geronimo and his Apaches had surrendered to our ever-pursuing cavalry. Arizona was still "Arizona." Cow ranches still raised cattle, cowpunchers were not yet "picturesque" and worked steers instead of dudes. Indians were still Injuns, and you could read in the pitiless eyes of Apaches the memory of burning buildings in the gray dawn and the long shuddering screams of torture. The prickly silent desert was still a place where you could get lost and die the terrible death of thirst; where 125-in-the-shade was still 125-in-the-shade, and a red earthen olla, swung under the ramada, was more essential than the most gadgety frigidaire can ever hope to be.

Arizona was still "frontier." Yes—men were few and not well thought of, and the citizens generally adhered to the precept: "So live that you can look every damn man in the eye and tell him to go to hell"—which they frequently did.

The business district of Prescott had been burned flat and upon my arrival the place was humming like a new mining camp. Stores, banks, saloons, and gambling places were doing business under pine boards and canvas. One citizen was pointed out to me as a good man not to monkey with. He was tall and wore a wide hat, his grey eyes were mild and sad, his moustache had a despondent droop and he sagged a little at the knees and shoulders. He wore a deputy's badge. It seemed that recently some enthusiastic lad had done a bank hold-up and was making a galloping getaway when the sad eyed man, at long range, nailed him with one shot. When complimented, he remarked, "I seldom miss." I glanced down the long pine bar. A dazzle of glassware and bottles showed you could buy any drink to be had in the most rococo thirst parlors of New York or San Francisco. From behind it, spaced at intervals in pairs, protruded the butts of sixshooters.

In those days in Arizona being an artist was something you just had to endure—or be smart enough to explain why. It was incomprehensible that you were just out "seeing the country." If you were not working for the railroad, considering real estate or scouting for a mining company what the hell were you? The drawings I made were no excuse; and I was regarded as a wandering lunatic.

In Phoenix at the Hassayampa Club I met some of the old timers. "Well, son," said one of them, "if you want to see Arizona, just put a box o' soda crackers and a jug o' whiskey in the back o' the wagon and you can travel from one end of the place to the other and never spend a dollar." Anyhow, it was then safe manners in the Territory to "set 'em up"—and ask no personal questions.

Torrid in its irrigated valley, Phoenix was no great city. Many of the buildings were adobe; wagons, buggies and saddled horses were tired before the wide awnings; Pima, Papago and Maricopa, arrayed in gay silks and calicos, squatted along the sidewalk, and "Chihuahua Town" was sizeable if not important.

The brown-skinned people fascinated me. In Tempe, then nine-tenths Mexican, I made many drawings of them; enjoyed their simple hospitality, and in starlit evenings learned to sing, in paisano style:

Mujer, mujer, mi corazon pierdese,
Mi triste pecho se encuentra apasionado.

Something *muy simpatica* in all this and to be long treasured in the memory.

My first desert camp was near Sacaton on the Reservation, and here I first met the saguaro. Close to my bed stood the tall shaft of one devoid of branches. All that long sleepless night it dominated me, a dark finger of doubt pointing ominously forever upward into an unknowable universe of stars. In the pale yellow light of sunrise a saguaro is only a giant cactus—but through all my longer acquaintance with them that night remains my strongest memory. Nor shall I ever forget a giant Pima who came at sunset riding a roan pony down a little slope, gazing straight into the sun, clad only in an undershirt stretched thin over the great arch of his chest, his long gray hair hanging straight down his back. Not a glance my way. He was all "Injun."

The Agua Fria Valley (really a high plateau) was my first look at mesa and benchland country, and the terrific drama of dark thunderstorm and cloudburst. It was then grass land, but at the end of the fourth dry year the plain was dotted with mummified carcasses of cattle. Here was a new world, full of great imaginings. And here I first saw cowboys of the Texas type: "rim-fire" saddle, tied rope, batwing chaps,—very different from the old Miller and Lux vaqueros of the San Joaquin.

Out of all this I made a large drawing of a cowpuncher on a starved-looking pony gazing ruefully down at a mummied steer, named it *Drouth* and sent it to *Harper's Weekly*. It came back with the comment, "Not serious enough." If the editor could have heard the Arizona comments on that drawing. . . . But that was forty-one years ago.

There were Apache—Tontos—at old Camp Verde; fierce hawk-faced people from the chaparral. It was not wise, the storekeeper told me, for a stranger to visit their camp alone. I made some sketches of them though; but quickly, and from safe concealment. How much of the cruelty I saw in those grim visages was of my own imagining? But they were the nearest thing to the wild fighting Injun I shall ever see.

Crawling through tiny rooms cut in the cream colored cliff of Montezuma's Castle (silly name)—picking up bits of pottery, dreaming of a far and forgotten past; the enchantment of moonlight on Montezuma's Well—and dreams, more dreams. Those dim Indian ghosts that I induced have ever since befriended me. I knew them again at old Oraibi, at Walpi, at Mishongnovi, at Shipaulovi and at silent Betatakin—and through them I have reached to something I cannot name, yet more than half believe. Somehow, it seems, you may not understand Indians until you make friends with the ghosts.

The Hopi—we called them Moqui then—in their prehistoric villages atop the mesas—were, it seemed to me, the living incarnation of those ghosts. The light, the color, the dusky interiors, the quiet murmur of their voices, the surrounding silence, all confirmed it. Four months at Walpi in lone association with this living past. I knew time no more; only seasons, and the world suspended in eternity. A little feathered Katchina and bits of turquoise hung against a pearl-white wall and my friend Namoki telling stories to his little naked son,—the swaying arc of costumed figures in the Basket Dance,—and deep chant of the Neman Katchina,—the moving sunlit poetry of the Flute Dance at Toreva,—all this and Broadway were under the same sky. I never worked at higher levels.

Thirty-three thousand Navajo they told me, in a vast remote country of mesas, plains and canyons, the all of which no white man knew. To a man on horseback, remember, or in a wagon, the world was on a scale unknown to motorists,—and roads then were trails or wagon tracks.

Ganado trading post, sixty-five miles from the railroad, was two days by horseback, one day with a good buggy team, and four days for the freight wagons—in good weather. Now two hours by motor car. Chinlee, twenty-five miles further, at the mouth of Canyon de Chelly, was really remote, and Kayenta, seventy miles more, was "a damn long way in any direction."

There were real trading posts—not small-town stores transplanted. Ganado was a solid mud-and-stone bastion—almost a fort—with barred windows and heavy double doors and ready firearms in every room. Here Lorenzo Hubbell, the elder, was jovial dictator, and from the head of his long dining table dispensed an endless flow of droll anecdotes and a fare of carne seca, frijoles, canned corn and sourdough biscuits to visiting sen-ators, traveling salesmen and Mexican teamsters alike with equal and unfailing courtesy.

Chinlee was a log house with extremely wide eaves, and mud floor, small dusty windows, with its corral and hay-stack isolated upon a bare knoll. Here Sam Day and his wife held the post with hospitality to all trav-elers and fair treatment to the Navajo. The walls, floors, and furniture were literally covered with an astounding assortment of Navajo weaving and Ute beadwork of all ages, kinds and conditions. It was "old-timey" to the limit. The Indians seemed wilder and even more primitive than at Ganado, and here I heard "railroad Indians" mentioned with disdain.

Thirty-three thousand Navajo—"Not hostile," I was told, "but better travel in a party. No, they would not kill you, but if they caught you alone they'd likely take everything you've got and leave you afoot; and getting back to somewhere might be plenty tough." In those days they had a little custom with strangers. Meeting you out afoot, they would run their horses right at you, all in a bunch, yelling and laughing as though to trample you into the ground—and the Lord help you if you ran. You might as well keep on running until you reached the railroad. They tried it on me once and I just kept on walking. Well, there was no place to run to.

These were the singing Indians. As they rode across the long valleys or though echoing canyons their high-keyed lilting songs could be heard from far off through the clean high air. With their sheep and goats and ponies, their little cornfields and shelters of juniper boughs; their igloo-like hogans; their pointed moccasins and jewelry of silver, turquoise and shell, their steep saddles padded with goat skins, and their slim grace of people forever on horseback; they made a world of their own. And was this also Arizona? It could have been central Asia.

Then the Yei Betchai. Sam Day should have known, for he had two sons taking part in the dance and he translated it "Giant Grandfather." Three thousand Indians in that camp, with their wagons drawn up around the great fires of the dance oval—and perhaps a dozen whites. The medicine men in full Navajo dress with their sacred meal and pollen; the masked and painted dancers; eagle feathers, turquoise and glinting silver in the firelight, the shrill high chant and chirring rattles; sweating bodies in the sharp November night. And there, behind those masks, singing out of a twilight past with the voices of eagles, coyotes, bear,—but wilder, fiercer—were my Indian ghosts again.

The age-old mystery of sun and shadow among the red cliffs of Canyon de Chelly, the rainbow miracles of color wrought by charging storms, the aromatic odor of piñon and juniper, the pale twinkle of cottonwoods beside acequias, the small campfire of greasewood and catclaw in a white desert wash, carefree cowboys riding the ragged ridges of the Sierra Blanca, all these can never be forgotten by any painter who has really known them.

Then came flivvers and irrigation projects—and the West changed. The Arizona of paved highways, big canals, citrus groves, dude ranches, cactus gardens, chambers of commerce and Ohio-Spanish architecture is not so dear to me. The Indians have cut their hair, the cowboys wear "association" clothes and most of the tang has gone out of the Mexican comida and yet. . . . And yet when you visit the home of some well-to-do business man you are very apt to discover the old saddle and boots in the back porch; there is a canvas-covered bed roll in the garage; his pet .45 and bridle ornament on the mantel shelf and you could not get the old branding iron from him for love or money. In spite of "promotion" there is still something of the old free and open way of doing things; there, if you will but look, are still the unbeaten mountains and unfathomable blue above.

In all the land west of the Rockies I know of none more wonderful and various in conformation, more marvelous in light and living color, more stimulating to the imagination. To me it has imparted something of an ancient mystery, of a stark and clear-cut reality, a pageant of ever-moving drama.

Here on the outskirts of Tucson the big studio window faces the changing grandeur of the Catalinas across the Rillito. Overhead in the blue the great gray birds of war roar westward to beleaguered islands. Inside the little patio is a spot of green oasis—orange and lemon and cottonwood, and iris bulbs growing; and outside the mesquite and cactus and catclaw come right up to the adobe wall, growing just as they always grew, for which we are glad. And why? Because—well, because it is still Arizona.

Maynard Dixon

Edward S. Curtis—"The Reburial of Chief Joseph" (Negative 613, Special Collections, University of Washington Libraries, Seattle).

~

Edward S. Curtis (1868-1952)

As George Catlin labored, often crudely, among the "wild" plains tribes, he often despaired of ever producing the rich pictorial record of American Indians the nation deserved. Then, a few years after Catlin's death, the son of a poor, disabled veteran of the Civil War began completing Catlin's dream, not with brushes, but with a camera.

For those who believe that artists must be weird creatures—half aggressive hustlers, half creative geniuses—to succeed, the career of Edward S. Curtis may seem bright with the catalyst of divine intervention. An avid but unknown photographer in Seattle, young Curtis bumped into a group of lost scientists huddled under a ledge during a snowstorm on Mount Rainier. Curtis led the men down the mountain to safety. Among the personages he rescued was George Bird Grinnell, the well-connected editor of *Forest and Stream*. Grinnell did more than encourage the youth's interest in photographing Indians; his influence led to incalculably valuable contacts with the likes of John Muir and President Theodore Roosevelt.

The upshot in this chain of good fortune was an introduction to financier J. P. Morgan. Known as a skinflint, Morgan fixed his glinting eye on Curtis—and was inexplicably pleased. His checks did more than fund Curtis' career; they supported the artist's lifetime work, *The North American Indian*. Appearing between 1907 and 1930, this lavishly printed, twenty-volume set became publishing crème de la crème, the most important visual record we have of our native peoples.

Curtis, however, was almost too late. The old life he sought to capture on film was fast fading. Nonetheless, he worked doggedly on, moving from tribe to tribe and often encouraged by aging Indians who gladly dug out their elaborate outfits from the days of wild buffalo hunts to pose for their amiable visitor. Others scowled as he plodded on, desperate to record what was almost gone. He was shot at four times; once, he wisely packed up and left, sensing that he would be blamed when an Indian girl died in an accidental fall (Weinberger, "Classic Images of Dying Nations Enjoy a Rebirth" 88).

In his essay "Vanishing Indian Types," Curtis struggles as his deep sense of humanity for a subjugated people wars with the insistent realism of his intellectual toughness. The two were irreconcilable. His father had been an itinerant preacher, and the missionary impulse is evident as Curtis strains to rescue what he can of disappearing cultures. On the other hand, he saw clearly what was happening in the cruel dynamics of demographic forces. Whatever his sentiments, as had happened time and time again on the earth, a Stone Age people was being ground up by a technologically superior and far-more populous invader.

These sentiments definitely leaned toward idealization of his subjects. Bob Kapoun argues that part of Curtis' emotional coloring is due to the nature of photographic art itself. Depicting everyday life may be the goal, but selecting the most dramatic images for publication can skew the viewers' understanding ("Introduction to the Photographer" xvii-xix). Nevertheless, the strongest element at work here was what Caspar Weinberger, Jr. calls Curtis' "warm melancholy" about the irredeemable old days ("Classic Images of Dying Nations Enjoy a Rebirth" 88). That in Curtis' view Indians lived "wild, care-free, picturesque" lives certainly is debatable, albeit the view was becoming current in Curtis' time among the younger Indians. They, no less than the whites, were beginning to see the past shaded in the tints of nostalgia.

Further Reading

Curtis, Edward S. *The North American Indian.* 1907-1930. Köln: Taschen, 1997. 20 volumes.

———. "Vanishing Indian Types: The Tribes of the Northwest Plains." *Scribner's Magazine* 39 (May-June 1906): 657-71.

Kapoun, Bob. "Introduction to the Photographer and His Unpublished Photographs." *Prayer to the Great Mystery: The Uncollected Writings and Photography of Edward S. Curtis.* Gerald Hausman, ed. New York: St. Martin's Press, 1995. xvii-xx.

Weinberger, Jr., Caspar. "Classic Images of Dying Nations Enjoy a Rebirth." *Smithsonian* 6.1 (April 1975): 82-89.

~

From "Vanishing Indian Types"

Edward
S.
Curtis

The Northwest Plains Indian is, to the average person, the typical American Indian, the Indian of our school-day books—powerful of physique, statuesque, gorgeous in dress, with the bravery of the firm believer in predestination. The constant, fearless hunting and slaughtering of the buffalo trained him to the greatest physical endurance, and gave an inbred desire for bloodshed. Thousands of peace-loving, agricultural-living Indians might climb down from their cliff-perched homes, till their miniature farms, attend their flocks, and at night-time climb back up the winding stairs to their home in the clouds, and attract no attention. But if a fierce band of Sioux rushed down on a hapless emigrant train the world soon learned of it.

The culture of all primitive peoples is necessarily determined by their environment. This, of course, means that all plains tribes—though speaking a score of languages—were, in life and manner, broadly alike. They were buffalo-hunting Indians, and only in rare cases did they give any attention to agriculture. Buffalo meat was their food, and the by-products their clothing, tools, and implements.

The plains tribes in earlier times were certainly true nomads. For a time, in the depths of winter, they camped in the shelter of some forest along the streams. Other than that, wherever roamed a herd of buffalo, there also wandered the bands of Northern Indians. The very existence of these tribes seemed bound to that of the buffalo. From the skins their lodges were built. With the hair on, the hides furnished the robes for the body, as well as mattresses and bed coverings. The meat, prepared in many ways, with the addition of a few roots and berries, furnished their entire food. Advancing civilization has swept these countless herds from the face of the plains, and left their human companions stranded.

In many despondent hours of pondering over the fate of these native children I have felt that perhaps if they, too, could have perished with the buffalo herd it would have been vastly better for them. But, no! Though thousands of years behind us in civilization, they are human beings. Their loves are like our loves; their affection for their children like our own, except that many ages of civilization have given us, perhaps, a little more self-control.

In a cabin on the plains of Montana three of us sat talking: an educated Plains Indian, a Government sub-agent, and myself. I was telling of the splendid advancement of the Apaches, and how well they would work. At the close of my story the agent turned to the Indian and asked him, "Why don't your people work like that?" All about the cabin, as a decorative frieze, was a row of buffalo skulls. The Indian looked up at those skulls, saying: "They tell you why. While those buffaloes were alive we did not need to work. Only niggers and white people farmed. We were a superior people and had nothing but contempt for those who worked. Do you realize that I, a comparatively young man, know the days when if we wanted food we had but to ride out on the plains, shoot buffalo, or other game, and the women would go out and bring it into camp? Do you expect us, in the fraction of a life-time, in the quarter of the age of an old man, to have changed our whole life, and even to have forgotten the days of the old freedom, when we were lords of all the great plains and mountains? In what way does your civilization benefit us? Before you had attempted to force your so-called civilization upon us we had every desire of the heart! An easy, simple, carefree life, and to the worthy and brave a certainty of a future life of plenty and comfort. What has your civilization done for us? Robbed us of our land, our strength, our dignity, our content. Even your religion has robbed us of our confidence in the hereafter. What have you given us in return? Desire, corruption, beggary, discontent. You have robbed us of our birthright, and scarcely given us a husk. You said we did not make use of the land as the white man would, so you took it from us and use it as you like. I could as well go to the man who has his millions loaned at three per cent. and say, 'You are only getting three per cent. for this. I can use it and make ten. I will take it because I will make the best use of it.'"

It is true that advancement demands the extermination of these wild, care-free, picturesque Indians, and, in the language of our President, we cannot keep them or their lands for bric-a-brac. The fact that we cannot, however, makes it none the less regrettable or hard on the people who are being ground beneath the wheel of civilization, and though we may be able to justify our claims that advancement and progress demand the extermination of the Indians, we can scarcely justify the method used in this extermination. As the years pass on and we are able to see the subject as history, stripped of its little local prejudices, we will be found guilty, as a nation, under the manipulations of crafty, unscrupulous politicians, of having committed more than "the crime of a century." In all our years of handling the Indians we have taught them one thing—the white man seldom told the truth. The relationship of the Indians and people of this country is that of a child and parent. We will stand convicted for all time as a parent who failed in his duty.

For once we have a commissioner whose hands are free. No senator or congressman may say, "You cannot," or "You must not"; and to appeal to the Chief Executive is to be told, "As far as the law permits, Commissioner Leupp controls the Indian Department, and I can give you no assistance." The present sane, straightforward handling of the subject is productive of great good, and it is to be hoped that many years of work can be carried on without a change of policy, as the continual changes of the department's so-called policies have been one of the Indians' greatest curses.

In June of last year I went into the hills of the Okanogan country in eastern Washington. The occasion of my going was the reburial of the splendid old Nez Percé chief, Joseph, and the erection of a man-fashioned monument of what it is hoped will be his final resting-place.

Matters dragged in the digging of one grave and the digging out of another. It was no small task, and, hoping to expedite matters, I dug, pried, tugged, and lifted in assisting to get that burial-chest out of one place and moved to another. It was what one might term a study in practical or applied ethnology. Many speeches were made. A college professor in frock coat and silk hat did part of the talking. Several chiefs and would-be chiefs in blankets and feathers did the rest. We did not have the regular Indian burial rite in the reburial. The Indians said: "Last year we buried him; this time just move him." A child died early that morning, and the Indians buried it in their own way late in the afternoon. In this there was no "Boston hat" or "Boston man's talk," but a most beautiful pagan ceremony. The mourners encircled the grave. A high-keyed, falsetto chant by forty voices, rising and falling in absolute unison, sent chills down our spines that hot June day, as does the dismal wail of wintry winds in the pine forests.

On the following day came the Chief Joseph potlatch—a Hi-u potlatch (Big Giving), in which every earthly possession of the old chief and his wife was given away. Through it all the wife sat by the side of the great stack of goods being distributed, handing out each article and trinket. At times when some article obviously dear to her heart was handed out great tears would roll down her cheeks. Two days were taken in this giving, and then the visiting Indians tore down the grand council lodge, and so closed the last chapter in the life and death of the most decent Indian the Northwest has ever known. No more will he beg of the Great White Father, and say: "All I ask is to go back to the old home in the Wallowa Valley; my father's home, and the home of my father's father." His troubled life has run its course, and one of the greatest Indians who ever lived is no longer a part of the white man's burden.

The Crows, of Montana, who call themselves "Absarokas," are one of the strong groups of the Northwest Indians. They did not take to fighting with the white settlers or soldiers, but from the earliest traditions have been constantly engaged in intertribal war with the Sioux, Piegans, and other tribes. At no time were they allied with the other tribes of the region, and, being fewer in number, their very existence was a fight for life. This fact kept them up to the height of physical condition. None but the strongest could survive. To this they perhaps owe the fact that of all of the Northwest tribes they are the finest in physique. They have a splendid reservation. It is allotted, and, so far as it is possible for Indians to get on in the battle to be self-supporting, they are doing well. But the remodelling of their life to meet the changed conditions forced on them by advancing civilization is solving the Indian problem for them, and at the present rate of decrease there will not be a living Crow in forty years.

The Custer battlefield is close to the Crow Agency. In a desire to know all that I could, at close range, of the tragedy of the Little Big Horn, I spent many days in going over the battlefield foot by foot, from where the troops left the Rosebud to the ridge where the men had made their last stubborn fight. White marble slabs mark the spots where they fell. In most cases the slabs are in twos, side by side. Strange how it is when it comes to the final end, we reach out for human companionship. There they made their last earthly stand, bunkie by bunkie.

Among the dozens of Indians I questioned of the fight was Curley, who is so often called the sole survivor of the Custer fight. He has been so bullied, badgered, questioned, cross-questioned, leading-questioned, and called, by mouth and in type, a coward and a liar by an endless horde of the curious and knowledge seeking, that I doubt to-day, if his life depended upon it, he could tell whether he was ever at or near the Custer fight.

I was particularly interested in getting the Indian point of view as to the bravery and respective fighting qualities of the different tribes. The Crows, in summing up the other tribes, claim that the Flatheads were the most worthy foes in intertribal fights, "as they fought most like us." On the other hand, they claimed that the Blackfoot was brave to recklessness, but was foolhardy and lacking in judgment; did not even know when to run. The Sioux were a worthy foe, and so greatly outnumbered the Crows that the latter could succeed in their fighting with them only by quick, bold strokes, and then back into their own country. Many a Crow war party went out to the land of the Sioux never to return.

One expects to find the highest development of the Plains Indians in the Sioux, but I question the fact. Physically they are not equal to many of the other tribes of that region. In legend and mythology the field is more sterile than with the small, isolated branches of the Algonquin stock, the Blackfoot and Cheyenne.

But it is among the Sioux that we find the greatest number of old historical characters. Each year cuts down their number, and soon these old fellows who know of the days before the coming of the white man will be no more. Red Cloud is, without doubt, the record holder of the living North American chiefs to-day. His home is close to Pine Ridge Agency. Ninety-one years old, blind, almost deaf, he sits dreaming of the past. No wonder he is irritated by the idle information seeker! Who would be called back from the dreams of his youth? Sightless and infirm, he is living over the days when in youth he sat his horse as a king, the pride of the great Sioux nation. To his ears must come the roar of the hunt as the countless bison herd, like a tidal wave, rolled by; and, again, the great day of his life, when his red-blanketed band swept down on the hapless Fetterman troop. Even now his heart must seem to stand still as he lives over again that day. And then that fearful day of the "Wagon Box" fight, when he hurled the pick of the Sioux nation against those thirty-two riflemen concealed in that corral, only to have his men mowed down by the repeating-rifles, with which this was the Indians' first meeting.

Intertribal Indian wars were, like most warfare up to a rather late date, war for plunder. Prehistorically there was little in the Indian life worth stealing, except the women. Later, after the Spanish invasion, there were the horses as well, which made marauding warfare far more worth while. The discouraging part of this sort of war was, that quite often the war party would fail to return to their homes, and in the camp of the enemy there would be a most merry scalp dance, with fresh scalplocks on the coup sticks.

In working with the Crows I gathered together a party of the men and

Edward S. Curtis

made a long trip across the reservation and into the mountains. My bunch of Indians were certainly a picturesque and interesting group. Two of the best characters were old Bull Chief, eighty-five years old, but still good for a forty-mile day in the saddle, and old Shot-in-the-Hand, quite a few years younger, but old enough to know a great deal of the old life. Our tents were the Indian lodges, and at night-time, around the lodge fire, the old fellows told me stories of the old Indian life. Bull Chief was the best Indian story-teller I have ever known. With clear, keen memory he traced back the Crow history through the lives of ten reigning chiefs. He was old enough to kill Buffalo calves with bow and arrow when he saw the first white man, and his people were still using stone axes. His picture of the first time he saw a white man and the things of white man's make was most vivid. A trader, whom the Indians called "Crane," from his slender build and great height, came up the Yellowstone in a canoe, stopping at the junction of that stream and the Big Horn. Think of it! Seventy years ago these people, pure pagans, saw the first white man, and to-day we quarrel with them because they are not equally civilized with us, with all our thousands of years of education.

Our camp was by a particularly beautiful mountain stream, in a deep, narrow canyon. One night the whole band of Indians was gathered by the lodge fire to listen to stories by old Bull Chief. Story after story had been told by him of the terrific fights with Piegan and Sioux. Many of the men had dropped off to sleep, when on the quiet air rang out two signal shots. Every Indian was awake and out of the lodge in an instant. Their conversation was low; all was nervous excitement. "Who was it? What could it mean?" You would have thought we were a war party in the land of the enemy. I had them fire shots in reply to the signal, thinking it might be someone in distress, but could get no reply. My attempt to allay their anxiety and get them to telling stories again was useless. No more stories that night.

But the old life, with its picturesque and romantic setting, like the war-ship with its white wings of canvas, has gone—passed on forever. The reservations have been cut down piece by piece. Now the Indian is accepting the inevitable and taking his allotment of a few acres. Across valleys and around hills they are stretching fences of wire. Along the edges of the valley, where a few years ago they hunted the buffalo, they are now digging irrigation ditches. On some of the reservations one sees marked evidence of advancement of the tribe, in so far as to become self-supporting as farmers. Among other tribes, through lack of proper management, or a resistance on their own part, no marked advancement has been made. A span of years between the extermination of the buffalo herd and the present has seen such management of many groups of Indians, however, as to demoralize and make beggars of them. The longer they are fed by the Government, without any effort on their part, the more worthless they become. A visit to the average Indian reservation means to go away discouraged. You find a lack of sympathy for the Indians by those who are responsible for their management. They say the Indian is lazy, irresponsible, dishonest; that the returned students are more worthless than the uneducated, and vastly more troublesome. Talk with the Indian, and he will tell you a story that is most startling. At the best, it is an accusation that the management of the reservation affairs is dishonest and corrupt; that the principal effort the employees are making is to keep their positions; that the returned students are given no opportunity to advance, but, on the contrary, are kept down, and that the Government at Washington is not keeping the promises of the past, nor those of to-day.

Edward S. Curtis

The outsider must read between the two extreme statements. He can see but little difference between the uneducated and the returned Carlisle boy, except that the latter is, if anything, more crafty. Also, as soon as you make a study of one of the educated boys or men after their return to the reservation, you see that education is not civilization, and are convinced that while you can educate an Indian in one generation, you cannot civilize him in so brief a period. As soon as his school uniform is worn out you cannot pick him out from the other Indians. To escape the ridicule of his own people, and following along the lines of least resistance, he lives as his tribe lives. If, on returning home, he finds his family sleeping on the ground, eating food squatted around the kettle in which it is cooked, he also sleeps on the ground, and joins the circle about the kettle, reaching in his fingers or spoon. What else can he do? As a matter of fact, there is little else for him to do.

As for the Indians' charge of mismanagement and incompetency, while there is much truth in their statements, it is certain that they overdraw their grievances. The department experiences great difficulty in getting capable men who have the moral strength and courage and the interest in the Indian to do the work. Generally speaking, if a man is capable of filling one of these places, he is worth more to himself than the Government pays. I can personally think of many agents who are doing all that any human being can do for the good of their people; even using money from their own salaries to help; and it is certain wherever you see an agent of that kind you see advancement. It may not be considered advancement by the people in the neighborhood of the reservation, but their point of view from self-interest is not broad enough to be considered. What they claim as knowledge is prejudice. In a recent conversation with an educated Indian, he wanted to know what I, after many years among the Indians, thought was the solution of the problem. "Your tribe is, perhaps, in the best condition of any of the Northwest Plains tribes. You have better farming lands. Your people are showing more progress, more energy, and a greater desire to accumulate property and become educated. You are decreasing at the rate of three per cent. a year. Take this pencil and figure out your own solution." At the end of a few minutes he looked up, with a surprised, wondering expression. "Why, if I live to be an old man there will be none of my people left." "Yes, my boy, there will be a few of your people left. It will be a survival of a limited few of you who are best fitted to meet the changes which civilization is forcing upon you."

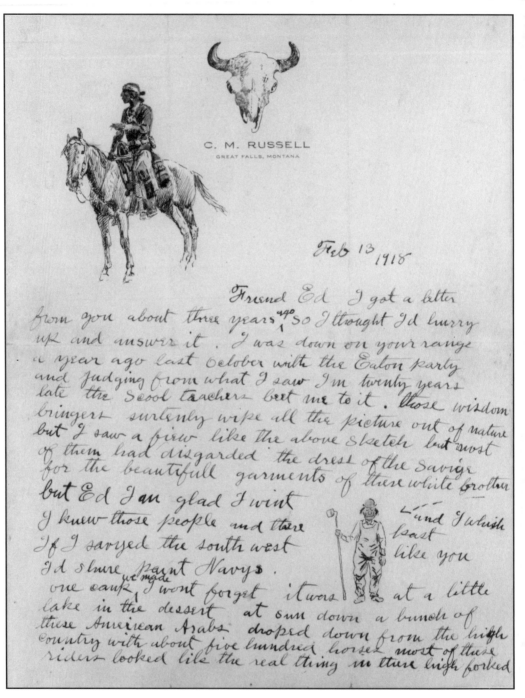

Feb 13/1918

Friend Ed I got a letter from you about three years ^{ago} so I thought I'd hurry up and answer it. I was down on your range a year ago last October with the Eaton party and judging from what I saw I'm twenty years late the scool teachers beet me to it. those wisdom bringers surtenly wipe all the picture out of nature but I saw a fiew like the above Sketch but most of them had disgarded the dress of the Savige for the beautifull garments of there white brother

but Ed I am glad I wint I knew those people and there If I saryed the south west I'd shure paint Navys. one cause I wont forget it was at a little lake in the dessert at sun down a bunch of these American Arabs droped down from the high country with about five hundred horses most of these riders looked like the real thing in there high forked

and I wish last like you

Charles M. Russell's illustrated letter to fellow artist Ed Borein, 1918 (the M. C. Naftzger Collection, Witchita Art Museum, Witchita, Kansas).

248

~

Charles M. Russell (1864-1926)

The legend of Charles M. Russell goes something like this: Charlie Russell was a homespun cowboy artist who realistically depicted the frontier West in his drawings, sculptures, and paintings.

Like many legends, the one surrounding Russell contains some truth as well as some fancy. Russell was, indeed, a Montana cowboy, though this was a role he consciously sought out rather than one that life thrust upon him. Born in St. Louis, the Charlie Russell who hit Montana in 1880 was green, sixteen, and primed for frontier adventures of the sort he had read about in yellow-back novels. The son of a wealthy manufacturing family that had given him the Montana trip as a birthday present, Russell was, in fact, nothing less than a classic remittance man come west to play cowboy. After a rocky start as a sheepherder, Russell eventually worked his way up to the not-very-prestigious job of night herder, a line of work that allowed him the freedom to paint during the daylight hours. He often gave away the artwork he produced to friends and acquaintances who reciprocated with a free drink or two. As a cowboy, Russell lent a hand in a few of the last big roundups in Montana, but he came too late to experience the glory days of the open range. He was also too late for Indian warfare, buffalo hunts, and a score of other frontier activities that eventually became subjects of his art.

In 1893 Russell decided to become a full-time artist. He got a few sketches published in national magazines, did some book illustration, and executed a painting or two on commission, but his artistic career did not really take off until his 1896 marriage to Nancy Cooper, an ambitious young woman who proved to be one of the shrewdest marketing geniuses the art world would ever know. For starters, Nancy cut back the time Charlie spent sitting on a bar stool and increased the time spent sitting in front of canvas. Next, she began marketing both the artist (colorfully decked out in his sombrero and red "half-breed" sash) and his art in places where Old West nostalgia and Big Money met: New York, Southern California, and London. Russell's art career flourished under Nancy's brilliant management, with his work becoming so prized that not long before his death he received the incredible sum of $30,000 dollars for two paintings commissioned for E. L. Doheny's California mansion. Not bad for an artist who once thought that the $400 price tag Nancy put on one of his early works was "Dead man's wages."

The focus of Russell's art was always on the vanished frontier, a fact that reflects his deep, even painful, nostalgia for a West he knew more through the stories of various white and Indian old-timers than through personal experience. So while Russell's artwork is thoroughly realistic in its carefully detailed depictions of animals, humans, and all the intricate trappings of frontier life, this realism is softened by a romantic view of the frontier that did not fade as Russell matured.

Along with his visual art, Russell produced a number of western stories (most of which are told in the colorful, colloquial voice of the artist's alter-ego, Montana cowboy Rawhide Rawlins) as well as body of delightful illustrated letters sent to lucky friends over the years. As with his art work, Russell's writings combine authentic details with a romantic view of the past. In the story "A Gift Horse," Russell shows off the sense of humor that won him a reputation as a storyteller who could hold his own with good friend Will Rogers, while the story "The War Scars of Medicine-Whip" demonstrates Russell's considerable respect for, and purposefully acquired knowledge of, American Indians. The letter to fellow artist Edward Borein describes a trip made to the Southwest and, like so much of Russell's published and unpublished writing, reflects Russell's persistent wish to have been born twenty years sooner, born in time to have known the dear, departed frontier that he tried all his life to capture in his artwork and in his writing.

Further Reading

Barclay, Donald A. "Charles M. Russell," in Steven E. Smith, Catherine A. Hastedt, and Donald H. Dyal, eds. *American Book and Magazine Illustrators to 1920: Dictionary of Literary Biography,* vol. 188. Detroit: Gale Research, 1998.

Dippie, Brian W. *Charles M. Russell: Word Painter: Letters 1887-1926.* Fort Worth: Amon Carter Museum, 1993.

Gale, Robert L. *Charles Marion Russell.* Western Writers Series 38. Boise, Idaho: Boise State University, 1979.

Russell, Charles M. *Good Medicine: The Illustrated Letters of Charles M. Russell.* Garden City, New York: Doubleday, Doran, 1929.

_____. *More Rawhides.* Great Falls: Montana Newspaper Association, 1925.

_____. *Rawhide Rawlins Stories.* Great Falls: Montana Newspaper Association, 1921.

_____. *Trails Plowed Under.* Garden City, New York: Doubleday, 1927.

Taliaferro, John. *Charles M. Russell: The Life and Legend of America's Cowboy Artist.* Boston: Little, Brown, 1996.

～

From "A Gift Horse"

Charley Furiman tells me about a hoss he owns and if you're able to stay on him he'll take you to the end of the trail. The gent Charley got him from, says he, "Gentle? He's a pet." (This man hates to part with him.) "He's a lady's hoss. You can catch him anywhere with a biscuit."

Next day Charley finds out he's a lady's hoss, all right, but he don't like men. Furiman ain't a mile from his corral when he slips the pack. Charley crawls him again kinder careful and rides him sixty miles an' he don't turn a hair. Next day he saddles him he acts like he's harmless but he's looking for something. He's out about ten mile. Charley notices he travels with one ear down. This ain't a good sign, but Charley gets careless and about noon he comes to a dry creek bed where there's lots of boulders. That's what this cayuse is looking for 'cause right in the middle of the boulder-strewn flat is where he breaks in two and unloads. Charley tells me, "I don't miss none of them boulders an' where I light there's nothing gives but different parts of me. For a while I wonder where I'm at and when things do clear up it comes to me right I forgot to bring the biscuits. How am I going to catch him? If I had a Winchester, I'd catch him just over the eye.

"To make a long story short, I followed him back to the ranch afoot. Walking ain't my strong holt an' these boulder bumps don't help me none. Next morning after a good night's sleep, I feel better. Going out to the corral, I offer this cayuse a biscuit, thinkin' I'll start off friendly. He strikes at me and knocks my hat off. My pardner tries to square it by telling me I ain't got the right kind. 'That's a lady's hoss,' says he, 'and being a pet, he wants them little lady's biscuits; it's enough to make him sore, handing him them sour doughs.'

"While I'm getting my hat, I happen to think of a friend of mine that's got married and I ain't give him no wedding present. This friend of mine is a bronk rider named Con Price. So while my heart's good, I saddle a gentle hoss and lead this man-hater over and presents him to Price with my best wishes.

"I don't meet Con till next fall on the beef roundup. He ain't too friendly. Next morning when we're roping horses, he steps up to me an says, kinder low, holdin' out his hand to shake, 'Charley, I'm letting bygones be bygones, but if I get married again anywhere in your neighborhood, don't give me no wedding presents. If you do you'll get lots of flowers.'"

From "The War Scars of Medicine-Whip"

I'd been over on Broken Bow, an' had seen many strange Indians in Long Pipe's camp; among 'em an old, scar-faced warrior that interested me. Knowin' Squaw Owens' acquaintance among these people, I enquire if he knows any such savage.

"From the earmarks you give me," says he, "it's old Medicine-Whip, my uncle by marriage; that Blood woman I had was his niece. When I'm a kid in Missouri I used to read yaller-back novels that was sure scary, but Medicine-Whip's history would make them romances look like a primer story. There ain't much pleasure for him since the Whites made laws agin killin' men for fun. His range is up on Belly River. I guess he's down visitin' some of his relatives, an' when an Injun goes visitin' it ain't one of them how-dye-do, how-are-you calls, where you stand awhile with your hat in your hand. It's a case of stay till the grub plays out. This social habit is one of the things that makes 'em hard to civilize; you'd as well try an' scatter a flock of blackbirds or make a bee live lonesome as to separate these people. 'Tain't their nature. In old times they bunched for protection agin their enermies, an' they've never got over likin' that way of livin'. Nature fed an' clothed her children an' taught 'em how to live, an' it'll take Uncle Sam some time to wean 'em from their mother.

"We'll say here's an Injun forty years old. He's had the dust of the runnin' herd in his nostrils, an' the clatter of dew claws an' hoofs are still fresh in his ears, when Uncle Sam pulls him down off a high-headed, painted buffalo hoss, an' hookin' his hands around the handle of a walkin' plow, tells him it's a good thing, to push it along. Farmin' is the hardest work on earth, an' when Uncle Sam saws off a job like this to Mr. Injun, a gentleman that never raised nothin' but hell an' hair, it's no wonder he backs away from the proposition. As far back as anybody knows, his folks lived by the use of their weapons. They sowed nothin' an' reaped nothin'. Barrin' a few roots an' berries the women gathered, Injuns were carniverous animals; meat was their strong holt, an' if they had that they asked for nothin' more.

*Charles
M.
Russell*

"But you were askin' about Medicine-Whip. That old savage is the real article, an' can spin yarns of killin's an' scalpin's that would make your hair set up like the roach on a buck antelope; that is, if you caught him feelin' right. I ain't never got him strung out but once.

"That's about four years ago; I'm huntin' hosses in the Ghost Butte country. One afternoon after ridin' since sun-up with nothin' to eat, I run on to a Blood camp an' I ain't sorry, for I'm sure hungry. This camp's pretty quiet; barrin' a few half-naked kids playin' an' an old squaw humped over, scrapin' a beefhide, there's no life in sight. It's one of these hot days that makes folks hug shadows; even the dogs, layin' in the shade of the lodges with their tongues lollin', don't no more'n glance at me. I ask the old woman where is the chief's lodge. She straightens up and points with her chin to one with queer-lookin' birds painted on each side of the door. Droppin' my reins to the ground, I slide from the saddle an' approach the gentleman's residence. Not wantin' to walk in too free, I say 'How' when I near the door. There's an answer of 'How! How! How!' from inside, an' stoopin' an' peekin' in, I see my old uncle.

"He's kind of half leanin' agin a willer backrest, cuttin' his smoke mixture of red willow an' tobacco with a long butcher knife. He never looks up from his work, but signs to me with his free hand to come in an' sit down. Readin' his face, you wouldn't think he knew I was there, but it's a safe bet he or some of his snake-eyed kids had me spotted before I discovered the camp. There never was an Injun camp without a lookout, an' when he sees anything it don't bother him none to let the folks know. A man that can get to an Injun camp without bein' seen has got a medal comin' for sneakin'.

"Well, after a mighty cold handshake, I sit down. He keeps choppin' away at his tobacco with no word of welcome. While I'm sittin' there, rollin' a smoke, he calls to a squaw outside an' tells her somethin' I don't catch. Pretty soon the lady shows up with some half-boiled beef an' a greasy bannock on a tin plate, along with a cup of tea, an' sets it on the ground before me. For looks it ain't very appetizin', but the way I'm hollered out inside, I ain't lookin' for dainties, an' I'm not long makin' a cleanup. While I'm feedin' I go to sizin' up Medicine-Whip. He ain't wearin' nothin' but a clout, givin' me a chance to look him over. The lodge-sides are rolled up all around, allowin' what little breeze there is to work under, makin' it mighty pleasant in there, while outside it's hot enough to pop corn. An' maybe you think my uncle ain't takin' comfort in his summer garments, while I'm clothed from heel to chin in clothes grimed with sweat an' alkali dust; but bein' civilized, I'm forced to stand it.

"Well, as I started to say, sizin' up this old killer, in age I'd guess him anywhere between seventy-five an' a hundred, an' he looks like he'll go that much more if somebody don't put his light out. For by the scars he's wearin', he's a hard one to down, an' it's a cinch he's packin' considerable lead under his hide right now. His hair, that hangs loose on his shoulders, is gettin' roan; there's a deep scar follerin' his wrinkled face from where the hair starts on his forehead down across his left eye, windin' up at the point of his chin. The way the bone of his cheek is caved in an' the crooked set of his jaw, this ain't no knife wound; it's a safe bet it was a tomahawk, swung by somebody that wasn't jokin'. His thin-lipped mouth looks like another scar under his nose; if he ever had a good feature, time, weather, an' fightin' has wiped it out. On his breast, just above the nipples, is several sets of scars. I savvy these; they're the marks of the Sun-Dance, where the skewers held him to the medicine pole, an' by the numbers, he's went through several of these sun jigs. Barrin' these, his body ain't marked up much, but his legs an' arms have sure had rough handlin'. He's a regular war map settin' up before me in his clout an' scars, but I can't read him. Knowin' Medicine-Whip to be a close-mouthed Injun, I'm wonderin' how I'll wring a story out of him. He ain't got no love for a man of my color; he hates a white man's tracks. He's fed me, but Injuns are liberal with grub, an' the chances are the beef I'm eatin' he downed on the range an' burned or buried the hide, or cut it up for moccasin soles. The Whites killed his cattle, an' he can't see where it ain't right to knock over a spotted buffalo now an' then. He'd do the same with the owner if the play came right. I don't doubt for a minute but this old uncle would down his lovin' nephew if he caught him lonesome. But even knowin' this I admire this red-handed killer. The Whites have killed his meat an' taken his country, but they've made no change in him. He's as much Injun as his ancestors that packed their quivers loaded with flint-pointed arrows, an' built fires by rubbin' sticks together. He laughs at priests an' preachers. Outside his lodge on a tripod hangs a bullhide shield an' medicine bag to keep away the ghosts. He's got a religion of his own, an' it tells him that the buffalo are comin' back. He lights his pipe, an' smokes with the sun the same as his folks did a thousand winters behind him. When he cashes in, his shadow goes prancin' off on a shadow pony, joinin' those that have gone before, to run shadow buffalo. He's seen enough of white men, an' don't want to throw in with 'em in no other world.

"Feelin' this way toward me an' my people, naturally it's hard for me to get confidential with him. He's smokin' his pipe, which he ain't never offered to me, when I break the ice of my visit by enquiring about them hosses I'm huntin'. He tells me he ain't seen or heard nothin' of 'em. Then I start fillin' him up about bein' a great warrior, an' I'd like to hear the story of them scars he's wearin'. I make this talk so smooth an' strong that he starts thawin' out, but's mighty slow loosenin' up his history. Finally, reloadin' an' lightin' his pipe, he hands it to me, an' I know he's comin' my way. Injuns are slow talkers, an' it's some time before he gathers his yarn to reel it out to me.

On the start he straightens up, throwin' his shoulders back, an' tells me his folks was all fighters. He ain't seen three moons when his mother is killed by a Sioux war party. She's gatherin' berries, an' the Sioux try to take her prisoner, but she gets noisy an' one of the party slips a knife under her left ribs, quietin' her for always. When her folks find her, the boy's asleep, soaked in his mother's blood. The old men an' women prophesy that he will be a great warrior; it will be bad for the Sioux that meets the boy that slept in his mother's blood. An' it's the truth, 'cuse before he's fifteen he downs an' scalps a Sioux, an' from that time on he makes it his business to upset an' take the hair of his enemy any time he meets one.

He's about twenty-five when he gets these scars I'm enquirin' about. Them days this killer's known as "Sleeps-In-Blood." He gets the name of Medicine-Whip along with these scars. It's about this time the Crows burn the Blood range, drivin' the herd south, and his people are forced to foller up for their meat. Sleeps-In-Blood, with about fifteen warriors, is in advance of the main band. The whole camp's hungry, an' you know empty bellies don't sweeten nobody's temper. This advance guard ain't joyous;

255

they're sure wolfy, with belts cinched to their lean flanks, an' it wouldn't be healthy for man or beast that runs into these hungry hunters. They're all rigged for war; lances, bows, an' loaded quivers. Most of 'em's packin' bullhide shields; a few's got smooth-bore flintlocks; their ponies 're feathered an' painted.

"They're joggin' along, bad-humored, when of a sudden Sleeps-In-Blood, who's a little in advance, pulls up his pony; his bead-eye has caught a pony track in the beaten buffalo trail they're follerin'. In a minute they're all down, studyin' the tracks. As near as they can figger there's about ten ponies, an' by the way the sign's strung out, they're packin' riders.

"The sight of these tracks sets this blood-hungry bunch warlike for sure, an' they ain't slow about strippin' their saddles an' sheddin' their extra garments. Every Injun pulls his paintbag an's busy puttin' on the finishin' touches; when they're through with their toilets, they don't look like the same bunch. Sleeps-In-Blood smears his left hand with vermilion an' slaps it across his mouth, leavin' a red hand-print under his nose, showin' he's drank the enemies' blood. To keep the hair out of his eyes he wraps his foretop in weaselskin. One or two of the party's wearin' war-bonnets, but barrin' eagle or hawk feathers, the bunch ain't wearin' nothin' heavier 'n paint. When everybody's striped and streaked till they look like hell's home guard, Sleeps-In-Blood lights a small warpipe, an' after a couple of whiffs holds the mouthpiece toward the sun reelin' off a prayer that would do a preacher proud. 'See, Father, I smoke with you,' he says. 'I've lit the pipe, an' Sleeps-In-Blood does not lie when the pipe is passed. Have mercy on your children, Big Father; our parfleshes swing light at our ponies' sides; already the babies cry with empty bellies. Our enemy has burnt the grass. Now that we have struck their trail make our medicine strong!' He winds up his long, flowery prayer by handin' the pipe around to his painted brothers, who take two or three draws apiece. Then it is shaken out, an' each Injun forks his pony.

"They don't travel fast; the tracks are plain enough in the trail, but in the grass they're hard to hold. The party ain't gone far when the leaders catch sight of dust. They savvy this; it's buffalo, an' it ain't long till they hear the rumble of the runnin' herd. It's an easy guess the enemy they're follerin's among 'em, an' raisin' the next hill they sight 'em. A glimpse shows they're Sioux, so busy gettin' meat they're careless, allowin' Sleeps-In-Blood an' his men to ride up in plain sight.

"The Bloods are wise an' don't jump 'em right away, givin' 'em time to fag their ponies. Then, slippin' into the dust of the herd, they go to work on 'em an' down three before the Sioux savvy what they're up against. But, as soon as they do, they ain't slow about quittin' the herd. Now buffalo runnin' is hard on hoss flesh; they ain't gone no distance till the Sioux ponies, plumb winded, throw their tails up. They're makin' a slow runnin' fight of it when Sleeps-In-Blood kills the pony under the Sioux medicine man, causin' his party to pull up an' bunch. They're pretty well heeled, most of 'em packin' guns, an' the way they handle 'em keeps the Bloods at a respectful distance. From what old Medicine-Whip tells me, the Sioux are sure makin' a good standoff. Twice they charge 'em, an' each time a pony comes back shy a rider. These charges ain't successful; they've lost two men an' have three cripples out of the fight. The Bloods are plumb buffaloed, an' it looks like it's goin' to be a drawn battle. Sleeps-In-Blood an' his men have pulled off out of range an' are bunched up, makin' medicine, when a Sioux starts shoutin' abuse to 'em in their own tongue. This might sound strange to anyone that don't know Injuns. In those times, women were counted as plunder an' were taken as such by war parties. The speaker is either a renegade Blood or his mother a stolen woman an' she's learnt her offspring the tongue of her people. He hollers to them that it ain't no credit to a Sioux to take the hair of a Blood: these trophies are only good to trim squaw leggin's with, or make wigs for dolls for the youngsters. He said that the Sioux, when they take Bloods prisoners, don't kill 'em, but keep 'em to pack water for the squaws. Then he starts pickin' on Sleeps-In-Blood, who is sittin' on his pinto pony.

"'That pony,' said he, describin' Sleeps-In-Blood's animal, 'is a war hoss. Why is he under a woman? No,' says he, shadin' his eyes with his hand, 'it's a maggot I see. Do the Bloods allow the flies to blow their ponies' backs? Come, pony, to a warrior who will clean your back before it rots. The smell is already bad on the wind.' The Sioux all laughed long and loud.

"This talk makes Sleeps-In-Blood madder than a teased snake, an' he hollers back: 'Has the liar said all? The Sioux call themselves hunters, but they lay in camp and eat their brothers, the dog!'

"You may not know it but the Bloods are one tribe that don't eat dog, an' say it is not good to eat those who guard your camp, an' howl at your door with lonesomeness when you're gone.

"'It's a poor hunter that eats his friends,' goes on Sleeps-In-Blood. 'If the liar has more to say, let him speak fast, for in less time than it takes to smoke the warpipe, his tongue will be stilled for always; for he you call the maggot will whip your medicine man like he would a bad woman.'

"With that he throws to the ground his bow an' nearly empty quiver. He has already got his rawhide rope wrapped 'round an' 'round his pony's belly, an' by shovin' his legs under an' crampin' his knees back with feet stuck in the rope below, he's as good as tied. This is often done by Indians when chargin' a dangerous place, knowin' if they are wounded or killed the pony will pack them out. If the pony is downed, the Indian takes a chance of cuttin' himself loose with his scalpin' knife. So, as I said before, he throws down his bow and empty quiver, an' flies at them. This sure surprises the Sioux: before you could bat your eye, he's among 'em.

"The feller that has been doin' the talkin' is standin' on the edge of the bunch, an' as Sleeps-In-Blood reaches him he shoves his lance up under the Sioux's ribs, hollerin': 'If I'm a maggot I give meat to my brothers!' The lance catches in the Sioux's carcass, and Sleeps-In-Blood loses it, leavin' him nothin' but his quirt an' bullhide shield, which he holds close over his vitals an' crowds in among the ponies. The last he remembers he's lashing the medicine-man across the back an' shoulders with his quirt. He's so fightin' locoed he don't feel the arrows that are piercin' his legs an' thighs. He's got 'em pretty well scattered with his quirt, when a Sioux beefs him with his tomahawk an' he flops over.

"This game charge of his rallies an' nerves up his own men so they're right at his pony's tail when he hits the Sioux bunch, who are so busy dodgin' the swing of his quirt they're killed before they come to.

"When Sleeps-In-Blood wakes up he's sure dazed. Lookin' 'round he don't seem to savvy what's happened, till one of his friends slips a knife into his hand an' tells him to go to work. Plumb locoed with the pain of his wound, he starts butcherin'. The Sioux are all dead an' scalped but two: the medicine-man an' the one that done the talkin'. They've held them two out for him to trim.

"The blood runnin' through Sleeps-In-Blood's eyes has set him mad. He couldn't have been more fiendish if he'd broke fresh from hell. He's satisfied with the locks of the medicine-man, but the way he trims that Sioux that calls him names is sure scandalous. Every cut he makes means somethin' to an Injun, an' as these people believe a man lands in the next world in the shape he leaves this one, it won't be hard, he thinks, to identify this Sioux as a liar an' thief in the happy huntin' ground.

"Reelin' off this yarn has warmed my uncle up plenty; it's brought all the savage in him to the surface, an' lookin' him over, I don't doubt his story. He's been a fighter all right, an' it's in him yet."

From *Good Medicine:*
The Illustrated Letters of Charles M. Russell

"C. M. Russell to Edward Borein"

Feb 13
1918

Friend Ed

I got a letter from you about three years ago so I thought Id hurry up and answer it. I was down on your range a year ago last October with the Eaton party and judging from what I saw Im twenty years late the scool teachers beet me to it. those wisdom bringers surtenly wipe all the picture out of nature but I saw a fiew like the above sketch but most of them had disgarded the dress of the savige for the beautifull garments of these white brother but Ed Im glad I wint and I whish I knew those people and there past If I savyed the south west like you Id sure paint Navys [Navajos].

One camp we made I wont forget it was at a little lake in the dessert at sundown a bunch of these American Arabs droped down from the high country with about five hundred horses most of these riders looked lik the real thing in there high forked saddles and concho belts silver ore turquis necklaces and year rings they were all hatless some wore split pants their shirts were Navyho make but its a safe bet if we could drop back in there history they would be shy the shirt they rode short sturrips an each packed a skin rope. They were not like the Indian I know but every thing on them spelt wild people and horsemen and in a mixture of dust and red sun light it made a picture that will not let me foget Arizona

I also saw a Yabachae dance of the Navys that was wild and scary I guess I benn telling you things you already know but I like to unlode on men whos likes are the same as mine I dont know when I will see you so I want you to write and tell me about the the big camp How is Marsh do you ever see that Terrapin Bill Crawford is Rogers still heeling fillyes at the follies does he still loap up to your camp quirting himself down the hind leg with a paper if he keeps that up hel get to be a ring tail. I wonder if Fred Stone when hes Lion hunting pulls that funny stuff of his if he dos tell him I dont think its squar to shoot the big cat while hes Laughing

with best regards to yourself and the bunch from my best half and myself

Your friend
C M Russell

Selected Bibliography

1. Western American Art

Andrews, Ralph W. *Photographers of the Frontier West: Their Lives and Works, 1875-1915.* Seattle: Superior Publishing, 1965.

Bruce, Chris. *Myth of the West.* Seattle: University of Washington Press, 1990.

Dawdy, Doris Ostrander. *Artists of The American West: A Biographical Dictionary.* Athens: Ohio University Press, 1985.

Dippie, Brian W. "The Visual West." *The Oxford History of the American West.* Clyde A. Milner, II, Carol A. O'Connor, and Martha A. Sandweiss, eds. New York: Oxford University Press, 1994. 675-705.

Ewers, John Canfield. *Artists of the Old West.* Garden City: Doubleday, 1965.

Getlein, Frank. *The Lure of the Great West.* Waukesha, Wisconsin: Country Beautiful, 1973.

Glanz, Dawn. *How the West Was Drawn: American Art and the Settling of the Frontier.* Ann Arbor: UMI Research Press, 1982.

Goetzmann, William H., and William N. Goetzmann. *The West of the Imagination.* New York: Norton, 1986.

Hassrick, Peter. *The Way West: Art of Frontier America.* New York: Abrams, 1977.

Naef, Weston J., et al. *Era of Exploration: The Rise of Landscape Photography in the American West, 1860-1885.* Buffalo: Albright-Knox Art Gallery, 1975.

Prown, Jules, et al. *Discovered Lands, Invented Pasts: Transforming Visions of the American West.* New Haven: Yale University Press, 1992.

Samuels, Peggy and Harold. *The Illustrated Biographical Encyclopedia of Artists of the American West.* Garden City: Doubleday, 1976.

Samuels, Peggy and Harold, Joan Samuels, and Daniel Fabian. *Techniques of the Artists of the American West.* Secaucus, New Jersey: Wellfleet Press, 1990.

Sandweiss, Martha A., ed. *Photography in Nineteenth-Century America.* Fort Worth: Amon Carter Museum/Abrams, 1991.

Taft, Robert. *Artists and Illustrators of the Old West, 1850-1900.* New York: Charles Scribner's Sons, 1953.

Truettner, William H. *Art in New Mexico, 1900-1945: Paths to Taos and Santa Fe.* New York: Abbeville Press, 1986.

Tyler, Ron, et al. *American Frontier Life: Early Western Painting and Prints.* New York: Abbeville Press, 1987.

Wade, Edwin L., ed. *The Arts of the North American Indian: Native Traditions in Evolution.* New York: Hudson Hills Press, 1986.

The West as America: Reinterpreting Images of the Frontier, 1820-1920. Washington, D.C.: Smithsonian Institution Press (for the National Museum of American Art), 1991.

11. Western American History

Cronon, William. *Under an Open Sky: Rethinking America's Western Past.* New York: Norton, 1992.

Etulain, Richard W. *The American West, Comparative Perspectives: A Bibliography.* Albuquerque: University of New Mexico Press, 1996.

Goetzmann, William H. *New Lands, New Men: America and the Second Great Age of Discovery.* New York: Viking, 1986.

_____. *Exploration and Empire: The Explorer and the Scientist in the Winning of the American West.* Austin: Texas State Historical Association, 1993.

Hyde, Anne Farrar. *An American Vision: Far Western Landscape and National Culture.* New York: New York University Press, 1990.

Lamar, Howard R., ed. *The New Encyclopedia of the American West.* New Haven: Yale University Press, 1998.

Limerick, Patricia Nelson. *The Legacy of Conquest: The Unbroken Past of the American West.* New York: Norton, 1987.

Merk, Frederick. *History of the Westward Movement.* New York: Knopf, 1978.

Milner, Clyde A., ed. *Major Problems in the History of the American West: Documents and Essays.* Lexington, Massachusetts: Heath, 1989.

_____. *A New Significance: Re-envisioning the History of the American West.* New York: Oxford University Press, 1996.

_____. Carol A. O'Connor, and Martha A. Sandweiss, eds. *The Oxford History of the American West.* New York: Oxford University Press, 1994.

Nash, Gerald D. *Creating the West: Historical Interpretations, 1880-1990.* Albuquerque: University of New Mexico Press, 1991.

Paul, Rodman W., and Richard W. Etulain, comps. *The Frontier and the American West.* Arlington Heights, Illinois: AHM , 1977.

Ridge, Martin. *Writing the History of the American West.* Worcester, Massachusetts: American Antiquarian Society, 1991.

Robinson, Forrest G. *The New Western History: The Territory Ahead.* Tucson: University of Arizona Press, 1998.

Smith, Henry Nash. *Virgin Land: The American West as Symbol and Myth.* 1950. Cambridge: Harvard University Press, 1970.

White, Richard. *"It's Your Misfortune and None of My Own": A History of the American West.* Norman: University of Oklahoma Press, 1991.

Wilkinson, Charles F. *The American West: A Narrative Bibliography and a Study in Regionalism.* Niwot, Colorado: University Press of Colorado, 1989.

Worster, Donald. *Under Western Skies: Nature and History in the American West.* New York: Oxford University Press, 1992.

iii. Western American Literature

Cracroft, Richard H., ed. *Twentieth-Century American Western Writers, First Series. Dictionary of Literary Biography,* vol. 206. Detroit: Gale Research, 1999.

_____. ed. *Twentieth-Century American Western Writers, Second Series. Dictionary of Literary Biography,* vol. 212. Detroit: Gale Research, 1999.

Erisman, Fred, and Richard W. Etulain, eds. *Fifty Western Writers.* Westport, Connecticut: Greenwood Press, 1982.

Etulain, Richard W., and N. Jill Howard, eds. *A Bibliographical Guide to the Study of Western American Literature.* 2nd ed. Albuquerque: University of New Mexico Press, 1995.

Gale, Robert L., ed. *Nineteenth-Century American Western Writers. Dictionary of Literary Biography,* vol. 186. Detroit: Gale Research, 1997.

Kowalewski, Michael. *Reading the West: New Essays on the Literature of the American West.* New York: Cambridge University Press, 1996.

Lee, Robert Edson. *From East to West: Studies in the Literature of the American West.* Urbana: University of Illinois Press, 1966.

Lyon, Thomas J. "The Literary West." *The Oxford History of the American West.* Clyde A. Milner, Carol A. O'Connor, and Martha A. Sandweiss, eds. New York: Oxford University Press, 1994.

Lyon, Thomas J., et al, eds. *Updating the Literary West.* Fort Worth: Texas Christian University Press, 1997.

Milton, John R. *The Novel of the American West.* Lincoln: University of Nebraska Press, 1980.

Rosowski, Susan. *Birthing a Nation: Gender, Creativity, and the West in American Literature.* Lincoln: University of Nebraska Press, 1999.

Taylor, J. Golden, Thomas J. Lyon, et al, eds. *A Literary History of the American West.* Fort Worth: Texas Christian University Press, 1987.

Index

THE EDITORS

Donald A. Barclay is a librarian at the Houston Academy of Medicine/Texas Medical Center Library in Houston. James H. Maguire is a professor of English at Boise (Idaho) State University. Peter Wild is a professor of English at the University of Arizona in Tucson. The three scholars have previously collaborated on *A Rendezvous Reader: Tall, Tangled, and True Tales of the Mountain Men, 1805-1850* (1997) and *Into the Wilderness Dream: Exploration Narratives of the American West* (1994).